MAHABHARATA

MAHABHARATA

WINSOME BOOKS INDIA

ISBN No. : 978-81-88043-76 -7

First Edition : 2015

Published in 2015 by
Winsome Books India
209, F-17, Harsha Complex, Subhash Chowk
Laxmi Nagar, Delhi-92
Email: winsomebooks@rediffmail.com
Website: www.winsomebooks.com

MAHABHARATA

R.S.SHUKLA

THE AUTHOR

R.S. Shukla has been the President of Noida Kanyakubja Samaj for the last ten years and Patron of this brahman samaj for the last two years. Hailing from a family of authors and ardent devotees of Shri Rama and Krishna, he has been engaged in many devotional activities for years.

The author represents a blend of tradition and modernity. With a background of Air Force and Industry, including a diplomatic tenure in the erstwhile USSY, he has concentrated in the last decade mainly on academic activities, authoring fifteen books and contributing a large number of articles to the national dailies on important contemporary matters-primarily management subjects and issues. A past President of Noida Management Association for two successive tenures, he is also a recipient of a prestigious national honour, the Vikas Jyoti Award for excellence incontribution to the Society. He has travelled extensively both in India and abroad.

INDEX

PREFACE

Mahabharata is an epic written by Bhagwan Vyasa, the great vedic scholar and rishi, nearly three thousand years before Christ, about a great dynastic war between Kauravas and Pandavas, the two branches of a single ruling family of India. The scene of its great battles was at the confluence of Ganges and Yamuna rivers near Delhi, the present capital of India. By the time the learned rishi wrote the epic, the stories of war had already become a part of legends and folk'lores of our people. The work of Vyasa, however, enshrined the story at a much higher plane, emphasizing not only the historical aspects, but also the moral, philosophical and spiritual values as well. Little wonder that, along with 'Ramayana' by rishi Valmiki, the two books have influenced and symbolized the essence of Indian culture of the preceding five millennia and will continue to do so for thousands of years to come.

The original Mahabharata has been aptly described as the mightiest single effort of literary creation of any culture in the world. In sheer size, it is more than seven times of 'Iliad' and 'Odyssey' combined. The size limitation of my book has resulted in my concentrating on the main story and a few other important ones only. The fact is that the original works embellished by hundreds of interesting tales and vedic stories which provide a social, ethical, moral and cosmological background to the central theme of the book that at first the evil might have an upper hand but eventually the good triumphs and that the adherence to 'Dharma', i.e. righteousness, leads to the victory.

Mahabharata also describes a highly evolved society in those days of India which had many autonomous as well as independent kingdoms. The education was imparted in Ashramas managed by great sages and located in sections of forest recesses. Women were actively involved in the work of their husbands and sons.They were educated and highly honoured. Its prime characters depict a great vitality and surprisingly not much different from India of today.

Originally titled 'Bharata', symbolizing the biggest battle involving almost all the armies of the land 'Bharata' i.e. India, the prefix 'Maha' was added at the instance of a conclave of celestial lords, the 'Devas', which concluded that the work was of a greater significance than all the four Vedas put together. For scholars, the epic has another name of the work, 'Jaya' , in its first invocatory verse. Some, who have been impressed beyond imagination, have described it as the fifth 'Veda'. On an aesthetic plane, Mahabharata is a brilliant piece of poetry. It is also more than an epic. Indeed, it is an astounding tale of romance – romance of heroic people, some of whom were superhuman and divine. The book, indeed, is a mix of mythology and history, wielding a much higher influence on the Indian mind and hearts, and the national character, than our actual heroes and events of history without a mythological mix. That is why it can be said that if one wishes to really know and understand the Indian culture, ethos and its way of life, reading of Mahabharata and Ramayana is an essential pre-requisite

NOIDA

R.S.SHUKLA

Chapter-1

LORD GANAPATI, THE AMANUENSIS OF RISHI VYASA

Rishi Vyasa, the man who compiled the four Vedas, was in deep in contemplation regarding his latest problem. The brilliant son of Parashar and Satyawati, who had acquired the divine powers of knowing past, present and future through his intense tapas, had conceived during the last three years a story on the epic and devastating battle fought between the descendents of the Kuru family, the Kauravas and Pandavas, involving practically all the Kings and Chieftains of the nation. As he sat in his hut deciding on how to find someone capable of writing his dictation, his room was lit up with a brilliant light. To his surprise, he found Brahma, the creator, standing before him.

After making him sit and paying the customary salutations, Vyasa found the Lord looking at him askance. Vyasa, holding his hands together, told Brahma, “Lord, I have conceived a great epic but am unable to decide on whom to ask for taking down the dictation. In size alone, the entire story is likely to run into more than twenty four thousand verses”.

“Invoke Ganesha and request him to be your writer. I am confident that this will be the one of the greatest epics ever written by anyone in the world”, Brahma said and blessing Vyasa, disappeared. Relieved that his problem has been resolved, Vyasa invoked Ganesha, the son of Shiva, and the most intelligent deva in the world. Ganesha immediately appeared in front of Vyasa, who promptly asked him to be his scribe.

“Why me?” Ganesha quizzed?

“Because you are the remover of barriers from all new ventures and the god of writers”, Vyasa responded and narrates his story in brief.

Ganesha was impressed, but laid down one condition. "You shall not pause. The moment you do that I will leave. I am pressed for time and your book is long".

"Agreed, but I too have one condition. If you do not understand what I have dictated, you should stop till you fully comprehend".

"Ganesha sighed, "Agreed. It is just that my thirst for knowledge is never satisfied".

Vyasa sat on a high seat with Ganesha looking up to take the dictation. Occasionally, he would pause to get to the meaning of what was dictated. Vyasa utilized this time to compose more verses.

A totally new problem suddenly surfaced. Saraswati, the Goddess of learning, was very annoyed that the task was not entrusted to her. Flowing in the form of a river next to Vyasa she made such a noise that Ganesha could barely hear what Vyasa was dictating. He looked at Vyasa who requested the Goddess to lower the noise level. Saraswati, however, was not ready to oblige.

The holy sage eventually became furious. He stood up and pronounced a curse on her. "A short distance away from here, you shall disappear from the face of the earth". The curse took immediate effect and the noise became a whimper. Vyasa resumed his dictation.

In no time, Saraswati, along with some other devas stood with folded hands.

She apologized for her mistake and asked to be forgiven again and again. When other devas also pleaded on her behalf, Vyasa calmed down.

He said, "I cannot withdraw my curse, but shall modify it. You shall disappear from here in Himalayas, but shall reappear far away at holy Prayag along with Ganges and Yamuna rivers to make a confluence of the three rivers".Ganesha sat chuckling to himself as he wrote the verses of Vyas. He had witnessed the powers of devas on a number of occasions, but was seeing the power of a Rishi, a learned sage, for the first time. With Ganesha writing on the leaves, the great epic “Mahabharata” started taking shape.Those were the days before the printing had been invented and the memory of the wise and intelligent was the sole source of information and knowledge.When the epic had been written, Vyasa taught the same firstly to his own son, the sage Suka and thereafter to some of his chosen disciples. Narada was the one who told the great story to devas while Suka narrated the same to the gandharvas, Yakshas and Rakshasas. The humans, however, were first told the epic by Vaisampayana in the presence of Vyasa during the Nag-Yagya (Snake-sacrifice) organized by King Janmejaya, the son of Parikshit and the grandson of Arjuna.

The great story describing the events and the teachings of Vyasa on dharma and other objectives of life were passed on thereafter from word of mouth to the humanity even far beyond the shores of India. Even now, stories of Mahabharata and Ramayan are told and even dramatized in many countries of the world. With the advent of ultra-modern printing technology, let us read, enjoy and benefit from reading the book in a small readable form.

Chapter-II

KING SHANTANU AND GANGA

The stories of Mahabharata begin from the king Shantanu of Hastinapur belonging to Kuru dynasty of the human race. Shantanu was a powerful king just like his illustrious ancestor, Bharata. Bharata, the son of king Dushyanta and Shankuntala, had a great reputation of being very strong and courageous. In his childhood, he was reputed to have been opening the jaws of fully grown-up lions to count their teeth. India derives its other and equally popular name 'Bharata' from this king.

Shantanu had been advised by his father that he would meet his future wife when the time came on the banks of river Ganges. Sure enough, one day when he was taking a stroll in the forests by the riverside, he saw an extremely beautiful woman. Shantanu, attracted by her radiant beauty, immediately fell in love with her. He walked up to her and immediately proposed a marriage to her. The woman was goddess Ganga in human form. She knew that Shantanu would come and propose to her someday. On hearing from him, she replied, "O King, I shall marry you only on some specific conditions. Neither you nor anyone else will ever ask me who I am or where do I come from. You shall not criticize or question me on any of my actions, however good or bad they might appear to be. You shall not admonish me or be annoyed with me on any count. If you violate these terms, I shall be free to leave you then and there. If you agree, it will be a privilege to be your queen".

King Shantanu was so enamoured and infatuated with the divine beauty that he accepted the conditions set forth by her without any second thoughts. Ganga proved to be an ideal wife, loving, affectionate and caring.

In due course, Ganga bore him seven children, but, to the extreme dismay and horror of Shantanu, she took each of the seven newly-borns to the river Ganges and consigned them to the rushing waters. Shantanu had followed Ganga on each occasion at a distance and, despite having a great desire to stop her from commiting such a heinous act, or at least querying her of the reason for such a strange and illogical behavior, he restrained himself from doing so, fearing that she would walk away from his life.

However, Shantanu's patience had totally exhausted when Ganga started walking towards the river once again with their eighth child. He shouted at her from behind, saying, "Stop; why are you murdering these innocent children of ours. Don't you have an iota of mercy or kindness for these little beings who should be allowed to grow and enjoy rather than be subjected to such a cruel death?

Ganga turned around and looked at Shantanu almost with regret, holding the newly born in her lap. After a pause, she slowly uttered, "O King, you have broken your pledge. Now I have to leave you. However, the child, your son, will remain with me for a few years till I return him to you as my gift".

Ganga continued, "Let me, however, explain the reason for such a seemingly irrational behavior of mine. I am Ganga, the river goddess prayed to and revered by all on the earth and in heavens. The eight infants, seven of them dead and eighth in my arms, were vasus, angels, who had stolen the beautiful looking cow, Nandini, from the ashram of the sage Vasishth. The vasus did, in fact, not need a cow but committed the unworthy act solely to satisfy the whimsical wishes of one of wives, who liked that splendid looking creature". Vasishth was away when the theft took place. On his return, there were anxious enquiries and searches by his ashram mates without any fruitful result.

The holy sage then used his divine insight to know the truth of the matter. In no time, the cow along with the eight vasus were in front of him. Vasishth was angry at the eight vasus who despite being immortal and having no need for a cow had no explanation for this senseless act done at the behest of a woman. He pronounced a curse on all eight of them ordering that notwithstanding their immortality, they would be born on the earth and spend one lifetime there".

"Thunderstruck, the vasus fell at the feet of Vasishth for mercy and forgiveness. Eventually, the anger of the holy sage subsided. He told the vasus that even though he had forgiven them, he could only soften the curse. The seven vasus, except the main culprit, Prabhasa, would be set free from their curse as soon as they would be born on the earth. However, Prabhasa, the main perpetrator of the crime, will spend his full life on the earth. Being a vasu in his previous birth, he would lead an illustrious life and would be respected and revered by everyone".

Ganga continued, "The vasus came running to me and prayed that I marry a man of dignity and substance on the earth, bear them as my children, one by one, and consign them to the water after their birth. I agreed to their request".Ganga looked at Shantanu and concluded, "Now that I have finished my work on the earth, I am going back to heavens, but shall meet you briefly when I return once again to give back our son to you. Being the eighth vasu, Prabhasa, he has to suffer the vicissitudes of a long human life, along with its pain and sufferings".

Shantanu returned to his palace, deeply saddened. He found it impossible to live without Ganga. Most of the time he sat brooding over the tragedy and his folly in not trusting Ganga and on breaking his pledge. His life was completely transformed from an highly energetic and interesting person to that of a recluse. Even the governance of the kingdom suffered. His only hope lay in waiting for Ganga to give back his son. His favourite pastime was to go to the banks of river Ganga and relive the memories of his wife. With years passing by, he was becoming more and more impatient for Ganga's return.

One day when he had gone for his usual stroll on the banks of the river Ganga, he noticed an extremely handsome and well-built teenaged boy. The boy was practising archery, carrying his own bow and a quiver full of arrows. In fact, he was trying to make a dam of arrows across the river in flood literally treating the river like an indulgent mother. An inner force attracted Shantanu to the boy who reminded him of Indra, the King of gods.

Shantanu, as if drawn by a powerful magnet, started walking towards the boy, when, to his great surprise, he found goddess Ganga emerging out of the river and walking towards the king.

Ganga smiled and said, "Majesty, this is your eighth son, whom I have come to return to you. He has been well brought up and taught the art of war as well as Vedas by the sage Vasishta. I have named him 'Devavrata'.Ganga then turned towards their son,blessed and embraced him, and said, "Go with your father. Make him proud and happy". She then walked and faded away in the river.

Shantanu, overjoyed at finding his son, led him to the palace. Devavrata had all the qualities of an ideal prince. Powerful, proficient and courageous, he lived up to his mother's parting advice to make Shantanu a happy and proud father. Soon, the king consulted his precepts and elders and decided to make him the crown prince. The coronation was performed in the presence of all the important people of his empire and the rulers of neighbouring and far-away kingdoms. Devvrata served his father well. His mother had not only made him a very powerful person, but had also made him mentally tough to be able to face the harshest of the tragedies and challenges of the life with courage, fortitude and wisdom. The king was getting daily reports of his acts of bravery and benevolence.

Once, the crown prince happened to be at the borders of his kingdom when he spotted a neighboring king who was marching stealthily towards Hastinapur along with a large army.Even though alone, he challenged the invading king, fought and defeated him and his army. He made the king a prisoner and brought him to king Shantanu. Naturally, the king was overjoyed at the valour and achievements of Devavrata.

Shantanu was a happy man, a happy father and a happy king. Yet he missed his wife, off and on, knowing that she will never ever come back. This was the only dark spot in his otherwise bright life.

Devavrata too missed his mother but somehow felt assured that she would always be around to love and protect him. Being near to his father was an additional gift.

Chapter-III

SATYAVATI AND DEVAVRATA

Satyavati was raised as a daughter by a chief of fishermen of king Shantanu's kingdom. She was extremely good looking possessing a regal bearing. Her beauty had become the talk of the entire region.

She, in fact, was the daughter of the king Uparichava whose kingdom lay in the south of Hastinapur. By a strange twist of fate, the king's vital seed had fallen on a leaf when he was asleep dreaming of his queen, in a forest while on a hunting trip. The leaf was carried by a hawk over a river where it had to be abandoned due to attacks from another hawk.The leaf fell into the river Yamuna and just as it touched the water, it was swallowed by a mother fish.

The fish swam upstream reaching Shantanu's kingdom. Months later, it was netted by the fishmen's chief. To the latter's surprise, on cutting the fish, he found a baby girl. He accepted her as a gift of the almighty and brought her up as his daughter. Satyawati grew up to be a beautiful maiden wandering in her boats and helping her father in his daily tasks. There was only one flaw in this beautiful girl. She smelled profusely of fish.

One fine day the famous and highly learned rishi Parashara happened to venture near the place where Satyavati was playing with water. The rishi, wonder struck by her beauty, went to her and offered his love. Satyavati agreed and both of them went inside the island where Satyavati happily surrendered. Before leaving, Parashara removed the obnoxious fishy smell from her and made her fragrant, smelling of the choicest flowers.

However, she stayed in the river island till she gave birth to a male child. Parashara took the child away to bring him up in his hermitage while Satyavati returned to her father.The son of Satyavati and Parashara grew up to be a great scholar, a rishi and a famous composer. He was Vyasa, also known as Veda Vyasa on account of his profound knowledge of Vedas.

As the time passed, king Shantanu's memory of Ganga faded away.He, however, still longed for a life companion and a few more children, as was the custom those days. Devavrata was his only child. Loss of lives through sickness or wars was not an uncommon occurrence. There was, therefore a rational explanation to have more than one child to ensure perpetuity of the race.

One day, when Shantanu was having a stroll at the banks of river Yamuna, he saw Satyavati who, in addition to bearing the choicest fragrances, looked ravishingly beautiful. The king immediately decided to make her his queen and went and proposed to her. Satyavati was overjoyed at such an offer. She, however, was cautious and advised the king to go and see her father to get his blessings.

The chief of the fishermen was a shrewd person. He knew about the King, queen Ganga and the crown prince Devavrata. In a polite but firm manner, he laid down the condition that if the king has a son from Satyavati, the new-comer would inherit the throne. To Shantanu, this condition was totally unacceptable. The rightful and most appropriate choice would have to be Devavrata. There was no question of denying him, an otherwise a deserving person, his due. Shantanu declined to make such a commitment. He went back to his palace alone. True, as a king, he could have ordered Satyavati to come with him and agree to the marriage. As the situation developed, he was not inclined to force the issue.

On his return, Shantanu lived like a sad man. He lost interest in the governance and mostly had Satyavati in his thoughts. Devavrata, noticed this change almost immediately. Being a competent administrator himself, he soon found out the reasons for the unhappiness of his father. He immediately ordered his chariot and set about to meet the father of Satyavati.

The chief of the fishermen could perceive the eagerness of Devavrata for alleviating his father's distress. Playing his cards shrewdly, he repeated his condition for agreeing to give the hand of Satyavati for marriage.

Devavrata immediately agreed to his condition stating that he would renounce his claim to the throne for all time to come. Satyavati's father, however, had yet another fear, what if the children of Davavrata press the claim on the throne.

Devavrata smiled. He remembered his mother's parting advice to him to look after his father well and to serve him loyally. Without any hesitation he told the father of Satyavati, "Not only I renounce all my claim on the throne for all time to come, but I also promise never to marry".

Wonder-struck, Satyavati's father handed her over to Devavrata still trying to come to terms with the unexpected windfall he had received. Seeing the steely resolve in the eyes of Devavrata, he was convinced that the latter would keep his word as long as he lived.

Devavrata brought Satyavati to his father in the palace and immediately solemnized the marriage. The King was pleasantly surprised and happy at the turn of events.

However, when Shantanu came to know about the stringent pledges of Devavrata, particularly about his life long celibacy, the euphoria about his marriage disappeared. He called Devavrata and asked him, "Why did you do it for me?".

"Majesty, I want to see you happy and serve you well. This was my mother's parting advice to me also. Neither
I wish to be a king nor to marry. I want to make the Kuru dynasty the strongest in the land of Bharata".

Shantanu did not approve of the pledges but he knew of Devavrata's resolute character and his loyalty to his mother and father. He knew that it would be futile to make Devavrata change or modify his vows. He felt sad at the thought that he was indirectly responsible for wronging Devavrata and abusing Ganga's trust.

He haved a deep sigh, pondered over the matter for a few moments and then spoke to Devavrata, "From this act, you have proved what I already knew. You have a resolute will and absolute loyalty to the Kuru throne. Devavrata, for this supreme sacrifice, you have my blessings and a gift. You will die only when you would yourself will to do so. Otherwise, you shall live as long as you decide to do so. Neither Yamaraja nor anyone else will be able to take your life away from you against your desire".

The news about the pledges of Devavrata gradually spread far and wide earning for him yet more widespread praise and respect. People also gave a new title to him, 'Bhishma', which meant 'extremely stringent'. Gradually, as the years passed and his stature was further elevated, he was affectionately addressed as 'Pitamaha', or 'Bhishma Pitamaha' by the descendents of the Kuru dynasty.

Queen Satyavati bore two sons to king Shantanu, named 'Chitrangada' and 'Vichitravirya'. When the king passed away at a ripe old age, Chitrangada inherited the throne. This rule was, however, a short one as he was killed in a battle. Vichitravirya, a minor, was coronated as the king under the guidance of Bishma. Satyavati consulted Bhishma on every minor as well as major matter. The latter had indeed acquired a rock-solid reputation of a source of wisdom and strength to the Kuru dynasty.

When Vichitravirya became a major, Satyavati started to look for a suitable bride for Vichitravirya. Just then, Bhishma received a rather upsetting news about a swayamvar, a groom selection contest, being organized by the king of Kashi for his three daughters, Amba, Ambika and Ambalika. The king had invited all the eligible kings and princes barring the king of Hastinapur. Apparently, he was nursing an old grudge against the Kuru kingdom.

Bhishma decided to teach the Kashi king a lesson and to fetch all the three princesses as wives for young Vichitra virya. He went to Kashi in a light chariot driven by four swift horses and entered the arena incognito. He was neither wearing any armour nor carried any royal insignia.

They all had assembled in the central area in their full royal regalia. The army of Kashi was up in the front poised to intervene and restore peace amongst the rejected suitors after the swayamvara. Bhishma had positioned himself in the rear area. As the cavalcade carrying the royal household including the three would be brides passed by him, Bhishma gave the required signal to his horses. The chariot was driven at the speed of the wind. Breaking the army cordon from behind Bhishma captured the three brides-to-be, putting them in his chariot. Turning around, he addressed the king and the assemblage of royalty, "Go home and feel happy. Just know that the Kurus do not wish to complete with your lot, nor they pine for an invitation from an unworthy host". Before anyone could move or reach for their armour, the chariot was gone, leaving the Kashi King and his guests in a stunned silence. Bhishma brought the three maidens to Satyavati and asked her to solemnize their marriage to Vichitravirya.

However, when Amba confided to Satyavati saying that she had already accepted King Salva of the Western region as her spouse and he too had done the same, Satyavati understood her predicament. She promptly arranged her journey to the land of Salva so that she could join her beloved king. Ambika and Ambalika were married to Vichitravirya. (Salva did not accept Amba as his wife. Their story is described later).

Years passed but the heir to Kuru throne was not in sight. Vichitravirya, too, was falling sick off and on. He had fallen victim to consumption and his health kept failing gradually. In the end, seven years after his marriage, he died without an issue.

There was a pall of gloom in Hastinapur. Death of the king at a young age was bad enough. What made the things worse was the absence of an heir to the throne. Many considered it as a sign of ill-luck. Satyavati felt extremely sad. On one hand, her father's conditions to ensure the perpetuity of the empire through Satyavati's offsprings debarred an ideal person, Bhishma, from the throne. On the other, both her sons had died without an offspring-one in the war and the other out of sickness.

Satyavati sent for Bhishma, she told him that in the interest of the empire, she was revoking her father's conditions and wanted Bhishma to take up the reins of Hastinapur.

Bhishma heard her, smiled, and said, "Mother, it is impossible. What will the world think of me, if I were to break my pledges for the sake of the throne. I hope you will understand my refusal. I regret, this is the first time in my life that I have to decline to your request".

Bhishma continued, "However, I have a suggestion. You have another son, the island-borne Vyasa. Call him and ask him to father two sons through Ambika and Ambalika. This is a perfectly legitimate solution under such conditions". In those days, a king was entitled to a
lawful heir through five other alternatives apart from a son through his queen/ queens.

Satyavati thanked Bhishma for providing a window of hope. The next problem was to locate Vyasa who was reported to be somewhere deep in the forests doing his tapa (penance). She invoked the power of her mind to call Vyasa and, on his arrival, explained the task to him. Vyasa agreed to do as he was bid by his mother.

He waited in a chamber for the first of the sisters, Ambika. To the horror of the sisters, Vyas' reputation for being an ugly-looking person, quite opposite of his profound knowledge, intelligence and wisdom, had traveled ahead of his meeting the princess. On entering the chamber, Ambika kept her eyes closed as long as she was with him.

Ambalika, too, was extremely apprehensive and scared. She decided to play a deception. Instead of going in herself, she sent one of her maids, whom she dressed up in a beautiful royal attire and sent her in. The maid did not feel any fear and was totally uninhibited. To Ambalika's bad luck, the queen mother discovered her deception. She ordered her to visit Vyasa herself. She had no choice but to go in. However, she was shivering and felt weak throughout.

When Vyasa came to meet his mother, he told her, "The first one, Ambika had kept her eyes closed throughout. Her child will be physically very strong but blind. Ambalika's child would be frail in health. The maid would have a perfectly healthy child and the most intelligent and the wise out of the three. The other two children will also be intelligent possessing a sound mind. Vyasa then took permission of his mother and returned to the forests.

Soon all the three maidens came into the family way. Within a year they gave birth to a son each. Ambika's son was named 'Dhristarashtra'. As foretold he was robustly built but blind. Ambalika's offspring was named 'Pandu'. Though possessing a frail health, he was fit and intelligent. The maid's son was named 'Vidura'. He was healthy, wise and a seeker of knowledge. Vidura was known by all as a great mahatma who was not only a great scholar and practitioner of dharma, shastras and governance, but totally devoid also of anger, attachment and other negative human emotions. In virtue, knowledge and wisdom, he was unparelleled in the three worlds. He was, in fact, the incarnation of Lord Dharma who had been cursed by the great rishi Mandavya to be born as a mortal in the world since the great lord had decreed a disproportionately large punishment to Mandavya for some minor mistakes committed by him in his childhood.

Bhishma kept all the three princes i.e. Dhritarashtra, Pandu and Vidura under his personal care and supervised their training and education as they grew up. Due to the blindness since birth, Dhristrashtra, despite being the eldest, was ruled out to be the king. Pandu thus became the king designate. Similarly, Vidura was being groomed as Chief Counsellor to the king. On reaching adulthood, Pandu and Vidura became the King and Prime Minister of Hastinapur respectively.

Bhishma, thus, ensured that the Kuru line of succession had been maintained while his own assurances and vows had not been compromised. Satyavati, too, was happy that she had not let down king Shantanu in providing him with the heir to the throne. Apart from being grateful to Devavrata for always standing by her side and advising her correctly, she had developed a great regard for him for adherence to dharma and remaining on the correct path despite great personal temptations. Many-a-times she felt sad that her father had demanded such a heavy price from the then prince Devavrata who had a full life ahead of him. But then, what had been done could not be undone. On her part she could only bless Bhishma and wish him well, which she did throughout her life.

Bhishma lived long in Hastinapur and chose the time of his death only at the end of the great battle of Kurukshetra. Revered by all, as the 'Pitamaha', the 'Pater Familias', he lived a glorious life and died at a time of his choosing.

Chapter-IV

AMBA' S PLIGHT AND A TERRIBLE REVENGE

Amba, the eldest princess of Kashi and the eldest amongst the three sisters whom Bhishma had brought from Kashi to be the prospective wives of Vichitravirya, had to go through a terrible ordeal which cast a dark shadow on her future life. Hers was also one of the rare few episodes of the life of Bhishma's otherwise impeccable character and fairest of the fair conduct which he always displayed towards one and all.

After being permitted by Satyavati to go to marry the king of Sanbala, Salva, Amba was sent under escort to him. On arrival there, she described to him what had happened. To her surprise and consternation, he refused to marry her. Since he had challenged Bhishma in Kashi and was defeated by the latter in everybody's sight, he rightly felt that she had since then become a charge of Bhishma and
Salva's marriage with her would add insult to injury. "Go back to Bhishma and do what he desires you to do", he said and added, "I certainly cannot marry you". He accordingly arranged to send her to go back to Bhishma.

Bhishma understood her plight and tried to be as helpful as possible. He explained to Vichitravirya her predicament and advised him to now take her as his wife. However, in those days, marrying a girl who had openly expressed her love for someone else was not an honourable matter. Vichitravirya was persistent in his refusal. In sheer desperation, Amba asked Bhishma himself to marry her. Once again, Bhishma's vows had come in the way of him obliging Amba, much as he sympathized with her and appreciated the force of her arguments. He advised Amba to go to Salva again and make yet another effort. Amba hesitated and vacillated. She knew it would be a futile exercise. Yet, hoping against hope, she went to Salva again. Salva, however, was as adamant as ever. His response was same as before.

Amba's sadness and despondency gradually turned her against Bhishma. Having won her in the Swayamvar, it was his responsibility to find a suitable husband for her, or else marry her himself. Her only wish now was that Bhishma should be punished, nay, killed for the way he had mistreated her.

She went from one prince to another, from one Kshatriya to another and literally from every pillar to the post. None, however, was willing to fight Bhishma despite each one amongst them agreeing that she had been wronged by the elder kuru and deserved to be punished.

Amba, in sheer desperation, went to Parasuram, the great ascetic and soldier, who was a known hater of Kshatriyas. He sympathised with her and expressed willingness to go to Salva and prevail upon him to take Amba as his wife. Amba, however, refused to accept this offer. Having been rejected twice, this would have been a humiliating exercise. She told

Parasurama that all she wanted was Bhishma's death. Parasurama went to Bhishma and castigated him for the wrongs done to an innocent girl and ruining her life. He challenged Bhishma for a mortal combat. What followed was a fierce combat between two greatest warriors of that era. It was a prolonged and almost equal battle, but in the end, even Parasurama had to acknowledge defeat and bow out. He told Amba of his helplessness and advised her to go to Bhishma and seek mercy. This was not acceptable to the princess.

Refused by every human, seething with rage and desperate to get her revenge, she decided to go to Himalayas to seek justice from Lord Shiva. Practising rigorous austerities, she prayed continuously for months till the Lord appeared.
Hearing her wish, he granted her the boon that, in her next birth, she would be the cause of death of Bhishma.

Satisfied with the Lord's benevolence and impatient to be borne again, Amba made a pyre and consigned her body to it. Even hell cannot match the fury of scorned woman.

In her next birth, Amba was born as a daughter to King Drupada. A few years thereafter, she had to be sent into exile in the forests because she had unwillingly worn a garland of never fading lotuses which was hanging on one of the walls of Drupada's palaces. For years it was hanging there without being touched by anyone since it had been ordained that the one who wore that would be the one who would be responsible for the killing of Bhishma. The king had to send her to forests because he did not wish to offend Bhishma and invite serious retribution.

The princess offered serious prayers and very stringent austerites in the forest. In another pre-ordained development, she underwent a sex-change and came to be known as warrior Shikhandin. Born as a girl with the later transformation into male, Shikhandin played a crucial role in the death of Bhishma in the Mahabharata.

Chapter-V

THE WIVES AND CHILDREN OF DHRITARASHTRA AND PANDU

The wives of Dhritarashtra and Pandu were all pious, religious minded, noble and devoted to the husbands. They possessed a sterling character and high moral values. In penances and prayers, they were unequalled.

Dhritarashtra was married to the princess of Gandhara and appropriately called Gandhari. Exhibiting a high moral sense, she blind-folded herself for life since Dhritarshtra, her husband, was blind by birth. She never took the band off her eyes except for one occasion in her entire life. This was when she wanted to bestow upon her eldest and most favourite son, Duryodhana, her yogic strength which required to be transmitted from her eyes.

Gandhari was blessed with hundred sons, with the eldest two being named Duryodhana and Dushasana respectively. In addition, whe was blessed with one daughter who was named Dushala. Dushala was married to the king of Sindhu, Jaidratha who played a prominent role in the culminating events of the war of Mahabharata. Dhritarashtra had another son, Yuyutsu through his personal maid who looked after him with extra care during the confinement of Gandhari.

In the tradition of yore, a king had to have more than one wife to ensure the progeny. For king Pandu, Bhishma had ensured that he (Pandu) had two wives, Kunti and Madri. Kunti, originally named Pritha, was the daughter of King Shoorsen, a Yadava chieftain of high repute and the grandfather of Krishna. She was extremely goodlooking as well as virtuous Since a close cousin of the king, Kuntibhoj, was childless, Shoorsen had consented Pritha to be adopted by him as his daughter. Pritha's name was thereafter changed to Kunti after her adopted father, Kuntibhoja. Coincidently, Kunti was also reputed to be having beautiful hair and the word 'Kuntal' meaning 'Goldilocks', further justified her name.

When Kunti was young, the famous sage Durvasa visited Kuntibhoj and decided to stay with him for a while. Kunti served the revered sage with so much of devotion, dedication and diligence that Durvasa extended his stay to nearly an year. He was one of the few who knew not only the present and the past, but the future as well. He was aware of the fate which was to befall Kunti after her marriage.

Before his departure, the learned sage called Kunti and gave her a 'Mantra'. He explained that by reciting the mantra and remembering any god, she could recall him to her and have a child from him.

Kunti was neither married at that time nor was desirous of bearing a child. Yet, possession of the knowledge of a powerful mantra made her curious and impatient to try it out just to confirm if it worked. Despite Durvasa's reputation as one of the greatest rishis, she was quite skeptical of the power of the mantra itself.

As days passed, she became more and more impatient, till one night, she decided to try out the mantra at midnight. As she chanted the mantra and willed the sun god to come, she was amazed to find the bright shining god right in front of her with a brilliantly lit aura of light around him.

Kunti panicked, 'Good lord, what have I done', she thought,. The thoughts of somehow extricating herself from that situation were racing in her mind.

The sun-god smiled at her and said, 'You do not have to worry or fear, but, bound by the mantra, I cannot return without giving you a son. However, unlike the normal humans, your period of pregnancy will be just one day. Also, after the child, your virginity will be restored soon'.

Next night, the son of the sun-god was born to her. To her amazement, he was wearing divine armour on his chest and earrings on both the ears. Much as Kunti loved the infant with the true motherly affection the situation demanded that she get rid of him quickly. Therefore, with a heavy heart, she put him in a basket wherein she had made his bed, went to the river, and consigned the basket to the waves of the flowing river.

The basket containing the child was noticed by a childless charioteer. He brought it to the shore and finding the child occupant, took him to his wife, Radha, who had been longing for a child for a long time. She was happy to get a son whom she reared with all the love and motherly affection.

The boy grew up to become one of the mightiest warriors of his day. Named as, 'Karna', he was also known as 'Radheya', i.e. the son of Radha. The other singular attribute of Karna was that if someone came to ask him for something, whatever it was, he never said 'No. He, therefore, was also referred as 'Dana-Vira Karna' or 'A knight amongst philanthropic donors – Karna'.

Pandu's second wife Madri was the princess of Madra and the sister of the then king. Pandu had a happy married life and guided by Bhishma and advised by Vidura, reigned over the kingdom well.

One day when Pandu had gone on a hunting trip to the forest, he shot at a male deer and grieviously injured it. The deer, in fact was a sage in disguise who had taken his wife also to the forest and was romancing with her. Pandu rushed to him on hearing a human cry. The injured sage was dying and before his death, he cursed the king and said, 'Sinner, you will also meet the death the moment you shall go to bed with your wife. 'Before Pandu could offer any clarification and remove the misunderstanding, the sage breathed his last.

Pandu was aghast at the curse of the dying sage. On return to the palace, he decided to retire to the forest with his wives for a long period. He entrusted the kingdom of Hastinapur to Bhishma and Vidura and himself lived a life of total abstinence in the woods. Many a times he worried and felt sad at the fact that he would not be able to provide a heir to the kingdom on account of the fear of the curse of the sage taking effect.

Kunti, knowing the agony of the king, confided to him regarding the son-giving mantra of the sage Durvasa. Pandu immediately suggested that Kunti should chant the mantra for Madri also. Both she and Madri should try for the offsprings of divine bodies. Thus, on invocation of the mantra, Kunti obtained sons through Dharma deva, Vayu deva and Indra deva whereas Madri invoked the twin Aswins for two sons.

The five were named Yudhishthira, Bhima, Arjuna, Nakula and Sahadeva respectively. Yudhishthira was the eldest amongst the offsprings of Dhritarashtra and Pandu while Duryodhana and Bhima were both born on the same day. The children of Dhritarashtra and Pandu were also referred as 'Kauravas' and 'Pandavas'.

The five Pandavas grew under the watchful eyes of Pandu and their mothers. They were also given adequate training by the ascetics on all the subjects considered essential for the princes.Pandu led a happy and contended life keeping in touch with the affairs of the state while remaining in his forest abode. Years passed quickly unnoticed till one day when the destiny dealt a cruel blow to the family and their happiness. Pandu was with Madri enjoying an exceptional weather under idyllic surroundings. Influenced by the salubrious weather in the forest, Pandu felt a great sexual desire towards the younger queen. Madri reminded Pandu of the curse of the sage pronounced many a years ago but Pandu's pent-up desires overcame him and he could not resist himself. Alas, as he was in the midst of his love making, the curse took effect and Pandu died immediately.

Pandu was cremated in Hastinapur, after his body was brought by the sages. The funeral was attended by Dhritarashtra, Vidura and all important people of the state. Madri was extremely sad blaming herself. She burnt herself on Pandu's funeral pyre after making Kunti agree to stay back and look after all the young ones including Nakul and Sahdev, who would become twice orphaned after the demise of Pandu and Madri.

The news about the death of Pandu plunged the kingdom of Hastinapur into gloom. Although Yudhishthira, being the eldest son of the departed king, had the right to succeed, but considering his young age, Bhishma decided that Dhritarashtra would act as a king temporarily till Yudhishthira came of age. Kunti continued to stay in the forest with children for

completion of their education. After some time, Kunti came back from the forest with her flock. The hundred and one Kauravas (including Yuyutsu) and five Pandavas made a merry bunch of youngsters playing,
fighting and frolicking together. Bhishma ensured that their training proceeded without any hinderance.

The signs of a future strife between Kauravas and Pandavas were dormant but could easily be forecast in their complexes and attitudes. Despite being the eldest, Dhritarashtra was not made the king on account of his being blind by the birth. The Kaurava youngsters were aggressive and at times mean while the Pandavas were much more balanced and fair. Dhritarashtra was a weak person and his excessive attachment to Duryodhana, his eldest son, resulted in him (Dhritarashtra) not checking Duryodhana at the very outset from planning and executing schemes to harm the Pandavas. This encouraged Duryodhana more and more.

Dhritarashtra also secretly desired and helped Duryodhana work towards the goal of becoming a Yuvaraj and have more and more control over the affairs of the state. The combination of a weak king, a doting father and an indulgent and ambitious son resulted in the Pandavas being treated unfairly and at times almost falling prey to a extreme evil designs of Kaurava princes which had the potential of being fatal or which would have resulted in excessive shame. As always happens, in such situations, other evil minded people also emerge to help and hatch the evil plans. One such was Duryodhana's maternal uncle Shakuni, who was a past master at intrigues and wrongdoings. He was the friend, guide and the philosopher for Duryodhana and his constant companion in bringing to fruition the schemes designed to harm Pandavas, at times even grieviously. Gandhari's brother would play a prime role in almost all the events leading to climactic war of Mahabharata.

Chapter-VI

THE TWO GREAT TEACHERS KRIPACHARYA AND DRONACHARYA

Under the general supervision of Bhishma, the Kuru children Kauravas and Pandavas) had the benefit of teaching by the two great teachers of those times, Kripacharya and Dronacharya. Both of them had a different career path.

Kripacharya had a steady rise to his exalted career. A very learned person, he took a considerable interest in all his pupils. He did not have any favourites and on balance, concentrated more in the vedic and other education and comparatively less on the weapons training.

Drona was a brilliant scholar right from the beginning. Amongst his illustrious colleagues at the gurukul, run by the sage Agnivesh and his good friend was one prince Drupada. Knowing that Drona was poor and short of means, Drupada always made promises to Drona that once he became the king, he would look after Drona if he ever came to him for help.

However, neither Drona's finances improved nor his determination not to seek undue favours from his erstwhile colleagues. He married Kripi, sister of Kripacharya and was blessed with a son who was named Ashwasthama. Drona was very attached to his son and felt really sad that he could not provide even the ordinary things for his son which his other friends had. Driven to despair, he decided to shed his self pride and go to see Drupada, who had become the king, and seek his help. He took his wife and son with him and was confident of Drupada's assistance particularly in the background of his promises when they were Gurukul mates.

Drona, was, however in for a huge shock. Drupada not only refused to recognize Drona totally but he also made fun of his requests to a King. Drona felt utterly humiliated since it all happened in front of all the courtiers of Drupada as well as his wife Kripi and son Ashwasthama. He left the palace seething with anger and made promise to himself to take an appropriate revenge from Drupada if he ever had an opportunity in future.

Drona's lot remained the same for a long time, an unjust reward for a brilliant man who deserved a far better life. It is truly said that a man can fight and overcome everything excepting the dictates of the providence.

However, the wheel of the misfortime turned full circle and the lady luck decided to smile on Drona.

It started with a simple incident. Drona was passing by a place where the Kuru children were gathered around a well with exasperation writ on their faces as the ball they were playing with had fallen in the well and all their efforts to retrieve the same were of no avail. In fact, Yudhishtira, the eldest amongst them, had also lost his ring which had slipped out of his finger and had fallen in the well in the process of the retrieval of the ball.

Drona told the children that he would help them in getting their ball. Using some weeds which were growing nearby, he made arrows which he shot at the ball and the rear end of each arrow. The boys were amazed to notice his accuracy and concentration as he shot the arrows chanting mantras. Soon a chain of arrows had reached the top and the ball was pulled out of the well to the joy of all. Drona used the same technique and mantras to retrieve the ring of Yudhishtira, which was lying at the bottom of the well.

Thoroughly impressed by the prowess of Drona, Yudhishtira requested Drona to come with him to his grand father, Bhishma. He described the whole incident to the Pitamaha (the grand father). As Bhishma talked to Drona, he became more and more impressed with him. He asked Drona to join Kripacharya in teaching the children and particularly concentrate on weapons training and the art of war. Drona, since then, had become 'Dronacharya' and progressed steadily to occupy the highest echelon of power in the Kuru Kingdom.

Chapter-VII

THE GOOD AND 'NOT SO GOOD' ACTS OF DRONACHARYA

The Guru Dronacharya was undoubtably the best teacher in Shastras as well as in martial sciences of his times. Years ago, when he was going through lean times, on hearing that Rishi Parashuram was distributing his riches, he had rushed to the great rishi's ashram. To his bad luck he found he was too late. The learned rishi Paashuram however, recognized the hidden talent and potential of Drona. He accordingly invited him to stay back at the Ashram so that he could be taught the martial sciences, the most effective use of weapons and tactics and strategies of war. On completion of this training under such a renowned person as Parashuram, he had indeed become one of the best teachers aptly suited for training the princes.

Amongst his Kuru disciples, Bhima and Duryodhana were very good in fighting with maces (gada). Bhima, in any case, was physically the strongest amongst them. However, in archery and general art of war, he rated Arjun as the best and gradually, Arjuna became his most favourite pupil. As it stood, Arjuna had already won the affections of Bhishma.

One day, Dronacharya decided to test the archery prowess of all the princes. He got a wooden bird made and placed it firmly on top of one of the branches of a tree. He then told all the princes that the bird was their
target and each one would have to answer some of his questions.

Yudhishthira was the first to come up for the test. Drona directed him to aim at the target and then asked him as to what did he see.

"A tree, its branches and the bird sitting on one branch", Yudhishtira responded, "

Drona, a shade disappointed, asked him to send the next student. The answeres of almost all his pupils, except Arjuna, were similar to that of Yudhishthira.

When the royal teacher asked Arjuna to aim and then asked him as to what was he seeing, Arjun said, "Only and only the eye of the bird". He then shot the arrow which hit the bird right in the eye.

Dronacharya was very impressed with the concentration shown by Arjuna. On that day, Arjuna occupied in the mind of Dronacharya as the best marksman amongst the princes. He also reconfirmed his position as his most favourite pupil.

Eklavya

Eklavya was a tribal boy who was a very keen archer and wanted to become the best amongst his contemporaries. He had heard of Dronacharya and, hearing of his reputation wished to learn archery under him. He accordingly traveled to Hastinapur, sought an audience with the famous teacher and explained his desire. Perceiving the keenness of Eklavya, Dronacharya wished to help the boy but this would have been a contravention of his known duties as the royal teacher where he could only teach the Kuru princes. Although he felt bad, yet he had to refuse the request of Eklavya.

Eklavya too understood the reasons behind the refusal of Dronacharya. He had, however, become so focussed on having Dronacharya as his guru that he picked up some earth from the place where Drona was standing and talking to him. Taking this earth, he went to an appropriate place in the forests where he wished to practice archery, made a statue of Dronacharya and installed it on a pedestral.

He did all his practice under the virtual guidance of Dronacharya. What was most surprising was that Eklavya improved in his prowess by leaps and bounds.

Then one day, a strange incident happened which changed the life of Eklavya. While he was practicing, a dog came and started barking at him. Eklavya tried to drive him away but the dog kept coming back at him barking ferociously. Eventually, Eklavya lost his patience. He aimed seven arrows at him and shot them at the dog's mouth from his bow. The arrows found their target and in a few moments, the dog's mouth was effectively sealed with seven stitches neatly woven on it. The dog ran away whimpering to the direction it had come from.

The dog had belonged to some of the Kuru children who had accompanied Dronacharya to the forest. When it came back with mouth effectively sealed through the mouth, they all were wonder struck at the neatness and precision of the act done. Dronacharya also wanted to meet the great archer. Separating himself from his pupils, he followed the paw marks of the dog and reached the place where Eklavya was still practicing archery. Dronacharya immediately recognized Eklavya. When the latter touched his feet and made obeisance to him, Dronacharya asked him as to who his guru was.

"You Sir," Eklavya replied. Then, pointing towards Dronacharya's statue, Eklavya explained his improvised arrangement. Dronacharya felt happy as well as sad.

Happy because he had found a disciple who possessed such an outstanding skill. He, however, became aware that Eklavya had the potential to become a formidable threat to Arjuna for whom the great teacher wanted the position of being the best archer in the world. He eventually made a decision after a considerable self-debate.

"Eklavya," he asked, "Are you aware that as your guru, I am entitled to a Guru-Dakshina?"

"Yes," Eklavya replied and added, "whatever you ask from me will be done or given by me".

Then give me your one thumb", demanded the Acharya. Eklavya, without batting even an eyelid, cut off his right thumb and presented the same to Drona. He knew that by doing so, he was sacrificing his entire career as an archer putting effectively an end to all his dreams and aspirations.

Till date, Eklavya remains an outstanding example of a disciple in the guru-shishya relationship. However, the demand of Dronacharya, only to promote his favourite pupil, is considered as blatantly biased and unfair by one and all.

Drupada

Dronacharya was enjoying himself. He was being paid a good salary and enjoyed a high status. He was also given a high degree of respect by all his pupils. He had forgotten the days of past when he lived under abject proverty. He also enjoyed a good health and pleasures of a devoted family consisting of his wife, Kripi and the son, Ashwasthama.

However, if there was one thing which kept on troubling him and always gnawing at his heart was the humiliation meted out to him and his family by his old friend, Drupada, son of Prishaka and the king of Panchala (Chhatravati). Dronacharya would continuously think of the insults almost every day. He had decided that when his disciples became well versed in weaponry, he would seek his revenge from Drupada.

One fine day, when Drona was convinced of the fact that his pupils had become masters of the weapons, he called the Pandavas. Drona said, "I have waited for this day for a long time. Now that you all have attained the highest level of competence in use of all weapons, I would like to demand from you my preceptional fee, i.e. the guru-dakshina".

The Pandavas spoke in unison, "Yes, of course. Anything you ask will be delivered to you or done for you".

Drona replied, "I want you to take away from Drupada his kingdom and deliver it to me".

The Pandavas set off immediately to fulfil their guru's wish. They defeated Drupada in a battle, took him and his ministers as their prisoners and brought all of them to Dronacharya.

For the Guru, this was the supreme moment of satisfaction. His pupils had carried out his instructions and had brought a prisoner, the man who had deeply humiliated him and since than, tormented him even in his dreams. However, Dronacharya did not wish to prolong the conflict. He said that he wanted Drupda as the king of half of his kingdom with the other half to be under Drona's rule. The region south of

Bhagirathi was to belong to former while that on the north would be Drona's. That way, Drona said, they both will be rulers of equal stretches of land.Drupada showed no signs of dissent and maintained a respectful attitude towards all. However, inside himself, he was seething with rage. He made a promise to himself. 'Drona will pay for this some day'. The shock, however, was much too much for him. After all, each of his subjects knew what had befallen him. Gradually it affected his health. What compounded his problems that he did not have a son bright and competent enough who could challenge the might of Dronacharya.

In quest of a competent Brahmana, superior and well skilled in yagyas (sacrificial rites) so that his objective for having a son who could do what his heart desired, i.e. revenging himself on Drona, Drupada travelled far and wide amongst many ashrams of Brahmanas. His efforts bore fruit when he chanced upon an ashram and found two Brahmana sages, Yaja and Upajaya. After some persuasion, Yaja agreed to perform a yagya for Drupada which would give him a child with desired qualities, one who would be invincible in war and who can overcome Drona. Upajaya promised to help Yaja in this task. The great childgiving Yagya was performed by the two sages. When the ceremony was over, Yaja requested the queen to come forward and accept the oblations informing that son and a daughter had arrived for her. Since she was not ready at that moment to accept the oblation, the two sages decided to pour the sanctioned butter on the fire instead for the desired result.

The whole assembly was spellbound to see a son emerge from the fire followed by a daughter. While the boy looked radiant and divine, the girl looked equally stunning. Everyone shouted with joy. The brahamanas named the boy as 'Dhrishtadyumna' on account of his defiant looks. The girl of perfect features with a radiant dark skin was named as 'Krishna'.

Dhrishtadyumna grew up to be a strong man and fighter. Drona sent for him when the time came and taught him all the weapons. In the great war of Mahabharata, he was the cause for destruction of Drona. Krishna, also known as Panchali as well as Draupadi, was the prime reason behind the tensions leading fo the war of Mahabharata in which many fighters had been destroyed. This also included all the Kauravas.

Chapter-VIII

KURU CHILDREN FROM CHILDHOOD TO MEN

After the death of Pandu and Madri, the sages brought Kunti and five children, including Nakula and Sahadeva, whose charge was given to Kunti by Madri before her death, and entrusted their responsibility to Bhishma. The last rites of Pandu were performed by Bhishma, Vyasa, Dhritarashtra and Vidura. Yudhistira was barely sixteen. Bhishma asked Dhritarashtra to act as the king with Vidura as his adviser till Yudhishtira came of age.

At this juncture, Vyasa came to Satyavati and said, "So far, you have seen mostly good things and enjoyed the company of the Kuru offsprings. That phase is likely to end soon and a prolonged period of sadness and miseries is likely to set in. It would be therefore advisable for the senior ladies to leave for the forest and offer penance in some hermitage in their last few years".

Satyavati understood and agreed with her illustrious son. She soon left Hastinapur accompanied by Ambika and Ambalika. In the forests, they settled down to the routine of an Ashrama, offering prayers and penances. Passing through the holy stages of ascetism they attained supreme bliss and moksha, unaware of what befell their off-springs.

Despite participating in sports, learning martial arts and wielding of weapons as well as playing of pranks together, it was evident that two groups were gradually emerging amongst the Kuru children; one led by Duryodhana and consisting of Kauravas and the other by Yudhishtira consprising of Pandavas. While Kauravas were unscrupulous and believed in the end justifying the means, Pandavas steadfastly adhered to the moral values and ethical conduct.

Duryodhana had been unhappy ever since he grew up enough to understand the interactions in the family. He deeply resented the fact that Pandu had been made the king, even though Dhritarashtra was elder to Pandu. (The honour to become the king was denied to Dhritarashtra because he was blind from birth).

Even after the younger brother Pandu had died and the charge of the kingdom was entrusted to Dhritarashtra, every one knew that this was temporary and once Yudhishtira came of age, he would be given the royal throne. Duryodhana deeply resented this fact and always thought of getting some thing done to ensure that the royal crown was retained with Dhritarshtra and he, Duryodhana himself would be pronounced as the heir-apparent – the Yuvaraj in due course.

From the early days, the Kaurava brothers had a unanimous dislike for Bhima. So powerful was he that he would regularly subject the Kauravas to physical manhandling which at times bordered on cruelty. Taking a couple of them under his armpits, Bhima would dive in the swirling waters of the river and stay under water till the brothers almost choked. Very early in their teens, Duryodhana hatched a plan to usurp the throne himself. He conspired with some of his senior brothers to poison and kill Bhima in an outing, arrest Yudhishtira and Arjuna and declare himself as the king.

An opportunity soon presented itself to Duryodhana. The Kauravas and Pandavas had gone for a picnic on the river side. The brothers played different sports in which Bhima was the most active participant. When they had
their meal after sports, he obviously ate the most. What he did not know that his meal was heavily drugged and poisoned by the Kauravas. Duryodhana had also arranged for planting of spikes in the river where he intended to throw Bhima's body after the drugs started to take effect. While everyone resumed playing after the meals, Bhima fell into deep slumber. Once he was alone, Duryodhana tied his body with the seaweeds and threw it in the river where he had planted the spikes. He then joined the brothers and played till they decided to call it a day and return. On the way, Yudhishthira did enquire about Bhima's whereabouts. He was told by the Kauravas that he had left early.

Fortunately for Bhima, the rushing waters of the river took him away from the place where spikes were planted. Another stroke of good luck was in form of rattle snakes biting Bhima whereupon the snake poison acted as an antidote to the poison already in his body. In a few hours, Bhima had woken up, broke his shakles and swam to the river bank. Shaking off his drowsiness, he too gradually trudged back to be with his mother and brothers, who were getting worried about his absence.

He recounted his story to them and it was evident that there indeed was a sinister attempt to poison and drown him. Kunti was worried and finding Vidura alone, shared her concern with him. Vidura agreed that a threat was emerging and advised her to be careful. He, however, assured her that there was no need to be unduly worried because all Pandavas had been destined to enjoy a long life. He also advised her against discussing the incident with others lest it should put the Kauravas on the guard and deepen the divide. Yudhishtira too had independently concluded that this was a sinister and deliberate attempt to kill Bhima. He told the brothers to be careful in future while simultaneously advising them not to discuss the incident with others. The Kauravas were obviously elated at the successful implementation of the first phase of their plan. There was a considerable rejoicing and feasting in the night after their return from the outing. They were, however, in for a rude shock when on the next day, they found business as usual in the Pandava circles. There was an utter confusion and disbelief when a little while later, they also found Bhima there along with his brothers.

Chapter-IX

KARNA – THE BROTHER WHO WAS'NT

While Kauravas and Pandavas played, frolicked and studied together, the eldest son of Kunti, Karna, had to fend for himself along with his foster parents, Adhirath – the charioteer and Radha, the wife of the latter. He grew up alone to become a tall, well-built lad. From the early childhood, it was quite clear that he was an extraordinary person. As it is, he was born with the earrings and chest-armour. Having been fathered by the sun – god his features too were god like with a face shining with brilliance. The beauty of his biological mother added to his looks.

Karna had an intense desire to be the best in wielding of weapons. He desperately wanted a competent Guru so that he could further improve and become more proficient and perfect. He went to Parashurama to learn from him the art of war. He did not tell the learned Brahmin that he (Karan) was the son of a charioteer, afraid that he would not be accepted as a pupil. He therefore told a lie that he was a Brahmin, Parashuram liked teaching him because he was an extra-ordinary learner who soon became highly proficient in use of all arms. Karna, indeed, had become a highly competent person, powerful, intelligent and one who was well versed in use of all kinds of weapons. Parashurama even taught him the mantra to invoke the Brahmastra, so happy was he with his favourite pupil.

One afternoon, however, it all changed. While Parashurama was having an afternoon nap, with his head in the lap of Karna under a tree, a scorpion fell on the thigh of latter and started biting him, burroughing under his flesh. Karna did not even flinch since he was afraid that movement would disturb the sleep of his guru.

When Parashurama got up from the sleep he was struck with the sight of the scorpion eating into Karna's flesh and blood oozing out of the wound. He instantaneously realized that Karna was not a Brahmin for a Brahmin could not bear so much of pain without flinching or crying. He asked Karna for the truth.

Karna admitted his subterfuge explaining the reason. Parashuram was not happy to hear of Karna's misdemeanour. He not only terminated Karna's training (which, in any case, was almost at the verge of finishing) but also pronounced a curse on Karna, stating that he would forget the mantra for invoking the Brahmastra at the time of its most critical need for him.

Karna learn't, on his own, the art of weaponry further. Through his sheer dedication and determination he progressed by the leaps and bounds, so much so that when he learn't that a public contest was being organized by Dronacharya and Kripacharya to show the mastery of the arts of weaponry by the Kuru princes on completion of their arms training, he too decided to go and if possible, participate.

Such events like a high profile weapon contest did not happen frequently and the people of Hastinapur were all agog with happiness and curiosity looking forward to witness the same. After all, this would be the first time they would see the Kuru princes show their skills on completion of their training by the two renowned Acharyas.

The royal games centre at Hastinapur, the venue of the contest and display, started to fill from early in the morning. In a special enclosure mean't for VVIPs, sat the Pitamaha, Dhritarashtra, Vidura, the queens and the other prominent ministers, chieftains and dignitaries.

Another block was earmarked for prominent and distinguished people. The rest of the stadium was filled with the general public. With the signal from Dhritarashtra, the contest and display commenced. Dronacharya asked his favourite pupil, Arjuna to step forward to show his skill of archery and then the shooting power.

Arjuna gave a brilliant display of the archery which left people with open mouth and breathless. There were many rounds of applauses from the gentry and the common public at each of his displays. . In the show of fierce shooting power and the fierce weaponry, Arjuna was simply superb. He shot one arrow on the ground which resulted in flames and fires. Some spectators sitting nearby prepared to run away, fearful of the fire reaching them. In the next moment, Arjuna shot an arrow sky-wards which brought the rain instantaneously over the flames and the scene of fire to douse the same. At the end, he got a standing ovation from everyone except Duryodhana whose eyes were full of envy. People admitted that they had witnessed the finest display of their life.

Arjuna's one-man show was followed by a mace – duel between Duryodhana and Bhima. Both were very strong but the latter was shade better and in every contest, it was he who was always the victor. Duryodhana on the other hand was scheming and employed even the very base acts of treachery – something which was not to Bhima's liking and certainly not in his own repertoire of mace – wielding skills.

The combat was fast-moving and fierce. Gradually it turned into what appeared to be a fight to kill and win. Fortunately, Ashwasthama jumped into the arena and made the two adversaries separate. Dronacharya announced the end of the combat.

Displays by other princes followed. The public was enjoying every moment of it. However, it was Arjuna's display which was foremost in their minds.

As the display was coming to a close, suddenly there was a flurry of movement at the entrance followed by a loud noise of slapping of arms on the body by a superbly looking warrior fully clad with a wild range of weaponry. His face flowed emanating brilliant light and the whole body exuded energy. As he walked to the main enclosure, all eyes were riveted upon him.

The young man stopped in front of Dronacharya, paid obeisance and said, "I seek your permission to replicate the display of Arjuna". Both the Acharyas nodded to him to go ahead.

What followed was a brilliant and dazzling display of shooting of arrows and weaponry with a casual and lazy brilliance. The audience was enjoying every moment of it. The display was as superb, if not better, than given by Arjuna early in the day.

A profound feeling of exultation ran through Duryodhana who realized that at last he had found a match for Arjuna, who was, till then, matchless. He advanced and embraced Karna with a big bear hug. Looking straight into his eyes Duryodhana said, "Excellent. The kingdom of Kurus is grateful to you for having given to us such a dazzling display. We welcome you and offer you whatever we have".

Karna responded, "I am indebted to you, oh king, and have only two wishes. Your love and affection and a one-to-one combat with Partha (Arjuna)"

Arjuna, the proud pandava, looked contemptuously towards Karna, rose to get ready for the combat. A hush came over the entire audience. At the very first sight, Kunti recognized her eldest son and felt highly elated at his superb performance. But, when Karna announced his challenge to Arjuna, fearing a disastrous outcome of a duel between two blood-brothers irrespective of the fact who won, Kunti fainted. Vidura asked one of her helps to look after her. She recovered a little while later but sat in her seat totally benumbed, praying for a divine intervention.

The crowd was inching towards the edges of their seats. In the sky, the presence of the two divine parents was evident with high wind and clouds at one end signifying the authority of Indra the lord of thunder clouds. At the other end, a blue sky with dazzling sun indicated the presence of Surya, the lord of innumerable rays. Arjuna went to Dronacharya to obtain his permission and then to his brothers, embracing and obtaining their best wishes, one-by-one He was ready, standing straight with a calm dignity. Karna, turning from the Kaurava brothers, strode towards Arjuna, facing him. Just when the contest was scheduled to commence, Kripacharya, the wise one who was conversant with all rules of combat, stepped in front and said, "Just a moment. The single combats are only allowed between two combatants of equal status. Partha here is the son of scion of Kuru vansh, Pandu and Pritha, who is the daughter of Sura, one of the best of yadava race. You are, however, an unknown stranger to us. Do reveal your parentage and race to enable us to allow your combat with Partha. You may not know but we cannot allow Partha to compete against unknown adventurers".

Everyone could see that Karna was feeling very uncomfortable to respond to Kripacharya's questions. Instantly, Duryodhana, who was known for quick decisions, perceiving the discomfiture of Karna and its likely reason, stepped forward and said to Karna, "What you have shown are the finest attributes of a fighter, expected from a royal scion. If there is a deficiency, it can easily be cured. I pronounce you as the king of Anga, I hope this will satisfy the learned Guru". Duryodhana then went to Dhritarashtra and Bhishma and obtained their consent. In a brief ceremony, Karna was officially pronounced as the king of Anga. He turned to Duryodhana and said, 'I am grateful to you for this fine gesture and shall always indebted to you". He then disengaged himself from the crowd and walked towards Arjuna".

It however appeared that the challenge would not fructify that day. When everything was all set and ready, Karna's foster-father, Adhiratha, a charioteer entered the area with a staff in hand and looking with a great deal of apprehension.

Karna, true to his sanskars, walked to the old man and paid a full obeisance to him befitting for a father. The old man embraced Karna, calling him his son with tears flowing out of his eyes. After all, Adhirath realized that Karna had achieved what he had always aimed for i.e. practice archery and mastry of weapons and be counted as a prince or a king.

Bhima clapped his hands and true to his brash nature, called out, "So you are the son of a charioteer? Why don't you take up your father's profession and be a charioteer, rather than fight Arjuna and lose your life. Also, give up your title as the king of Anga as a bad dream. Just remember your birth and lineage".

Karna looked down, sad and dejected. He also looked at the setting sun and sighed – Not enough time was left for the contest to be held. Duryodhana too was upset on hearing Bhima's harsh words. He exclaimed, "This is not fair, Oh Vrikodhara (Another name of Bhima), you have seen from your own eyes the competence, control and precision with which this person has wielded all his weapons. His body, face, demeanour and artistry of handling of weapons surely indicates that he is the very best, not only in this region but in the world". He then called his chariot and taking Karna with him drove away. Inwardly, he was extremely pleased with the day's preceedings. After all, he had with him, a prize catch who would be a veritable asset in any situation.

The crowd melted away, discussing the events of the day and inevitably comparing Arjuna with Karna. Some favoured Arjuna while others favoured the challenger Karna.

Kunti was relieved that the blood bath was avoided. Either way she would have been the loser. Happy as she was to discover that Karna was alive and well, she was also apprehensive of the fact of Karna joining Kauravas.

The lord of lords, Indra, was also a shade worried. He had seen the prowess and mastery of Karna. Knowing that Karna never refused whatever was asked from him (Karna was also referred as 'Danavira') he went to him a few days later, dressed as a Brahmin and asked for the alms. When Karna agreed to give him whatever was asked, the Brahmin asked for his earrings and chest guards, the armour, the two things which were a gift of his father and his chief protect. In fact, Bhaskara (The sun god) had earlier warned him that some day Indra would want to take them away on some pretext or other. However, since he had already given his word to the Brahmin, whoever he might be, he allowed him to take the two items from his body.Indra, deeply impressed and feeling a bit guilty, revealed himself and asked Karna if he wanted something in return.

Aware that he had been tricked as his father had predicted, Karna decided to make amends. He asked Indra to give him his most powerful weapon which would kill anyone at whom it was directed.

Indra readily gave him the 'Shakti' but with the condition that he could use it only once. "Once you have used it on someone, it will no longer be available to you, but will return to me", Indra explained.

Karna remained totally loyal to Duryodhana till the end of his life. He supported Duryodhana in all his good or bad acts. His valour was immense and known to everyone. In Mahabharata war, he took command of the Kaurava Army after Bhishma and Dronacharya. In the end he lost his life due to two prime reasons – Non availability of Indra's 'shakti' when he needed it most as he was made to use it on some one other than Arjuna – his eventual target. The second factor was the curse of Parashurama, which made him forget the use of 'Brahmastra' when he was in dire need to use the same. He remembered it till the last moment but his mind went blank when his life was in mortal danger from Arjuna.

Chapter-X

THE DEEPENING DIVIDE

With every passing day, the people of Hastinapur were asking questions which begged answers but were not coming from Dhritarashtra or Duryodhana. The people had seen the Pandava princes in the recent contest. They were all now grown-up adults and had acquired the reputation of being extremely fair and devoted to the 'Dharma' The consensus was developing on Yudhishthira being crowned as a king to replace Dhritarashtra, who was brought in as a caretaker king at the time of Pandu's death. For the ambitious Duryodhana, this would be unacceptable, so used he had become in running the Kingdom on behalf of his blind and doting father. Duryodhana was additionally getting concerned with the increasing physical strength of Bhima and dexterity of Arjuna. Duryodhana's closest advisers, the maternal uncle Sakuni and Karna, were constantly urging him to do something fast before the situation went out of control.

They devised a scheme to get rid of all the pandavas at one stroke while making the deaths appear to have happened due to an accident with no links to kauravas. They decided to persuade the Pandavas to shift to a place called Vernavrata, which was not only famous for its scenic beauty, but also for an yearly Siva festival for which people came from all parts of the state. One of the closest aides of Duryodhana, a minister named Purochana, was entrusted with the task of proceeding immediately to Vernavrata and getting a palace, befitting of an abode for royalty, constructed. Purochana was secretly directed to ensure that the palace was built with inflammable material like lac and wax so that when it was set on fire at a later stage, all the accupants and most of their belongings would be burnt and destroyed. Idea was to get the Pandavas settled there and then send the instructions to Purochana on the exact time and date when the palace was to be set on fire.

The trio and their closest aids also set upon a plan to influence indirectly the pandavas to go and stay at Vernavrata to enjoy the beautiful place and be part of the religious fair. Additionally, Dhritarashtra had to be discreetly advised on the merit of getting the Pandavas away from the capital.

Dhritarashtra had always been on the horns of dillema. His wisdom suggested that Yudhishtira must be given his due and the kingdom's rule be entrusted upon him. However, having got used to the comforts and authority of a king and his most beloved son running the kingdom with the virtual authority of a Yuvaraja, his heart also desperately searched for a solution that will maintain or formalize the status-guo.

And so, Duryodhana, after carefully rehearsing his impending discussions with his father, went to him and laid bare his heart. He came out with his personal foreboding, if Yudhishtir was to be handed over the reins of the kingdom, which should have belonged to Dhritarashtra from the very outset, all the power would be wrested from Kauravas for good. He then proposed the shifting of Pandavas to Vernavrata (without disclosing his intentions of burning the palace down). Since any solution which postponed the transfer of power was welcome, the king gave a quiet assent to the plan.

Suddenly there was a change of attitude of Duryodhana and his close aides towards Pandavas which even took the latter by surprise. Those people praised Vernavrata and surroundings and particularly, the impending Siva fair. Simultaneously, these very people would go to near Dhritarashtra to convince him on the dangers from the close relations and the need to keep them away. When in a subsequent assembly, the name of Vernavrata was mentioned, Dhristarshtra himself recommended to Pandavas that they should plan a visit there, attend the fair and if they so desired extend their stay. The unsuspecting Pandavas readily agreed. Since Dhristarashtra was not a party to the sinister plan, he even ordered that Yudhishtir would attend the fair as 'Yuvaraja', the crown prince. Duryodhana was overjoyed to get the news of the departure of Pandavas. He had already received the news that Purochana and his men had completed the wax palace and were ready to receive the Pandavas.

Thus, when Pandavas with mother Kunti left for Vernavrata, Dhritarashtra, Duryodhana and most of the gentry of Hastinapur came out to see them off. Some even went upto Vernavrata to see them off. Pandavas were overwhelmed to see this kind of farewell.

Vidura, however, was not called 'the wisest one' for nothing. He could perceive that there was more to it than what met the eye. He had made his own private investigations and came to know of the entire plot. Prior to parting, Vidura gave to Yudhishthira a veiled warning, which only the latter could understand. "Yudhishthira", he said, "beware of a scheming enemy and forestall his sinister plans. The dangers can come from sources other than steel weapons. A forest fire can, for instance, be devastating – yet not for a rat which hides in a hole or a porcupine which burrows in the earth. Hide, if you have to and learn your directions by looking at the stars".

Yudhishthira understood the message and later passed on the same to Kunti and Bhima. They also decided to act as if nothing was suspected and let the frolicking and reveling go unchecked. After watching them closely for a few days, Purochana concluded that Pandavas had not
suspected anything. Knowing that it might involve a long wait, he settled down to the normal housekeeping activities.

Duryodhana, in the meantime, set about to strengthen his hold on the people and the leadership of the pressure groups. Ashwasthama was already in his kitchen cabinet which ensured that the two acharyas were on the kuru side. He was in no hurry to send the signal to Pruochana. His first priority was to tighten his grip on Hastinapur. If Pandavas gave any sign of wishing to return, Duryodhana felt confident that he would have enough time to issue orders to set the wax palace on fire. After all, the royalty would take quite sometime to pack and move, if they decided to return. As it stood, all reports to Duryodhana indicated that the Pandavas were enjoying the stay at Vernavrata and might stay there for months, or even years.

Yudhishthira, as warned, found that the whole palace was like a box or dry wood, ready to burn. Built of wax, lac, jute and other combustible material, all disguised and coloured as legitimate building material, would ensure that the entire palace would burn to ashes quickly on being set on fire.

Soon a person who was an expert in digging tunnels, arrived with a message from Vidura. Yudhishthira took other brothers also in to confidence and they decided to burrough a hole and build a tunnel across the house in the night. The exit was planned at some unobtrusive place away from the palace.
With everything set, Pandavas gave the indications of their impending departure. Purochana also decided to set the palace on fire during the night before they had planned to leave. Kunti gave a sumptuons feast to all the servants and even some labourers on the evening before. Having eaten to their full satisfaction, they all went to sleep in the servant quarters located in the palace itself. Pandavas gave finishing touches to their final preparations.

As expected, Purochana waited till around midnight and then set the palace on fire. In no time the palace was a huge ball of fire. Having underestimated his own capacity to build the inflammable palace, the fire was so huge that even he, could not escape and perished in his quarters. Also burnt alive were the palace staff and the casual labours who all ran helter skelter in the palace looking for an escape point but failed to find the same. Only the Pandavas, armed with their escape plan, quietly slipped out and disappeared from the palace in the wilderness in the dark. (In another version, it has been said that, once the tunnel had been completed, the Pandavas themselves forced the issue. On the appointed night, Bhima entered Purochana's quarters and killed him. Thereafter, having ensured that the rest of the Pandavas were safely out of the house, he set the palace on fire before being the last one to get in the tunnel and escape).

People living in the adjoining places rushed in to help or rescue but found that it was a lost cause. Purochana's charred body was found in his quarter while inside the palace, there were a number of dead corpses charred and burnt beyond recognition. It was logical to presume that those were the remains of the Pandavas and the servant staff of the palace.

The news spread like a wild fire and a pall of gloom descended on Varnavrata. Kunti and Pandavas were revered by the entire populace. Their sudden death by burning of the palace was incomprehensible. Urgent messages were sent to the king informing him of the unfortunate event.

Hastinapur went numb with the shock on hearing the news. It was a huge tragedy and a tremendous loss since Kunti and the Pandavas were looked upon with respect by one and all and people were looking forward to the day when Yudhishtira would be crowned as the king. Dhritarashtra was genuinely sad for his beloved brother's family. Yet, even though he had not wished it to happen that way, the way being cleared for his favourite son, Duryodhana, was one consolation. Duryodhana himself was immensely overjoyed though he maintained an outwardly picture of being devastated, sad and unhappy.

Hastinapur was in a state of mourning with the royalty too observing the rituals of shedding royal robes and observing penance. Duryodhana, Shakuni and Karna, the trio who masterminded the scheme were overjoyed, mainly because no one appeared to suspect a foul play. Outwardly, they were a picture of grief stricken relatives and friends. In a way they were happy that Purochana too had perished. His death had removed the only outsider, who knew the secret who could have been a future source of problems.

The last rites of Kunti and Pandavas were performed with all solemnity. Many citizens and courtiers were sad. Some even wept openly. Vidura's demeanour , however, was solemn,but hardly sad. People accepted this attitude as a philosophical one, as was expected from an intellectual. Little did they knew that Vidura knew much more than they did. He had already got the news of the safe escape of Pandavas. In due course he also told the entire truth to Bhishma in confidence. Pitamaha was relieved immensely and distressed to know of the complicity of Kauravas. He kept the secret to himself, knowing that letting the same out would harm only the Pandavas.

Chapter-XI

THE WANDERERS WITH A DIFFERENCE

Having escaped safely, the Pandavas set out for a predetermined place on bank of the river Ganga where they had arranged a boat to cross to the other side. The going through the forest was, however, tough on Kunti who was not used to such strenuous journeys that too in a dark night. It was also irksome for young Nakula and Sahdeva who were yet to grow strong and big. Bhima being the strongest, carried Kunti on his shoulders and Nakula and Sahdeva on his hips. They took rest mainly when Kunti wanted to even though there was a slight risk of their being discovered and the news reaching Kaurava. However, nothing of the sort had happened. Everyone slept except Bhima who stood a guard. With the dawn, everyone got up while Bhima took a nap to freshen himself.

After a while, they went to the bank of the river Ganga, found the boat and getting into the same, rowed themselves to the other bank and to relatively more safer surroundings.

They walked during the day, resting in short intervals till the night descended. Despite being thirsty, (at times) they slept without drinking water because it had to be fetched and they were quite tired and not prepared to wait. Bhima kept a watch while others slept.

Once, during the watch, Bhima strolled around and was surprised to find a fresh water pond. Having quenched his thirst to the full, Bhima carried some water for his mother and brothers. He, however, decided to wait, since they all looked to be in deep deep slumber.

The area they were in was the territory of a demon named Hidimb. He lived there along with his sister Hidimba.

The duo was feared by the people living in the surrounding areas. That evening, Hidimb was resting on a tree having had a sumptuous dinner of two bulls he had killed. However when he perceived the typical human smell, his appetite was once again aroused. He woke up Hidimba and asked her to go and investigate the source of smell and report back to him.

Hidimba too was excited at the smell of humans and on reaching near the resting place of Pandavas was thrilled to find that there were a number of men and a woman too. However, when she looked at Bhima, who was standing guard, she instantaneously fell in love with him. Bhima's massive stature, the muscular body, the rippling muscles and shining face floored her completely. She transformed herself into a beautiful looking woman through her maya and went to Bhima playing the part of a coy maiden completely in love.

Bhima looked at her, liking what he saw, and enquired about her being in the dark jungle so late in the night. She told her the complete truth about herself and her brother belonging to the demon race. She also informed Bhima about the impending threat to him and his family from her brother and advised him to shift to some safer place away from thejungle. Bhima laughed and told her not to worry. He had started liking her too and they both started talking to each other.

Hidimb was, in the meanwhile, getting impatient and eventually got down to go and check the things himself. Looking at Hidimba in the garb of a woman and talking intimately with Bhima, he understood the situation immediately.

Hidimb yelled at her, "You worthless demoness. Instead of obeying orders, you are chit-chatting with this despicable human being. Shame on you". He lunged at her to give her a massive blow. To his surprise, the blow was stopped in the mid-air because of Bhima's arm had come in the way. Hidimb felt as if his fist had hit a massive stone. With a huge roar, Hidimb turned his attention towards Bhima and launched a full scale attack on him. Pandavas were fully awake now ready to join the battle if a need arose. They, however, were confident that Bhima would be able to deal with the assailant alone. Bhima defended himself from all the blows with alacricity taunting the demon. Suddenly, Bhima's fighting changed the gears and he launched a ferocious counter-attack. Hidimb was totally outclassed. In a few moments he was down on the ground, panting and reeling. Bhima killed him with a final blow on his chest. Hidimba, who had taken cover behind some trees was not unhappy to see the death of her brother, but rather relieved and happy to see Bhima winning the duel.

The brothers decided to leave the place immediately as they rightly concluded that the news regarding, Hidimb's death would spread like a wild fire and his merciless killing could possibly be linked with Pandavas, particularly Bhima. The last thing they wanted was the discovery of their being alive.

However, as they walked briskly away, in an effort to put in as much distance between them and Hidimb's dead body, Kunti noticed a beautiful looking woman following them, keeping a bit of distance between them. Kunti was curious and hence called her to come to her. She asked about her and the reasons for following them.

Hidimba was polite, frank and forthright, "I am a demoness, belonging to the rakshasa race, and sister of the demon killed by him". She pointed towards Bhima and continued, "My brother was named Hidimb and I, his sister, am Hidimba. From the very first tme I looked at him pointing at Bhima, I fell in love with him. After seeing his mighty valour and strength, while fighting with my brother, I have resolved to be his wife and of none else. My decision is regardless of the fact whether I am accepted by you and him or not. And now I await your decision".

Kunti appreciated her frankness. She looked at Bhima and found him also keen and willing. She told Hidimba, "I have no objection to this alliance. You can come with us as long as we are in the forest. However, since Bhima stands guard over us in the night, you can only be with him during the day time".Hidimba was happy with the arrangement she stayed with Bhima during the days and did all the chores for him and the brothers. In due course, she came into the family way delivering a very healthy looking and strong baby. They named him 'Ghatotkach'. He had all the makings of growing into a great and powerful fighter.

Deep into the forest they also met Rishi Vyasa. Paying deep regards and obeisance to him, they narrated their experiences to him, expressing their frustration at being on the receiving end despite doing all acts ordained as per the religious texts. Vyasa cosoled them saying that even the best people who had committed no sin and performed good acts consistently had their share of grief and sorrow. A person's destiny was governed by not only his present but the acts of the previous lives. In any case, nothing was permanent in the life. The happiness was bound to follow the bad times. He advised them to go to a village named ekachakra and live there as Brahmins for sometimes. After some time, Rishi Vyasa left them wishing them good luck.

As they came to the end of the forest Bhima bade goodbye to Hidimba and Ghatokacha promising Hidimba
not to forget her. He asked her to look after Ghatokacha well and bring him up as a worthy son. "If we need him sometime in the future, we shall summon him to join us", Bhima added and left the two in the forest.

Chapter-XII

END OF BAKASURA

After leaving the forests,the Pandavas headed for Ekachakra, as advised by Maharishi Vyasa. After a long while, they were seeing villages in place of forests. They reached Ekachakara after a few days. Dressed as brahmins, they took shelter in the house of a brahmin, who along with his wife and a small daughter and an infant son, led a moderate existence. In the daybreak, the Pandavas used to venture out and beg for alms. On their return all of them would hand over their alms to mother Kunti. Kunti would pool them up and gave half of the pooled material to Bhima, befitting his size. The other half would be divided and shared between the remainder. Despite this, Kunti could see Bhima losing weight and getting thinner by the day.

One evening, however, their mind was distracted by the sound of loud crying and lamentatious from the portion where their host lived. Thinking that some tragedy had befallen on the family. Kunti tip-toed to the room where the sounds of weeping, sobbing and discussions were coming from. It did not take much time for her to grasp the situation and the serious problem faced by the family.

Ekchakra had been hounded by a demon named Bakasura. The ruler of Ekachakra was an incompetent person and unable to stop the onslaught of Bakasura. As he had run away to a distant place unable to stop the indiscriminate attacks, the villagers went to Bakasura to stop the same. In return, they promised that they would regularly send adequate foodstuff and one human being to him at fixed periods. They had agreed between themselves that each house will send one human sacrifice by turn. Bakasura, in return, promised complete peace to the village. (The arrangement was akin to the protection rackets being practised in many towns/localities these days). Kunti learnt that the next instalment for Bakasura was due on the next day and the turn of the host family to offer one human sacrifice had come. There were serious discussions between the husband and the wife, and even their small child, a daughter, as each of them wanted to go, sparing the others.

Kunti entered their room and offered to send Bhima to Bakasura in their place. The offer was flatly refused by the Brahmin stating that they were their guests and sending one of them would be unthinkable.

Kunti, on the other hand, had decided that she would send Bhima to exterminate Bakasura, an act which was considered as a repayment in gratitude to the Brahmin family. In strict confidence, she told the family of their true identity and assured them that this was the least they could do for them. She, however, extracted a promise from the family that they would keep their identity an absolute secret.

Bhima was elated at his mother's desire to send him to fight Bakasura. The villagers had already prepared a cartload of foodstuff and placed the cart in front of the house of the brahmin by the evening. The brahmin was expected to drive the bullock cart out of the village early next morning to Bakasura. His place would now be taken by Bhima.

Bhima set out very early in the morning to meet Bakasura, driving the bullock cart. One additional reason for his happiness was that he would be able to have a rightful claim on the food being sent for Bakasura. Ever since they had come, Bhima could never have his appetite fully satisfied since they had to depend totally on what he and his brothers could get on their daily outings to seek alms. Even though Bhima was
always given half of the combined collection of the day, he still finished quite hungry.

He reached the appointed place to wait for Bakasura, and did what he had decided to do when he started from the village. He started to eat the foodstuff brought for Bakasura.Bakasura was gradually climbing down the hill where he had his cave. When he spotted the cart, he was satisfied and quickened his pace. However, his happiness gave way to anger as he neared the cart because he spotted the driver eating the foodstuff brought for Bakasura.

Closing in on the cart, Bakasura uprooted a huge tree and threw it straight towards Bhima. The latter looked at the demon but did not take any evasive action. The tree hit Bima without any effect as if it had hit a boulder.

A bit surprised, Bakasura lifted a huge boulder and threw it towards Bhima while simultaneously closing in on the cart. Bhima deflected the boulder and advanced towards Bakasura. Before the demon knew what was happening, Bhima lifted him with the lightning speed and threw him high up in the air. Bakasura fell with a deep thud and died immediately without a whimper as his back was broken hitting the ground.

Bhima went back and resumed eating the food. After his appetite was fully satisfied he drove the cart back tying Bakasura's body with it. He left the cart and Bakasura's body just outside the village and rejoined his family conveying the happy news to them as well as to his landlord.

The landlord kept his promise to Kunti to keep their identity a secret. Hence, when the happily surprised villagers came to him, after seeing dead Bakasura, the Brahmin told them that a stranger who was proficient in
the practice of mantras and had sidhdhi, had stayed with them on the evening before and had volunteered to take the cart to Bakasura because he was confident of killing the demon. He added that the stranger must have left the village, after killing Bakasura and dragging his body to the outskirts of village, as it was his practice not to stay in a place where he had accomplished some formidable act.

Despite elaborate and successful subeterfuge, Pandavas were uncomfortable lest their cover was blown up. They also remembered the advice of Rishi Vyasa where he had recommended that after Ekachakra they should attend the swayamvara of Draupadi, the beautiful daughter of Drupad which was imminent. After a few days, they took leave of their gracious host and his family and left Ekachakra for Panchala with the intention to attend the upcoming swayamvara of the drupada princess.

Even though the Pandavas could have gone to Hastinapura after the escape from the lac-home of Vernavrata, they did not do so because they wanted to gauge the intentions of Duryodhana. His ambitions were already known. Also, his intolerance, jealousy and hatred of Pandavas – specially of Bhima and Arjuna were no secret.

Prior to their departure for Vernavrata from Hastinapur, Vidura's parting message had also hinted of their remaining incognito for some time and for remaining watchful and vigilant. Despite all precautions, there were, at times, incidents like killing of Hidimb and Bakasura, which required the Pandavas to leave for the next place with added haste.

Otherwise, even without the absence of luxury to which they were used to, Pandava brothers were a happy bunch – more so because their mother Kunti was also with them.

As they walked towards Ganges to cross the river at a suitable place, there was yet another incident involving some delay in their journey, it was early morning and Arjuna was leading the group as a torch – bearer to show the way to the river. All of a sudden, they heard clattering of the hoofs and the sound of a chariot approaching towards their group. Arjuna signaled to his group to halt and prepared to meet the stranger in the chariot. Since it was still slightly dark he could not recognize the stranger and other passengers in the chariot when it came to a screeching halt in front of him.

The person, sitting in the front in the chariot spoke in a loud and threatening voice, "Halt and go back. If you do not, you all will be killed. How dare you venture ito the property belonging to some one else".

Arjuna kept his cool and replied, "We were proceeding towards the banks of the Ganga. The holy river is accessible to everyone and is not the personal property of any particular person. Please allow us to proceed".

The dim figure of the chariot replied back in an irritated voice, "You seem to be new to this area. This is the time for the divine races like Gandharvas, Yakshas and others to take bath in the river and none else is allowed in this area". Advancing a bit further, he added, "I am the Gandharva king, Angaraparva. The area on both sides of the river belong to me and even angels and devas cannot come here without my permission. Leave this place immediately or else you will be punished for your insolence and be killed. This is no place for ordinary humans".

This was enough for Arjuna to lose his patience. He shouted at the king and said, "Enough, it appears that you have not met a competent human being so far. Or else, you have some very wrong notions about the superiority of the divine races. Even though it is much too early in the morning. I accept your challenge and intend punishing you for your haughtiness and arrogance".

King Angaraparva, thoroughly infuriated on hearing Arjuna's words, jumped down from his chariot with a sword in his hand. Taking a few steps in the front, he threw the sword at Arjuna. The latter parried the sword with his torch and in return, sent his torch itself towards the king and his chariot after invoking a mantra to enhance its destructive capability.

In no time, the chariot was fully ablaze. The queens who were sitting in the rear seats jumped out on the ground. Arjuna rushed towards the dazed king and catching and pulling him by the hair, dragged him down to mother Kunti and his brothers.

Shocked, disgraced, baffled and defeated, the king was a picture of misery. Moments before, he was a picture of over-confidence and arrogance, but now that he had been humiliated in front of his own wives by a mere mortal, he looked miserable. The wives understood the gravity of the situation. They rushed towards Kunti and Yudhishthira and begged for forgiveness.

Yudhishthira, always a kind person, took pity on Angaraparva and told Arjuna, "There is no higher disgrace than being humiliated in front of one's own wives. Let him go". Then, turning towards Angaraparva, he said, "The divine people are known for their supernatural powers. But, at no times, they should let these powers get into their head. If they do, sooner or later they stand to get disgraced with disastrous consequences".

One look at the five glorious figures and Angaraparva knew that he had met people who were more than a match for himself. Arjuna turned towards the Gandharva chief and told him, "Angaraparva, as directed by my noble brother, I forgive you".

Angaraparva was relieved to hear those words from Arjuna. He and his wives were a picture of extreme gratitude. With folded hands, he turned towards the Pandavas and said, "We are extremely thankful for your kind and magnanimous gesture. I want to remain your friend. As a token of my gratitude, I wish to gift to you a divine power named 'Chakshusee'. This will enable you see any thing anywhere in all the three worlds. Besides, I also wish to gift to you hundred gandharva horses. These animals never age and will run at the speed you wish".

Yudhishtira thanked the Gandharva king for the gifts and requested him to keep them on their behalf. The Pandavas promised to call for them when the need arose. Angaraparva nodded in affirmative and drove away along with his wives in another chariot which had arrived in the intervening period.The Pandavas crossed the river Ganga and resumed their journey towards Panchala. They joined some other parties which were also proceeding to the same destination. The most talked about topic was the swayamvara of Draupadi and the high praises of the beauty and sterling moral virtues of the princess of Panchala.

Chapter-XIII

DRAUPADI'S SWAYAMVARA

Pandavas reached Panchala a few days prior to swayamvara. They stayed at a potter's house who was happy to have hosted a brahmin family who had come to witness the big event. The whole town was agog with conversation mainly centred around the coming big event. The whole area was decorated. Pandava brothers went around for sight-seeing. They were immensely impressed. As usual, people in small and big groups mainly talked about the royal family, Draupadi (also called Krishna) and the swayamvara of this beautiful princess of extremely noble qualities. With many rishis, sages, Brahmans and kshatriya chieftains, kings and princes reaching Panchala one by one, the citizens every day had new things and people to talk about.

Soon the appointed day for swayamvara arrived. The venue started filling from early morning itself. There were different places nominated for different categories of people. The royalty was in full bloom with kings and princes flaunting their armour. The rishis, sages, precepts sat in a separate enclosure. Pandavas arrived as brahmins and sat along with other brahmins in their special enclosure. The gentry of Panchala was also present in full numbers. Krishna and Balrama also came to attend the function. After taking their seats. they surveyed the whole crowd. For a moment, Krishna's gaze rested on Pandavas and then moved on. He mentioned about their presence to Balrama.

King Drupada, accompanied by his son, prince Dhrishtadyumna and other courtiers arrived at the enclosure. They greeted the important personages and talked to some of them. Soon they had settled in the royal enclosure.

Dhrishtadyumna came to the centre of the arena and addressed the participants, "Distinguished participants, as you are aware, we have gathered here for the swayamvara of my sister, Draupadi. My father has laid a few conditions to chose a winner of my sister's hand".

Dhrishtadyumna continued, "As you can see, a pole has been erected here. On top of the pole,there is a revolving wheel which has a fish fixed on one of its spokes. On the platform by the side of the pole is placed a bow, an arrow and a tray full of oil. The aspirant has to string the bow and mount the arrow on it. He should then aim the arrow at the
revolving fish, looking down at the reflection of the fish in the tray of oil only. One who can successfully pierce the eye of the fish, wins my sister's hand".

With a buzz the contest commenced. There were many famous names, Duryodhana, his borthers, Karna, Shalya and scores of others. However, soon it became evident that the conditions were very tough. Many aspirants could not even string the bow. They all rose and approached the bow looking very confident with a beaming face. Once they failed in their effort, they returned to their seats looking dejected and gazing towards the ground.

All Kaurava brothers tried but failed. Others also followed suit. Already murmurs could be heard that may be there would be no winner after all becuase the terms to qualify were too difficult. The Kaurava crowd was egging Karna on to take up the challenge. Eventually he too got up and went to the centre. In a smooth single action, he lifted the bow and strung it. There was a hush in the audience.

As Karna prepared to put the arrow on the string and take aim, some of the royal participants raised an objection. Someone shouted “This contest is for genuine people and certainly not shamsters and imposters”. “Yes, yes, the contest is only for the royalty of blue blood, how can a weaver’s son be a participant?”, someone else shouted.

Karna’s face was showing visible signs of agitation. It is not that he did not have any support. The kaurava princes were very vocal in advocating his claims. On the other side, in Drupad’s enclosure where Draupadi was seated, the latter looked askance at Krishna and found him gesturing in the negative.

Draupadi got up and announced, “Even if he might have been made a king by some one, I shall not marry a weaver’s son. On hearing this, Karna put down the bow and kicking the ground below, stormed out of the enclosure despite efforts of Kaurava princes to persuade him to stay back.

Some more members of the royalty went and tried their luck, but failed to do the needul. King Drupada was showing signs of anxiety, possibly regretting his decision to stipulate such stringent conditions to win the hand of his beloved daughter. Some one from the audience said, “Had Arjuna been alive and here, he would have won the contest hands down”. Others also echoed that sentiment.

Arjuna was getting restive. He looked at his brothers all of whom nodded and gestured to him to step out and take up the challenge. As he got up, the other brahmins looked at him with disbelief. “How can an unknown Brahmin succeed where the famous kshatriyas have failed?". was the unanimous question. Some even advocated stopping Arjuna from entering the contest.

There was a counter-lobby as well. Many of the Brahmins were hugely impressed by Arjuna's perfect physique and quiet confidence seen on his face. Many even ventured to suggest that the young man be given a try in the hope that he might bring glory to the brahmin race.

Arjuna bowed towards the enclosure where the sages were sitting. He then took position in front of the platform where the bow was kept. Lifting the bow with ease, he strung it in one smooth movement. This resulted in a gasp from many while all of them moved to the edge of their seats. Drupada, who till few moments ago, was a picture of dejection and disappointment, was also all attention. Draupadi glanced at her mentor, Krishna, who smiled and gave an almost imperceptible nod.

Arjuna had put the arrow on the bow and was pointing it at a revolving fish while looking at the oil tray and fixing the aim. Suddenly, the arrow shot out with a swish and went straight into the right eye of the fish on the revolving wheel. There was a spontaneous applause from the bulk of the audience excepting from the participating royalty.

Most of the royalty, were on their feet. Some doubted Arjuna's credentials as a proposer. Others said that he was not a warrior. Some others shouted that Arjuna's hit was a 'fluke', a shot in the dark, which, by accident, hit the target on account of a pure chance.

Arjuna smiled and gestured towards the protestors to show patience since he intended to repeat the performance.

He took his aim again looking at the oil tray. While everyone held his breath, the arrow was shot by Arjuna, once again going towards the target with a swish. Lo and behold, the arrow hit the fish on its left eye.

Once again, there was spontaneous and loud applause all around. Gradually, it turned into a standing ovation as it was an outstanding exhibition of excellent marksmanship. Arjuna had won the challenge and without any hesitation Draupadi walked upto him and put the garland round the neck. The chests of all the Pandava brothers swelled up with pride. (In. another version, aspirants were required to shoot the fish with five successive steel arrows through the revolving mechanism. while the majority of princes failed to even string the bow, a very few managed to do so but were way off the mark, when they tried to hit the target. Even Karna, whom everyone expected to win the test with ease, missed the fish by a hair's breath. This started a string of murmurs where the royal visitors expressed the view that such a test, which none could pass, was too harsh and stringent. These murmurs, however subsided as quickly as they had started when Arjuna hit the target fish in five successful attempts. In this version also Arjuna was the sole winner of the contest and was accepted by Draupadi as the winner of her hand when she put the garland around his neck).

What followed was something which was reprehensible something which indicated the darker side of kshatriyas of not accepting defeat in the proper spirit. A large number of them ganged up together criticising Drupada and his son for allowing Draupadi to garland Arjuna and acknowledge the latter as the winner of her hand. They also advanced many other arguments, important amongst which was that the swayamvara was a practice amongst kshatriyas, and not brahmins.

Situation was getting ugly. Krishna and Balarama tried to assuage the feeling of those who were very angry and vocal. The troops of Dhrishtadumna had already been alerted. Bhima too, uprooted a tree and had pruned it to use it as an effective weapon – to use it like a thunder-bolt. Seeing the situation getting under control and tension petering out, Yudhishthira, Nakula and Sahadeva rushed to Kunti to tell of the happy tiding. Arjuna too, with Darupadi on the tow, left for their place of stay. Bhima stayed a bit longer and left when things were near normal.

Dhrishtadymna followed his sister surreptiously from a distance. He had a nagging feeling that there was more to that which met the eye. After seeing Draupadi, the five supposedly brahmin brothers and Kunti Devi, he was convinced that this was the Pandava clan which was rumoured to have been burnt alive in the lakshagraha at Vernavrata. Kunti's face was radiant and bright and the bearing regal – one which could only belong to a woman of royal descent. The way she received Daaupadi and commanded the respects of her sons was indeed like a queen would have done.

After staying for a while to further confirm his suspicions he rushed back to Drupada his father, and told him of his firm conclusions.

"Father", Dhrishtadumna said, "I am convinced that they are the missing Pandava brothers and their mother Kunti who had presumed to have lost their lives in the lac-house burning tragedy at Vernavrata and the person who won the competition at the swayamvara, is none other that the great Arjuna himself. As soon as he had shot the target five time in five successive attempts, I had a faint inkling that this could only be Arjuna. No one else, a kshtriya or a brahmin, could have the strength a nd the skill to perform such a stupendous deed. Now, having watched Draupadi with them and Kunti, I am totally convinced of the fact".

Drupada could not believe the words of his son. The information was something he had always hoped, aspired and dreamed of. Ever since he had to part half of his kingdom to Drona, he had hoped that if some-how he could have Arjuna on his side, he would take revenge from the great precept. With the lac-house tragedy, his dreams had disappeared. And now, out of blue, there stood a chance of his wishes coming true. He asked a number of questions from Dhrishtadyumna who was totally unwaivering of his conclusions.

Drupada was excited and euphoric. Yet he, however, felt the need of a firm confirmation of what his son had felt so convinced of. He accordingly requested to meet Yudhishthira.

On meeting Yudhishthira, Drupada enquired about their real identities. The Dharmaraja, famed for his truthfulness, told Drupada about their being the missing Pandavas and their mother being the famed Kunti, the wife of the deceased king Pandu. As expected, Drupada was extremely delighted.

The good news was, however, followed by a bad one, which shocked Drupada. Yudhishthira informed that the five brothers had decided to conjointly marry Draupadi.

Yudhishthira explained that once, in the face of great adversity, the five brothers had made a pact of jointly sharing the adversity as well as gains in common in future. He confirmed that the joint marriage had also the sanction of their mother.

Drupada was aghast on hearing this. Such marriages, in his view, did neither have social nor religious sanction. He told Yudhishtira that he considered his daughter marrying the five brothers together as preposterous.

Yudhishthira explained that examples of polyandry have been few, but none the less prevalent under special circumstances. Some communities even practiced it on a regular basis. As far as they were concerned, the brothers' pact and their mother's sanction was enough to sanctify the marriage.

Not convinced fully, Drupad wanted to consult some more knowledgable people. To his good fortune, Maharishi Veda Vyasa happened to be visiting Panchala. He sought an audience with him and explained his predicament. Veda Vyasa endorsed the views of Yudhishthira and further added that Draupadi's marriage to the five brothers had a prior divine sanction.

In her previous birth, she had carried out a deep penance praying to the Lord Mahadeva. When the Lord was satisfied and asked her for a boon, she had repeated the request five times for a husband of great virtues. The Lord had ordained accordingly that she would wed the five Pandava brothers, each of whom was a great virtuous person possessing special skills.

Convinced of sanctity of his special marriage, Drupada invited Kunti and the five Pandava brothers to stay in the palace where the marriage was celebrated with all the pomp and show. Draupadi, in any case, was totally convinced of the veracity of her marriage. In addition to the concurrence of Kunti, the marriage had the total support and endorsement of Krishna, in whom she had total faith.

Chapter-XIV

RETURN OF THE NATIVES

The news of Pandavas being alive, Arjuna's feat in winning the challenge in swayamvar and the marriage and celebrations spread like wild fire and reached Vidura in Hastinapura. No confirmation was needed since Vidura already knew that Pandavas were alive and were moving towards Panchala.

Vidura went to Dhritarashtra and told him that princess of Panchala had become part of their family after the swayamvara. Dhritarashtra, at first, misunderstood the news and jumped to the conclusion that Duryodhana had won the challenge and the hand of Draupadi. He became very excited and started eulogising the prowess of Duryodhana. Vidura hastened to correct the king and gave him the full news of happenings in Panchala, of Pandavas being alive and their marriage to Draupadi. This was a double blow to Dhritarashtra although he did not show it to Vidura. Outwardly, he showed great pleasure and asked Vidura to inform the others too of happy tidings.

Inwardly, the king, though happy to hear that the Pandavas were alive, was upset that his position and authority as the king and of Duryodhana as the crown-prince was under some threat. Dhritarashtra himself was not a part of the conspiracy of the wax-palace. He was also genuinely aggrieved when he heard about Kunti and her sons being burn't alive. However, it was also the fact that the death of Pandu's wife and children had confirmed Dhritarashtra in the position of a king not in an acting capacity, but in a totally confirmed position. Similarly, none could question the ascendancy of Duryodhana whose power and prestige had expanded way beyond that of the crown prince.

Dhritarashtra called Duryodhana and broke the news to him. Karna was also with the latter. They were very surprised to know that they could not recognize the Pandavas at the swayamvara. In the back of the mind of Duryodhana was the imminent threat to his unquestionable total authority. Karna also expressed the view that the new development had a potential of damaging their authority.

Barring Karna, the others were a confused lot. Some very stupid and childish strategies were discussed to divide Pandavas and weaken them, but were all found out to be counter-productive. Duryodhana was frank to confess that he had no credible strategy.

Karna, the 'Hawk' and a person fiercely loyal to Duryodhana, was the only one who from the very beginning was advocating a military solution. He said, "The schemes suggested by Duryodhana would not be effective. Before they left for Vernavrata, the Pandavas were an extremely close knit bunch. I am quite sure that now they are more so. Hence, any attempt to divide them will be foolhardy. The best alternative would be to attack the Pandavas and kill them in the battle. No doubt, they will be supported by the army of Drupada. We are capable of dealing with them. If we act swiftly, the element of surprise will be with us. Krishna will not be able to call the Yadava army from Dwarka".

Karna continued, "A lightning 'Putsch' will have the advantage of winning the war and also getting the endorsement from our people. We can spread a lot of disinformation on them, like from questioning to their being genuine Pandavas to the fact that the fire at wax-palace was conceived and planned by Pandavas as part of the greater conspiracy to usurp the kingdom. In any case, with all the key people and pressure groups on our side and under our firm control, we do not have to fear a backlash from the people".

Dhritarashtra, was, as usual, an indecisive person caught between the two forces, one of the love of his Pandava kins and the other being his blind love for Duryodhana. He therefore summoned Bhishma for advice.

Bhishma had known all the essential facts which had been given to him by Vidura from time to time. His advice was clear and unequivocal. "Your people have a considerable love, affection and respect for the Pandava brothers. There is already some talk of the foul play behind the burning of the wax house. In order to stop this loose talk and ensure fair dispensation, you must invite them to come to Hastinapur and bestow half of your kingdom to them. This is the only way to keep peace and keep your subjects happy and satisfied".

A shade non-plussed, Dhritarashtra called for Dronacharya and asked for his views. Karna and Duryodhana were also there. The learned precept also fully endorsed the advice of Bhishma. When Karna made some snyde remarks at the Acharya implying that he was being disloyal to his paymasters, Dronacharya flared up and told him, "Foolish people like you can only think of fights, battles and war. You do not possess any foresight. If the advice of Bhishma is not followed, there would be war and devastation and we all will be the sufferers".

Vidura, the Prime Minister also gave the similar opinion. Dhritarashtra himself became convinced of the logic of the proposed solution. It was much better to divide the kingdom in half and give one-half to Pandavas, who were the original inheritors of the entire territory. The other alternative, denying them anything was fraught with fearsome consequences and backlash. He therefore asked Vidura to go to Panchala and bring Kunti and Pandava brothers back to Hastinapur. Vidura arrived at Panchala carrying many priceless gifts for king Drupada and others. When he met Drupada he conveyed felicitations of Dhritarshtra and conveyed his request that Pandavas be sent to Hastinapura along with the new bride, princess Draupadi.

Drupada was not comfortable on hearing this request. He was quite aware of Duryodhana's virtual control on the kingdom and his jealousy and hatred towards Pandavas. Dhritarashtra's indecisive nature, his blindness and intense love for Duryodhana, which made the king take partial and biased decisions were the folktales of Hastinapur.

Drupada was convinced that the request was prompted by some ulterior motives. Yet he realized that he did not have the authority to refuse the request. After all, Pandavas were being requested to return to their homeland. He, therefore, finally relented and said, "It is upto Pandavas to decide". Vidura went to Pandavas and prostrated before Kunti. After exchanging courtesies with everyone, he turned to Kunti and repeated Dhritarashtra's message and request.

Kunti was skeptical of Dhritarashtra's intentions. She knew for sure that given the vile manners and scheming natures of the Kaurav children, some bad things were sure to follow. She told Vidura, "As dear and righteous brother of Pandu you have always looked after me and my children. Even though I am not sure that the return to Hastinapura is safe, I shall abide by your advice".

Vidura assured her, "You and your children will be safe and protected by the God. They will live long and rule this kingdom. There will be problems from time to time, but be assured that the final outcome will always favour the Pandavas". Kunti and Drupadi gave assent to the return to Hastinapura. They returned to Hastinapur amidst a lot of celebrations and rejoicing. The homecoming was as much a source of happiness to them as to the people of Hastinapura. The city was decked up and people lined up on both sides of the roads through which they passed.

Dhritarashtra, in a solemn ceremony, informed everyone of his decision to declare Yudhishthira the king of half of the kingdom. He was duly crowned and handed over the reins of the newly carved out territory.

Before his departure from Hastinapur, Yudhishthira, the new king was called by Dhritarashtra and told by him, "Your father ruled over Hastinapur with a great ability and dedication. He made this kingdom rich and prosperous. He was also a wise brother who sought and gave wise counsel from and to me. I am expecting the same relationship from you".He then added with an expression of total frankness, "Unlike the five of you, my sons are arrogant and wicked. This settlement has been made with the assent of other elders so that there is no bad blood between you and them. Make Khandavaprastha your new capital and rule from there.

Our ancestors, Pururvas, Nahusha and Yayati ruled the kingdom from this ancient place. You have my total blessings to re-establish the new place and be successful and famous.

Pandavas shifted to Khandavaprashtha and started renovating and rebuilding their new capital. It was renamed as 'Indraprastha'. For more than three decades, thirty six years to be precise, they ruled from there adhering to the tenets of Dharma and fairness. Their kingdom prospered beyond imagination. The people were very happy and contented. This period was indeed the one devoted to consolidation,growth and good governance.

Chapter-XV

GROUND RULES FOR HANDLING DRAUPADI'S POLYANDRY

Marriage of Draupadi to five Pandava brothers had worked smoothly mainly on account of excellent understanding and mutual relationship between the brothers. It was, however, clear that the informal arrangements required to be changed to formal ones to ensure a durable and smooth relationship. A pointer to this was provided during the visit of the wandering sage Narada to Indraprastha.

While discussing various issues with the brothers, the wise and wily sage described the story of two demon brothers, Sund and Upsund who fought each other over a beautiful woman Tilottama and died fighting.

After Narada had departed, the brothers discussed the matter between themselves. They concluded a pact between themselves to ensure a harmonious domestic arrangement over a long term. According to the pact, each brother would live with Draupadi for a month in the term. During this period, the other brothers will not visit her room under any circumstances. The brothers also devised a penalty clause if the pact was violated. As per this, the guilty brother would have to go in exile for twelve years. Although there had not been any problem so far, a formal arrangement was considered as a welcome gesture to eliminate the likelihood of any possible problem occurring in future.

However, destiny, as is said, chalks out a different path which at times can never be predicted. Of all the people, Arjuna, the noblest of the tribe, became an unfortunate casualty and a person guilty of violating the pact of brothers.A brahmin had come to the palace in an agitated state because his cow had been stolen. On seeing Arjuna, he implored him to intervene in the matter so that the cow was restored to him. It was a simple matter but the brahman was highly agitated and requested Arjuna to act urgently. Arjuna had a practical problem. His bow was kept in Draupadi's chamber and he could not go in it since this was the month in which only Yudhishthira was allowed to visit and be with Draupadi. As the brahmin's pleas became more strident, and also knowing that both Yudhishthira and Draupadi were not in the chamber, Arjuna decided to go and fetch his bow. He went with the brahmin and ensured that the cow was restored to him.

On his return, however, Arjuna realized that technically he had violated the pact and must bear the stipulated consequences. He, therefore, announced his intention to proceed on exile for twelve years. Although his brothers, as well as Draupadi, tried to convince him that because of the accompanying circumstances, his act did not amount to a serious violation of the pact and an exile for twelve years was much too harsh, Arjuna did not agree and proceeded on exile.

Twelve year period is not a short one. Arjuna trecked through many forests and other areas, till he reached the land of nagas (snakes). In fact the story goes that the naga princess, Uloopi had exercised her tapa powers to attract Arjuna making him come to that area. She had heard a great deal about him and had been told that he had gone to exile and was likely to be in the nearby region. Uloopi fell in love with him at the first sight. Very soon she proposed to marry him. Arjuna too liked her and married him. Multiple wives was an accepted thing in those days, particularly amongst the warrior class. After a few years, Arjuna wanted to move on. Uloopi gladly accepted his wish and allowed him to leave. She being the princess of the water-life, bestowed a boon on her husband to the effect that he would enjoy the protection and friendship of all water-borne creatures.

Arjuna moved on till he reached the kingdom of king Chitravahana. Aware of his fame as a warrior and a superb archery, the learned king invited him to stay as the royal guest in his palace.One day, the king's only child, princess Chitrangada saw him and immediately fell in love with him. She too expressed a wish to marry Arjuna. Arjuna had no objections. He went to king Chitravahana and sought his persmission for the marriage. The king happily gave his consent to the proposed alliance, but stipulated one condition. After their marriage, the couple would give their son for adoption by the king. This was because the king did not have any son and only had Chitrangada as his daughter. Both of them had no objection. The marriage was solemnized with usual pomp and show. Soon Chitrangada came into the family way and was blessed with a son. As per their agreement, he was given to the king for adoption as a prince and the heir-apparent. With permission and knowledge of all, Arjuna left Chitravahana's kingdom leaving his wife, Chitrangada behind.

Moving on, Arjuna travelled southwards. The exile had given him a splendid apportunity to meet different people, see their diverse way of living and observe the flora and fauna of different lands. He also observed as to how, despite different beliefs, customs and mores of all lands, they had followed the same broad culture and major religious tenets. Even in those times the essential unity in diversity of the great Indian nation was all too visible.

On the way Arjuna came across a dense forest, at the centre of which there was a clear land and huts and cottages. Arjuna learnt that a number of sages were there where they were practicing penances, prayers and other austerities. They were happy to meet the great warrior and imparted to him many gems of wisdom. The brahmins had a request of their own. Located nearby were five water reservoirs which were their only source of water. However, since each tank was occupied by a ferocious crocodile; getting water was not easy due to the terror of these crocodiles. They requested Arjuna to rid these tanks of the ferocious creatures. Arjuna gladly accepted their requests. One by one, he entered each tank and catching hold of the occupant hermaphrodite by the tail, flung them on the surrounding land. Armed with the special powers given by the Naga princess, Uloopi, he was neither threatened nor did he have anything to fear from these creatures.

What came as a pleasant surprise to every one, was that, on being flung on the ground all the five crocodiles were transformed into five heavenly beauties. The first one explained that all five of them were transformed into crocodiles as a consequence of a curse of a sage. After their pleas of mercy they had been informed that they would regain their original status when Arjuna would come and get rid of their crocodile form. They had to wait for nearly a hundred years. All the five heavenly angels bowed towards Arjuna and the sages and flew away skywards. Arjuna was blessed by the holy men for eliminating the threat of crocodiles from the five excellent reservoirs of water. He then asked and received their permission to move on to other lands on his wanderings. Arjuna reached Prabhasa region and was happily surprised to meet Krishna there. Both of them had a close affinity to each other. After some time in Prabhasa, Krishna brought Arjuna to Dwarka and asked him to stay in the palace as his guest. Krishna and Balarama had a beautiful looking sister, Subhadra. When Arjuna saw her, he instantaneously fell for her.

When Arjuna met Krishna next time, he confided to him regarding his liking for Subhadra. He said that he would like to ask for her hand for marriage. Krishna told Arjuna "Warriors don't ask for their beloved's hand, they just take them away". Arjuna got the hint and, at the first opportunity, eloped with Subhadra.

Balarama was livid with rage when he came to know of Arjuna's action. He was a highly temperamental person. He immediately planned to lead a contingent of soldiers to capture Arjuna. As usual, Krishna retrieved the situation. He was the only one who could argue convincingly and make Balarama change his decisions taken in an agitated state.

"Bhaiya," said Krishna, in his usual highly persuasive tone, "Just think about it with a cool mind. Where would you get a groom like Arjuna for our sister. Why, if you ask me, he is the best. An outstanding family, an outstanding warrior and an outstanding man.I feel you should forgive him and accept him in our family".

Balarama had cooled down and understood the logic of Krishna's arguments. He also secretly suspected that Krishna might have had a hand in it. However, the logic of Krishna's arguments was much too strong this time. He eventually gave consent to the alliance. They sent messengers in all directions to convey to Arjuna that all was forgiven and he and Subhadra should come back.

They came back and were welcomed with open arms by one and all. Their marriage was performed with all the pomp and show.

After a few days, they took leave of Balarama and Krishna and left Dwarka to see some other places. Eventually they reached Pushkar where they spent the remaining period of their exile.

Arjuna and Subhadra returned to Indraprashtha after the expiry of the exile term. Everyone in Indraprastha, from Yudhishthira to the common man on the street was extremely happy to see the Pandavas' most respected and competent warrior back. As to Subhadra, she was also welcomed by Kunti and Draupadi with open arms. Her humility was the most endearing quality of hers. The fact that she was the sister of Krishna, a person very close to all of them including Pandava brothers, Kunti and Draupadi made her much more acceptable. Once they had settled down, Balarama and Krishna arrived from Dwarka with customany gifts to confirm the marriage of their dear sister. Yudhishthira threw a great reception to commemorate the great occasion. Balarama returned to Dwarka after a few days but Krishna took former's permission to stay for some more time at Indraprastha. His closeness and friendship with Arjuna was well known to all.

In due course Subhadra gave birth to Abhimanyu while Draupadi became the proud mother of five sons, Pratibindhya, Shrutkarma, Shrutsena, Sutsena and Shataneeka.

All the young Pandava siblings were given proper education and training in use of arms, as they grew up. Their progress was excellent and they all became the darlings of the citizens of Indraprastha.

The stories narrated in the Mahabharata, Puranas and other vedic literature are a happy fusion of nature, imagination, enlightenment and education. It is not possible to narrate all the interesting episodes of

Mahabharata in this short book. However, all incidents and stories having direct relevance to the main theme of Mahabharata have been included. In addition, a few others, important and interesting, have also been carefully chosen and included.

Chapter-XVI

THE BATTLE OF GODS ON EARTH

One hot summer day, Krishna and Arjuna had gone to the cool banks of a nearby river. They quenched their thirst by drinking the water of the river. As they relaxed under a tree in the nearby forest, a brahmin appeared in front of them with folded hands.

Krishna and Arjuna looked at each other and then at the brahmin with a quizzical look. The brahmin said, "Please help me in getting my food. I have been denied my food for a very long time and I am genuinely starved. My requirement is very large because I am a voracious eater".

Arjuna was genuinely amused. He enquired, "What is it you wish to eat and how much of it?".

On Arjuna's query, the brahmin shed his disguise and appeared in his original form, that of the fire-god. He kept his hands folded and said, "I am not a brahmin. I am the fire-god. I am generally satisfied by eating the fire from a cluster of trees. However, ever since I set my eyes on this Khandawa forest, I have been denied my food. Wherever I start a fire in any corner, Lord Indra, the god of rain produces heavy showers to douse the fire and my hunger remains unsatisfied. Indra does it to protect his friend Takshakraj, the king of snakes.

"What I would request you two, who I know are divine people is to use your power to stop the showers of rain once it starts. This will enable the fire to spread without any interruption and my apetite will be satisfied."

Arjuna responded to the fire-god, "We do have some extraordinary powers but they are not enough to take on a formidable person like Indra. We wish to help you but without additional powers or weapons, it cannot be done.

The fire-god appreciated the logic of the argument advanced by Arjuna. For the first time he understood that stopping the rain would amount to challenging Lord Indra. He accordingly decided to help the duo and enhance their powers. He invoked the water-god and on latter's appearance, requested him to provide appropriate weapons for the to enable them to counter Indra.

The water god reappeared after a while. He gave to Krishna and Arjuna one powerful bow with a quiver having inexhaustible number of arrows. Also, he provided one chariot each to both of them.

The fire god also presented Krishna with the Sudershan Chakra and a mace. He explained "This divine disk with cutting edges on the circumpherence can be used against even the most powerful gods and demons alike. Your can order it to go and exterminate the adversary. It will carry out your instructions and will return to you on its own".

"The mace", he continued, "will enable you to fight with anyone. It is as strong as the 'vajra' of Indra".

Armed with the added weaponry the two expressed their readiness to the fire-god. Arjuna had an additional reason to undertake the mission. Khandawa forest had become a dreaded sanctuary of criminals, anti-social elements, thiefs and dacoits and they were already contemplating some strong action from the side of the state. Helping fire-god would serve the dual purpose.

They gave the signal to fire god to go ahead and commence the operations. The fire god did not need a second word. In no time the fire was started and the forest was a blazing inferno. The flames were leaping high and the heat even reached the skies. The fire-god was satisfying his appetite. All the criminal elements perished in the fire. Lord Indra came to know of the fire. He ordered some of the gods to proceed to the area. He remembered Taksharaja and sent immediate showers on the burning forest. However the fire was so fierce that the showers were converted to steam much before they could reach the fire.

Indra lost his patience. He summoned Airavata, his favourite elephant and armed with the Vajra in hand, descended on the scene. Seeing Arjuna and Krishna did not help matters.He remembered the ignominy suffered at the hands of Krishna in the Goverdhana episode at Gokul. As he braced up for a fight, the other gods who were present, stiffened, expecting a furious battle. Knowing the powers of Krishna and Arjuna and seeing their new weapons, most of them looked for a chance to flee.

However, soon there was a loud voice from the skies. “Listen Indra, do not embark upon a fight with Krishna. Your friend, Taksharaja has already fled from the Khandawa forest and is safe and sound. The fire has destroyed criminals and fugitives who deserved death anyway. Seek peace with Krishna ask for his pardon and return to your abode”.

Indra realized his mistake and after seeking the forgiveness of Krishna, returned to heavens along with his fellow-gods.

As the fire was still raging in full fury from one corner of the forest came the Maya demon galloping and gasping with the fire-god after him. Seeing the two, he leapt at the feet of Arjuna and entreated to be saved. Arjuna took pity and told the fire-god to spare him. The fire-god stopped chasing him and turned his attention over other objects. Fire could have killed the demon and Maya realized that his life had been spared only on account of Arjuna's dispensation. He was profusely thankful. He gave his full introduction and requested Arjuna to ask him for a return gift. Krishna, hearing that Maya was highly proficient at building houses with beautifully designed illusions, suggested that he build a great palace for Yudhishthira with great illusions in Khandavaprastha. Maya happily accepted. In due course the magnificient palace was ready. It was really a masterpiece – a unique one in the world. What was most remarkable were the large number of beautiful structures of the palace, each better than the other one. Many magnificient illusions had been created. In some places what looked like a floor was a water pond. In other, reverse was true.

There were places where one would get in and get lost, not knowing how to get out.

His task over, Maya acknowledged the gratitude of the Pandava family. He, however, confessed that he felt that he had not done enough to repay the debt he owed to Arjuna for saving his life. He gifted a diamond studded mace to Bhima, as well as a beautiful looking conch-shell named 'Deva Dutt' to Arjuna. He then took their leave. On account of his excellent and devoted work, the Pandavas granted to him their protection at any place wherever he stayed.

Once the formal religious ceremony for the entry/occupation ceremony of the palace had been held, the Pandavas and their guests occupied various rooms therein. Because of the brilliant illusory designs of Maya demon, the occupants took more than normal time to get settled and used to in the palace. The palace became a show-piece and added another exhibit to the hall of fame of Pandavas.

Chapter-XVII

HIGHER AMBITIONS

With the prosperity and reputation of Yudhistira's kingdom growing by leaps and bounds, it was inevitable that the people around the king would clamour for a higher status for their king. Many courtiers suggested that it was the opporture time for Yudhishtira being acknowledged and proclaimed as an emperor. They suggested that a Rajsuya yagya be performed. The general consensus was that the strength and valour of Pandavas and their armies was mighty enough to defeat any king of the region who might object to this venture. The Pandava brothers, specially Bhima and Arjuna were extremely thrilled about the whole idea.

"What is the point in being so prosperous and powerful, when you continue to remain just one of the many kings". Bhima opined, "If we are the strongest", he added, "let us declare so and let others acknowledge the same". Arjuna too supported the proposal to hold a Rajsuya yagya for declaring Yudhishthira the Emperor.

Yudhishthira was aware of the matter. He was not unenthusiastic on the issue but wanted to tread with caution. He was confident that the Kauravas will not oppose the move even though Duryodhana and his brothers would not be happy about it. There were, however, other kings in the region, whose attitudes ere unclear. The idea was that once the yagya was announced and held, it should be concluded successfully without a dissenting opinion or a formidable challenge from some unexpected quarters. It was therefore necessary to elicit an unbiased opinion of some knowledgable well-wisher. In such a situation, who could be a better adviser than Shri Krishna. Accordingly, the king sent a message to Krishna to come to Indraprastha for urgent consultations. As expected, Krishna arrived in Indraprastha within a few days. Yudhishthira and the other Pandavas sat together and explained to Krishna the idea of holding the Rajasuya yagya to declare Yudhishthira the emperor of the region. Krishna was requested for his views on the whole matter.

Pandavas had full faith in Krishna, his wisdom and tact. He and Arjuna, in particular, were very close to each other and it appeared to have been so from the previous births. Krishna was also the nephew of Kunti and always held her in high regard. Likewise, he was one of the closest friends of Vidura who himself was not only one of the wisest ministers of Dhritarashtra, but also a staunch adherent of 'Dharma', i.e. right action and right conduct all the time above all, Krishna was one person in whom Draupadi had supreme trust, confidence and faith. To consult Krishna was therefore the most logical thing to do in such a critical matter.

Krishna pondered over the matter and then spoke. "I feel it is an excellent idea and Yudhishtira deserves the honour you all are speaking of. However, one must weigh the pros and cons carefully. With me and Drupada, along with our respective armies, being your key allies, I do not foresee any problem from many quarters. Even though some of the Kauravas might be envious and hence resentful of this venture, they would not openly oppose the move. However, one person from whom I expect a definite opposition and an extremely strong resistance is Jarasandh, the king of Magadha."

"Jarasandha is strong and formidable. Even I fought a war for three years against him, but could not win and had to acknowledge defeat and consequently retire and retreat from Mathura to Dwarka. He nurtures his own ambitions which would come in conflict with our proposed plans. Hence my own advice is that we tackle Jarasandha first and then only hold the Rajasuya yagya".

Krishna continued, "Jarasandha has been assiduously engaged in moving against the kings and chiefs of his neighbourhood. He has imprisoned them and has been treating them in a very cruel and inhuman manner. As of now, he has eighty-six kings as his prisoners. He plans to capture fourteen more and then sacrifice all the hundred of them in a special ceremony. All the kshatriyas are scared of him. These also include some mighty warriors including my cousin Shishupal.

"I therefore feel that we have to eliminate the threat from Jarasandha and then alone think of the Rajasuya. We should avoid engaging his army, but instead try and kill him by employing some guile. Bhima, Arjuna and I myself could be part of this venture. Once we succeed, we can free the unfortunate prisoner-kings. The additional advantage would be that all these eighty six kings would be forever grateful to us and become our allies. By using the strength of Bhima, the finer martial prowesses of Arjuna and my full support, we have a very good chance achieving success".

Bhima and Arjuna immediately applauded the proposal but Yudhishthira was not so keen. The idea of exposing his two closest brothers, and even Krishna, to extreme peril just to attain the glory of the title of Emperor, was not so appealing. He expressed his serious reservations. Bhima and Arjuna, however, were unanimous of the view that for a kshatriya, it was necessary to engage in risky ventures to achieve his ambitious. They were all for implementing Krishna's plans and for seeing the success of Rajasuya yagya after elminitating Jarasandha.

After more discussions, Yudhishthira had to withdraw his objections and agree to let Bhima and Arjuna go and act against Jarasandha. Another reason for Yudhishthira agreeing to the venture was that on account of high expectations generated due to the public demand for his elevation, his own subjects would be very much disappointed if the yagya was not performed. Yudhishthira himself was a true kshatriya and a fighter, but the responsibilities of the king and that of the eldest brother, made him follow the 'Discretion is the better part of valour' policy. He eventually gave a go-ahead signal, but advised fool-proof plans and preparations.

Chapter-XVIII

REMOVING ROADBLOCKS - KILLING OF JARASANDHA

Jarasandha was the son of an illustrious warrior. Brihadratha, who commanded three regiments of Magadha apart from being its ruler. He was held in high regard by the people. He had two wives, the twin daughters of the king of Kashi. However, he remained childless till the old age. Eventually, he decided to hand over his kingdom to his ministers and himself, accompanied by his wives, retired to the forests to engage himself in prayers, penances and austerities. To his good fortune, he happened to visit the great sage Kaushika and served him with sincerety and devotion. When the learned sage enquired about the reason behind his all-too visible sadness on his face, he explained the source of his unhappiness i.e. not having had a son and a heir. Just then a mango fruit fell in the lap of the great sage. He picked it up and gave to Brihadratha saying that the fruit would give him the fulfillment of his wishes. Since Brihadratha always treated both of his wives impartially and with equal favours, he cut the mango in two equal halves and gave one portion each to his two queens.

Both the queens came into family way and delivered after the confinement. However, to their horror, both delivered pieces were found to be the portions of a child in two exact halves from top to the bottom. In sheer horror, the two portions were quietly disposed off and thrown in a garbage trash outside the town. These pieces would have been devoured by animals and birds, but for the fact that a rakshashi (demoness) chanced to pass by and noticing the flesh pieces, collected them to eat them herself. However, a very strange thing happened. As the rakshasi held the two pieces together in one hand, the pieces joined together and got converted into a live bubbly boy. The surprised rakshasi did not have a heart to kill the infant. She changed herself into the garb of an ordinary woman and took the child to the king relating the entire incident. Brihadratha immediately recognized his son and gratefully accepted him from the woman. He named his son as "Jarasandha' named after the demoness 'Jara'. The boy grew up to be a supremely powerful person. In due course, he took over as the king of Magadha. His power and fame spread far and wide. However, his sky rocketing ambitions also turned him into a cruel tyrant. The eighty-six kings languishing in his prisons bore testimony to this trait.

Krishna, Bhima and Arjuna had decided to manoeurve the things in such a manner so that Jarasandha could be engaged in a single combat. They wanted to avoid any confrontation with the army. Accordingly they disguised themselves in ochre robes and entered the Magadha capital. Jarasandha was known to honour the visiting sages and regularly hold dialogues with them. The trio were taken to the royal household and accommodated in the place specially earmarked for these people. Since Krishna had let it be known that Bhima and Arjuna were observing silence till midnight Jarasandha had indicated that he would visit them after they broke the silence i.e. midnight. He was a shade restless as well since a series of bad omens were indicating something bad was going to happen.

The king came to their chamber after midnight and started talking to them. However as the conversation proceeded, Jarasandha's suspicious regarding their true identities grew more and more. Eventually he could not control himself and challenged them to come out clean. The trio admitted that they were not sages and disclosed their true identities. They also challenged Jarsandha for an individual combat with any one of their group. According to the tradition in those days, a kshatriya could not refuse a duel, if challenged.

Jarasandha was an immensely powerful person who had not been defeated so far. He chose Bhima for the combat and declared that the combat would be without arms or weapons.'Krishna', he said, 'is not a kshatriya, just a cowherd and Arjuna is too young for me'.

Thus began the duel. Very soon, it was evident that the two adversaries were evenly matched. The fight was intense and continued for thirteen days with no result. Only on the fourteenth day, Jarasandha showed signs of some weakness. Sensing an opportunity to finish the fight Bhima lifted Jarasandha in the air and, whirling his body for a hundred times, banged it on the floor with a huge thud. Without losing any time, he took hold of both the legs and tore the body in two halves. Since Jarasandha had been made of the two equal parts since his infancy, the body was split in two equal parts, exactly the way they had been joined decades ago.

Bhima gave a victory shout but was amazed to see that the two parts suddenly joined together and a revived Jarasandha stood in front of them to resume the fight. Bhima was incredulous.

The combat resumed with Bhima once again gaining the upperhand. He was however at a loss to devise the best way to kill his adversary. Suddenly, he saw Krishna picking up a grass straw, splitting it into two parts and throwing the two pieces in two opposite directions i.e. the piece in the right hand to the left and the one in the left to the right side.

Bhima understood the gesture. He again lifted Jarasandha's body, whirled it around and banged it on the ground. Tearing the body in two pieces, like he had done earlier, he threw the pieces in two opposite directions. The pieces did not rejoin and Jarasandha this time was dead for good.

They made Jarasandha's son the king of Magadha. The eighty six royal prisoners were released from prison. All of them remained grateful to Pandavas and Krishna for saving them from a sure death. The three then returned to Indraprastha to join Yudhishthira.

Chapter-XIX

THE RAJSUYA YAGYA AND THE AFTERMATH

With the elimination of Jarasandha, the decks had been cleared for Rajsuya yagya. The date and time had been decided by the family priest. He had also compiled a list of invitees consisting of important rulers, rishis, pandits and prominent citizens of Indraprastha. Invitations had been sent to these people. Yudhishtira sent Sahdeva to Hastinapura to invite his near and dear ones.

Indraprastha was all decked up and decorated and looked magnificient. Gradually the invitees started coming. A big contingent came from Hastinapura. It consisted of Dhritarashtra, Bhishma, Vidura, Drona, Kripacharya, many kaurava princes and many other familiar faces. Dhritarashtra had got many magnificient gifts for Yudhishthira, other Pandava princes, Kunti, Draupadi and Subhadra. Hastinapura was in a great festive mood.

The Rajasuya yagya began in time and conducted with proper rituals. It was an impressive ceremony. The sight of all the powerful people, the kings and wise men of kingdoms far away from Hastinapur acknowledging the supremacy of Yudhishthira was inspiring, bringing credit to the pandava king.

On completion of the yagya, only one ceremony was left. Traditionally, one person amongst the gathering was named as a 'Special Person' on account of his outstanding achievements and qualities. Yudhishthira requested those present to suggest an appropriate person. Naturally, such a name had to have a popular endorsement.

The king of Magadha, son of Jarasandha, Sahadeva, proposed the name of Krishna for this unique honour.

Krishna's name found many popular supporters. It was formally seconded by Bhishma and Dronacharya.

There were, however, some dissenting voices as well. This was not unusual for such a vast gathering. While some had personal preferences due to special relationships and mentioned those persons, the others were unhappy with Krishna for one reason or other. There was not much support for the either group.

However the group unhappy with Krishna found Shishupal, Krishna's cousin and king of Chhedi very vocal with his criticism.

Despite being the first cousin of Krishna, Shishupal was opposite of the latter in personal qualities. Shishupal had been jealous and highly critical of Krishna from the early days. His mother was the sister of Krishna's father, but that was where the similarity ended. As Krishna's reputation of a highly respectable, wise, human person having divine powers grew, Shishupal's animosity towards him grew by equal proportions. On a large number of occasions, he had been downright mean, vulgar and antagonistic towards Krishna, but Krishna forgave him or ignored him. He had, in fact, made a promise to Shishupal's mother, his aunt that he will ignore as many as hundred acts of misdeeds, commissions and omissions by Shishupal. That number had long been surpassed.

On that day of Rajsuya, Shishupal was however, most vile and abusive. He not only criticized Krishna as 'much hyped', 'good for nothing' cowherd, but also took on the Pandava brothers, Bhishma and Vidura, criticizing them in choicest words. He even questioned their lineage calling the same as doubtful and low. Why, he asked, the assembly could not select a better person like Dronacharya, Rishi Vyasa or even Bhishma, who had the experience, wisdom and seniority.

Krishna listened to Shishupal's vile ranting and allowed it to go on in a true democratic tradition although he did frown and look agitated when the elders were criticised. Shishupal was in the meantime, getting more and more abusive. Bhishma intervened after enough was said. He rubbished Shishupal's description of Krishna and people who actively endorsed his nomination. Krishna, he said, was wise, brave and a follower of dharma. He was respected by his people and others for his sterling virtues. The criticism levelled by Shishupal was, therefore, grossly unfair and uncalled for. Majority of the assemblage indicated their agreement with Bhishma's views.

This further infuriated Shishupal who became personal using choicest uncomplimentary words for the grand sire. He even called him senile, mindless and stupid. Once again calling Krishna an incompetent fool and Bhishma a stupid imbecile, he staged a walk-out from the gathering. A sprinkling of those present also joined him in this act.

Krishna then rose and spoke, "I regret that Shishupal has chosen this auspicious and sober occasion to come out with what I can best describe as a dirty diatribe. I have been tolerating his bad manners and misdeeds only out of consideration of my aunt, his mother. But today, in criticizing and abusing senior and highly respected people, he has crossed all limits and needs to be punished.

Krishna then called out to Shishupal and asked him to apologise for his unworthy behaviour. On his refusal, Krishna unleashed his sudershana chakra which chased Shishupala and finally sliced his neck neatly cutting his head which fell on the floor. Those who were with Shishupala, quickly retreated to avoid retribution for siding with the evil. All were visibly scared.

Krishna was then honoured as the best person by Emperor Yudhishtira. He was blessed by all elders and congratulated by others.

This marked the end of the famous yagya which went off perfectly excepting the unhappy episode of Shishupal. Yudhishthira than thanked everyone. In a few days, everyone had departed carrying appropriate gifts and happy memories of the event, the people, the palace, the city and its wonderful well-mannnered and sweet-spoken people.

Rishi Vedavyasa also announced his intention to retire to his ashram in the forest for his penances and prayers. Yudhishtira came to him for a final audience with the grand old sire of the family. Every moment with him was worth its weight in gold. After paying his respects, Yudhishtira expressed his satisfaction that the yagya had been held successfully in the presence of all the prominent people of the entire region. He expressed his hope that this yagya will usher in a new eva of peace, happiness and prosperity, not only for his kingdom but for Kauravas and others as well.

Yudhishthira continued, “There are some wise men who had forecasted terrible events to come. I hope that phase has ended with the death of Shishupal and we can look forward to better times from now on”.

The progenitor and the guru responded, “Dharmavira, you have been crowned as an emperor. Discharge your duties conscientionsly to bring glory to the kuru race. However, the answer to your last comment is this. Yes, this whole region is in for a major catastrophe and the next thirteen years will be full of sorrow and suffering culminating in a major war which will result in the near total annihilation of the kshatriya race. You and your brothers and allies will be on one side while the Kaurava princes and their supporters will be on the other. My only advice to you is that during this period, you must steadfastedly stick to righteousness. Let the destiny prevail, but do not stray from the path of Dharma”.

Yudhishthira touched the feet of the rishi who then departed for his hermitage. The emperor then returned to his court. On meeting his brothers he shared with them the conversation he had with Veda Vyasa and asked them to be prepared for inhospitable events, if and when they occurred.

Yudhishthira declared, “I intend to be just, follow righteous path and not to stray from truth and dharma. I shall also ensure that we maintain the best of relations with the Kauravas in Hastinapura in order to ensure that we do not give them any provocation to start a conflict. If after doing all this, something happens, then that is God’s will, the destiny. We all know that the destiny rewards some who are wrongdoers and at times punishes the best of the people”.

Arjuna interceded, “you are the emperor and everyone knows we have been fair, just and truthful. There is no need to worry about the events in future too much. We shall worry about the bridges when we come to cross them. In the meantime, let us concentrate on the present and what is ahead in the immediate future.

Chapter-XX

DURYODHANA'S LAMENT AND ANOTHER PLOT

The hostility of the Kaurava princes towards their Pandava counter-parts had been a known fact from their childhood days. Small petty acts to serious acts with the intention to cause serious harms culminating in the Lac-house incident had been occurring at regular intervals. Bhishma and Dhritarashtra had thought that by giving half of the kingdom to Pandavas, both the factions would be happy and satisfied and be able to coexist.

However, Duryodhana and his brothers had a different mindset. Right from the childhood they had resented Pandavas. Their father, Dhritarashtra being denied the kingdom, despite being the eldest of brothers, had been the prime factor to fuel the negative emotions. It was difficult to reconcile to the fact that this was due to the fact that Dhritarashtra was blind by birth. Success of Pandu in governance and of Pandava children in their superior conduct, knowledge and skills further increased the jealousy. Decades of pent-up emotions could not be wished away by giving half of what Hastinapur had. Winning the hands of Draupadi in the swayamvar and the resultant alliance with Drupada was another feather in the Pandavas' cap. The tremendous prosperity and strength of their kingdom was indeed seen to be believed.

Those dormant feelings of envy and jealousy came to the fore during their visit to Indraprastha. The glitter, glitz and glory was all there to be seen. The great gathering of elite wise men and warriors, the yagya itself, acknowledgement of Yudhishthira as emperor, the snuffing of mighty Shishupal and above all, the palace designed and built by Maya contributed to the aura of magnificience. All this had the depressing effect on Duryodhana. What made it worse was that they were laughed at by Draupadi and the palace staff when they committed some stupid mistakes when going around the palace which was full of illusions. Having his maternal uncle, Shakuni, by his side, did not help Duryodhana either. The former played a perfect foil in arousing the anger and resentment of Duryodhana.

So strong were the feelings of Duryodhana that he even mooted waging war with Paṇḍavas and ḍrive them out of their kingdom. Duryodhana was brash but Shakuni was cunning and careful. He cautioned Duryodhana against any idea of direct conflict with Pandavas in the battle field.

"A direct conflict with them will be prolonged, bloody and counter-productive because you shall be striking at their strength", said Shakuni. "I would not advise that, dear nephew. Rather, I would like to strike at their weakness. For instance, I know that Yudhishtira is fond of gambling and is not particularly adept at it. In a game of dice between Yudhishtira and yourself, with me throwing dice on your behalf, Yudhishthira will be like a lamb ready to be slaughtered. That way, we can win from them all things, which you wanted to win through a bloody conflict. Let us go back to Hastinapura after taking leave of Pandavas with all the goodwill and gratitude. We should then persuade your father to invite the Pandavas to Hastinapura. Once they accept the invitation and arrive at your capital, you leave the rest to me. This, dear nephew, I can assure you, will be an infalliable plan".

Duryodhana realized the merit of Shakuni's arguments and agreed to his suggestions. They parted after praising the Pandavas for the splendid yagya and the entire function. Carrying a smile on their faces, they left Indraprastha for home with their heart burning with hatred, envy and jealousy.

Back at Hastinapura, Duryodhana poured out his heart to Dhritarashtra. He described the grandeur and prosperity of Indraprastha. He followed it up with the details of outstanding gifts, jewels, diamonds, brought by scores of kings who had come to attend the function. He summarized his conclusions that while the Pandavas have progressed beyond imagination, and were doing so with every passing day, the Kauravas were decaying. Unless this trend was reversed, they were bound to become menials. Duryodhana even threatened to take his life rather than face that ignominy.

Duryodhana then described the new palace of Pandavas built by Maya demon. Describing some of the outstanding features, the likes of which could not be matched by all the grandeur of the buildings of Hastinapura, he also described the humiliation suffered by them when they fell in the illusory pond of banged their heads unknowingly against the palace wall and the way the Pandava brothers, Draupadi and other women and even menials of the palace laughed at them when those incidents took place. He reiterated his views that unless they did something drastic to take away this prosperity and reversed the growth, Hastinapura would become a laughting stock because it was bound to be compared with Indraprastha sooner or later and mocked at with contempt by one and all.

Dhritarashtra, like many earlier occasions, was torn between his heart and his wisdom. He could understand the hurt felt by his son, because he himself felt the pangs of jealousy when told of the progress and achievements of Pandavas. However, he also realized that such adverse emotions were uncalled for.

He tried to persuade Duryodhana that comparisons were not called for because Pandavas were their brothers. There was enough for him and the Kaurava brothers to support a comfortable and luxurious likestyle befitting the royal family. Besides, a confrontation with the Pandavas would have disastrous results affecting both the sides. He therefore advised Duryodhana to change his views and attitudes towards the Pandavas and not to harbour any evil intentious towards them.

Duryodhana, however, was not convinced. He had always been an obstinate and aggressive person. He countered his father's arguments by saying that it ill-behoved a king who chose to remain happy and contended. Quoting Brihaspati, the great teacher of Devas, he repeated, "Forebearance and contentment, though the duties of ordinary people, are not the virtue of kings. A Kshatriya's duty is that of constantly seeking the victory. Pandavas are doing just that while we are decaying and remaining stagnant. Very soon, we will be laughed at by them, like they did in their palace at me".

Despite the sterling qualities of Dhritarashtra and the deep knowledge possessed by him, he had two major weaknesses. The first was his love for his son which made him blind to reason. This had happened a number of times in the past. The second weakness was that he still nursed a deep hurt of on account of Pandu having been given the throne in preference to him. Even though he knew that the blindness by birth bebarred him from the coveted honour, yet being the eldest and not being given the crown had hurt him and had continued to trouble him. Duryodhana and even others were aware of it and always took advantage of this.

Shakuni interjected in his ever-persuasive voice, “Bother-inlaw,”he said, “since I was constantly with Duryodhana at Indraprastha, I fully agree with the sentiments and hurt expressed by Duryodhana. I also agree with you that as far as possible, any bloodshed should be avoided. Rather, we should maintain good relations with the Pandavas. However, what Duryodhana is suggesting can also be achieved in another way which otherwise will be peaceful. Let us invite them for a gambling match. A game of chance, offering equal rewards to the participating parties has always been a favourite pastime of kshatriyas. If the Pandavas accept our invitation and come to play here, I am sure that, playing on behalf of Duryodhana and throwing the dice, I can win all which Duryodhana desires. Neither the pandavas nor any of their supporters can say that the game was unfair. I am confident of winning because compared to me, Yudhishtira is a mere non-entity in a game of dice. Gambling is possibly his only weakness and most important, he does not know when to stop”.

Dhritarashtra appreciated the merit of Shakuni's arguments. He felt that there was nothing wrong in inviting the pandavas for a gambling match. He knew that Shakuni could win the wagers on behalf of Duryodhana. If, however, he found the Kauravas losing, he could always stop the game in between. This was also one way to satisfy the demands of Duryodhana.

He, however, told the duo that he would consult Vidura on the matter before a final decision, just as he did on all important matters. Duryodhana immediately told his father that if he did that, the venture would be doomed as Vidura, a stickler for fairness and morality, will reject the proposal. They left Dhritarashtra asking him not to consult Vidura, but apply his own mind independently.

Dhritarashtra, however, quietly called Vidura and described the proposal of Duryodhana and Shakuni, "Vidura, as expected, opposed the idea in totality. He knew what has prompted Duryodhana and Shakuni to propose the game of dice. They had recently returned from Indraprastha and were seething with jealousy. Instead of working for development of their kingdom, they were resorting to the gambling route to get one up on Pandavas. He told Dhritarashtra, "Oh King, gambling has never benefited anyone and has ruined many kings and families. I would advise you not to permit it. If you do, then, it would open up the gates of hatred and strife, something which we wanted to avoid by giving the Pandavas half of the kingdom. It will indeed spell the ultimate doom to the kuru race".

The king had already been told about the expected reaction from Vidura. He, therefore, decided to go ahead with the proposed game. He ordered the construction of a hall of games and instructed Vidura to go to Indraprastha when the hall was ready and invite the Pandavas for a game of dice. He thought that Vidura was making too much of a simple game. After all, a game of dice was an accepted form of sport between the kshatriyas. Once again an ageing and doting father possessing a weak will gave in to the desires of a demanding son, much against a saner advice.

Much against his wishes Vidura went to Indraprastha when he met Yudhishthira, he conveyed the message of Dhritarashtra. "A magnificient hall of games has been constructed at the palace in Hastinapura. The king Dhritarashtra has invited you all to come for the inauguration and a game of dice. After playing the game, you can return to Indraprastha". said Vidura.

Yudhishthira did not find the usual warmth and cheerfulness on Vidura's face. He looked askance at

Vidura. Vidura said, "I have performed my duty of conveying the orders of the king Dhritarashtra. I would, however, advise you not to play the proposed game since pastimes like these never end up in happiness and good relations. Decision, however, is yours".

Yudhishtira, decided to go. It was indeed an honour to be invited by Dhritarashtra for whom he had high regards (Yudhishthira, for that matter, being a good person himself, had high regards for all elders). Secondly, he had just recently decided not to do anything which might displease Kauravas. Lastly, gambling was a weakness of his and he felt that he stood a decent chance against Duryodhana if pitted against him.

They reached Hastinapura a day prior to the start of the game. Yudhishtira rested during the day. Next day, accompanied by his brothers, Yudhishtira reached the hall of games. The hall was full. All the high and mighty were there. Bhishma, Vidura, Drona, Kripacharya and many others were already there. Dhritarashtra had stayed back at his chamber. There was also an undercurrent of tension because the general feeling was that the outcome of the games, regardless of which side won, would not be a happy one.

Soon the sheet of cloth on which they were expected to sit and gamble had been spread. Shakuni invited the participants on to the floor. Yudhishthira and his brothers also took their place. Before the start, the young emperor, suffering possibly from a pang of conscience, blurted out.

We have been advised that gambling is not good. Scores of wise rishis, well-versed in the affairs of the world have advised against it since it can be used by some who can resort to deception. One does not win by power, wit or merit. He does it either through mere luck or deceit. Either way, the winner does'nt deserve it all and the loser's loss might not be totally fair". Yudhishtira said the above based upon what his mind had been conditioned and trained to accept. But his body language was telling something different. He was known to be quite fond of gambling which was accepted as a legitimate sport amongst kshatriyas.

Shakuni was quick to perceive this inner conflict writ clearly on Yudhisthira's face. He countered, "What is wrong in playing a game of chance. It offers equal opportunities to all participants. I don't find any difference between a battle or a witty discussion between two scholars or two musical talents and this game. The person with better skill and wit, and of course luck on his side has more chance to win. If you wish, you need not play but for heaven's sake, do not quote outdated views".

A bit flushed, Yudhishthira said, " I shall play. Between whom is the game and who decides the stakes?".

Duryodhana replied, "From my side, I shall arrange the stakes and uncle Shakuni shall throw the dice on my behalf".

Yudhishthira again quizzed with raised eyebrows, "Isn't it rather unusual for one person to arrange the stakes and someone else playing on his behalf and throwing the dice?"

Shakuni replied, "Not at all. It has happened before if all the participants agree. Is this another ploy to withdraw from the game?

Yudhishthira hesitated and then said, "We will play".

Chapter-XXI

THE GAMES AND THE ULTIMATE SHAME

With the ground rules cleared, the game began. Despite the reservations expressed by Yudhishthira regarding Shakuni playing on behalf of Duryodhana, he had agreed to play. He was quite aware that Shakuni was an expert on throwing dice and he had practiced this art for days and months to perfect the art. The gamblers' streak in Yudhishthira made him feel certain that the lady luck was bound to smile at him as well.

What Yudhishthira was not aware that the dice itself was loaded to ensure that it favoured the call of Duryodhana, when thrown by Shakuni. The result was that Yudhishtira lost continuously, game after game.

First he lost jewels, then the gold and silver. This was followed by all his precious possessions, e.g. chariots, horses, elephants, armies, personal servants. This was followed by the villager, territories, cows, sheep, cities and their personal ornaments.

Yudhishthira was sad with tears in his eyes. He did lose in the past, but he won too. This unfortunately was one-way street. In his desperation and stupid obstinate thought that the good luck was round the corners, Yudhishthira staked his four brothers and later even himself but he lost them all.

There was a stunned silence in the entire hall. At last, it was broken when Duryodhana proudly proclaimed that all the five Pandava brothers had been won by him and they had become his slaves. They all stood with their eyes glued to the floor. Bhima started saying something critical of Yudhishthira when Arjuna stopped him from doing so warning him not to fall a victirm to opposition's ploy of sowing the seeds of dissention between brothers.

The game, however, was not over as far as Shakuni was concerned. He was a past master in manipulating emotions in a game of dice. He looked at Yudhishtira and said, "There is one very precious thing which you might still like to pledge. But......may be you might not".

Yudhishthira looked at him and asked as to what was Shakuni suggesting, because he had thought that he had lost all his precious possessions, his brothers including himself. Shakuni replied that he could continue the game by offering Draupadi as a wager.

A desperate Yudhishtira hesitated for a moment and then said 'I pledge her'.

A hush fell on the whole hall followed by murmurs of condemnation.Shakuni threw the dice with total concentration. Suddenly there was a shout in the Kaurava camp as Shakuni announced, "We have won".

The elders sat in a stunned silence. Most of the Kaurava princes, barring a handful, rejoiced loudly. A beaming Duryodhana turned to Vidura and said, "Go and fetch Draupadi. From now on, she is our maidservant. We will make her clean and swab the palace".

Vidura, shocked beyond comprehension, shouted at Duryodhana, "Have you gone mad. Drunk with your success, you do not realize that you are at the brink of abyss. If you pursue this path, the Kuru race stands to be decimated. Yudhishthira, after losing himself, has lost all his liberty and rights and hence he cannot pledge Draupadi".

Duryodhana, however, was on cloud nine. He told Vidura that although he professed to work for the Kauravas, he was jealous of them. He was also scared of Pandavas. He (Duryodhana) then turned to his charioteer, Prathikami, and asked him to go and bring Draupadi without any delay.

The charioteer went to Draupadi and told her the shocking news, giving the full details of the gambling rounds. Draupadi upset in the beginning, had regained her composure. She turned to the charioteer and said, "Go back to the assembly and ask the person who had pledged me as a stake, in front of the whole assembly, whether he had lost himself first or his wife?"

Prathikami returned to the hall and asked Yudhishthira as bidden by Draupadi. Every one heard the question. Yudhishthira stood there speechless and motionless.

Duryodhana was losing his patience. He asked the charioteer to go back to Draupadi and ask her to come and question Yudhishtira herself. The poor servant, caught between the two did what he was ordered to do. But, once again Draupadi asked him to go once again to Yudhishtira and ask him her original question once again loudly and clearly in front of the entire assembly.

Prathikami again repeated the earlier question. In the meantime, Duryodhana had lost his patience. He turned to Dushasana and said, 'This fellow is scared of Bhima and his brothers. Go and get Draupadi here even if you have to drag her here'.

Dushasana was to happy to receive these instructions. He rushed to Draupadi's chambers. Shouting with glee and announcing to Draupadi that she had become their maid servant, he asked her to accompany him immediately. When Draupadi wanted to run away from there to Gandhari's palace, Dushasana rushed at her and grabbing her by the hair he dragged her to the hall of games.

The elders sat glued to their seat feeling ashamed at this sad spectacle. It was clear that the crown prince was exhibiting his worst arrogance.As she was dragged on the floor, she rushed to the elders' enclosure and appealed to them. "How could you permit myself to be pledged by my husband who had already lost his freedom in this game in which he has been cheated by people who are experts at manipulating dices; something which is known universally I appeal to you to spare me this
humiliation. If you believe in Dharma and God, and have had mothers, wives and sisters, have pity on me.

There were many even in the kuru camp who showed dissent at what was happening. Yuyutsu was one of them. Another son of Dhritarashtra, Vikarna, was also very clear and forthright.

He said "I am young and am not expected to speak when such a galaxy of elders is available. But I am compelled to do so on account of sheer unfairness in this game. Firstly, Yudhishthira is tricked into playing this game where a person who is putting up the stakes is not throwing the dice. Rather, he is represented by some one who is a known expert in the art of throwing dice and is a giant when compared to the Pandavas in terms of this skill. Secondly, Yudhishthira is asked to offer Draupadi as a stake when he, having already lost his freedom himself, had no right to play the game. Again, we are all aware that Draupadi is married to all the five brothers and hence Yudhishthira alone had no right to pledge her without consulting the other brothers".

Warming up, Vikarna continued, "All the rules have been violated and yet none has objected to this gross unfairness. As per the rules of the game a specific pledge, cannot be suggested or demanded. Yet, Draupadi's name is specially mentioned".

Taking a brief pause and addressing the elders, Vikarna said, "I appeal to the elders to be dictated by the tenets of Dharma and cancel this game. Besides, games like these are held to promote good relations with our neighbours and more so with Pandavas, who are our first cousins. What we are seeing here, is an empress being dragged by her hair on the floor and turned into a maid. Karna intervened to cut him short. "Enough", he said," has been said by a person who should only hear and not speak. He has neither experience nor the age to take upon himself to criticize the elders. Shakuni has won the stakes and that is settled. Dushasan, take off the clothes of Pandavas and the robes of Draupadi since they are now our property.

Red-faced, the Pandavas took off their upper garments and handed over to Dushasana. Emboldened more, Dushasana put away those clothes and turned towards Draupadi to disrobe her. With her appeal to the elders falling into deaf ears, she shivered at the prospect of what was to happen.

Closing her eyes, she remembered Krishna, the Lord of Lords and appealed for the divine interventation. As Dushasana started disrobing her, everyone could hear her chanting her prayers. In the background, Duryodhana, Karna, Shakuni laughed, rejoiced and clapped with glee. In desperation, she made a knot of her robe and held it tight between her teeth. Dushasana, however was too strong for her. He wrenched it free with a bit of struggle. Not able to bear the shock Panchali (Draupadi) fainted, chanting Krishna's name. There were loud murmurs. Suddenly, everyone became aware that in the hall of games Hastinapur a miracle was unfolding. Every-time Dushasan disrobed one layer of clothes, they were replaced by a new set on Draupadi. He did it with extra-ordinary swiftness and energy initially enjoying the act like most of his brothers. However, as the time dragged on at the never-ending act, he could be seen tiring. Eventually, he collapsed on the floor totally exhausted, while Draupadi, recovering from the faint and realizing that her honour had been protected stood with her lips moving in prayers by the side of the big heap of the glittering and resplendent garments. The Kaurava brothers were quiet for a change while others in the hall were overwhelmed at this marvel. Many good men praised the almighty and openly wept.

Bhima, standing bare-chested with his huge body with a face writhing with emotions, announced in a clear, loud and baritone voice, "I, Bhima, vow not to join the blessed above,my forefathers, till I break the breast and drink the blood from the heart of this wretched Dushasana, the shame of the bharat race".

An eerie silence followed in the stunned hall, something unreal was happening. The silence was broken by the howling of jackals and dissonant voices of braying of the donkeys and cacophony of voices of eagles and crows from the top. These were decidedly bad omens, sending shivers down the spine of those present. In the meantime, Dhritrashtra, accompanied by Vidura had also arrived in the hall. Vidura had rushed to his chambers and reported the whole incident. The king realized the need for doing some thing decisive to diffuse the crisis. He called Draupadi and made her sit near him. He told her, "You are sinless and blameless. Forget this whole incident and forgive those who have wronged you. Take back all which was lost here, go back to Indraprastha".

The pandavas got up and prepared to head back to Indraprastha. A bit shell-shocked from the events of the day, they were still trying regain their composure and come to terms with the events. Two miracles happening on the same day was too good to be true. Or was it?

On the subject of Dhritrashtra closing his eyes on undue demands, misdeeds and misadventures of Duryodhana, the queen Gandhari, had been steadfastly warning Dhritarashtra that his failure to be firm with his son would spoil him more and more and would result in a very serious catastrophe one day. Dhritarashtra always agreed with her but everytime such a situation arose, he gave in to Duryodhana's demands due to his sheer misguided affection for the latter.

Far away in Dwarka, Rukmini, the head queen of Krishna was observing Krishna (in human form) lost in intense concentration. She knew that, even though he was sitting next to her, his mind was on something else – a thing too serious. Unable to restrain herself, she asked Krishna, "what is it?". Krishna replied, "A devotee of mine is calling me for help. She is being disrobed and stripped naked". Rukmini queried, "Then why don't you do something. Help her, she needs it immediately".

Krishna replied, " I shall, but only after she surrenders herself totally to me. Right now she is depending on her teeth, clutching her robe between them to save her". He remained in acute concentration for some more time and then opened his eyes. Looking at Rukmini, he said, “I have responded”.

Chapter- XXII

ANOTHER ROUND

A huge sigh of relief could be discerned in all those present. A major crisis had been averted. However, new fissures and cracks had come up in their relationships which would take time a long time to heal, if at all, they did heal. While the elders were unanimous in approving and applauding the actions of Dhritarashtra, the younger Kaurava clan and

Shakuni were visibly dissatisfied. A major battle and the booty had almost been won if the gains had not been gifted away by the king.

Karna looked at the Pandava brothers and Draupadi. He said, "I do not agree with what the elders said or did. However, this is a fact that you all are very fortunate".

Duryodhana was still fuming. He said, "Whatever has happened here today will cast long shadows for years to come. It is the king's prerogative to annul the results. My challenge, however, still remains unfulfilled".

Dhritarashtra faced Duryodhana and said, "As the crown prince and the virtual king, you have much much more than what you need. Now, what is it that you want? Anyone else in your place should feel happy, totally satisfied and well contended".

Duryodhana responded, "Majesty, I am what I am. I believe that a kshatriya is not worth his name if he does not want more than what he has. After today, we are virtually enemies. I had not wanted half of the kingdom to be given to Pandavas at the first instance. I still want it back. I assert once again that my challenge still remains unresponded". After the events of the day, the proper thing for Dhritarashtra should have been to say no to any request for the game of dice specially on that day. Once again, the heart prevailed over the head. The king waivered and asked Duryodhana, "What do you want"?

"I propose just one more game of dice", Duryodhana said, "If Pandavas lose, they would have to go in exile for twelve years and live totally incognito in the thirteenth. If during the thirteenth year, they are discovered, they repeat the cycle of twelve plus one year once again. If they complete the thirteenth year without being discovered, they can come back and claim their kingdom back".

Duryodhana continued, "And in case I lose, the same will apply to us. I, Dushasana, Karna and Shakuni will go in exile for twelve years followed by an year in total oblivion. If we are discovered in the thirteenth year we will have to repeat the thirteen year cycle once again".

Yudhishthira queried, "And will you play with new set of dice and who shall throw them"?.

Duryodhana said, "I shall throw the dice and we will play with a new set".

Dhritarashtra looked at Yudhishthira and asked, 'What do you say"?

Yudhishthira replied, "A game of dice is an accepted pastime amongst us kahatriyas. We accept the challenge, success or failure will come to us at the bidding of the providence whether we are in Hastinapur or away from it'.

The stage was set for another round with tension all around. Duryodhana called for new set of dices and threw his three.

'Seven' said Bhima. Yudhishtira threw his three.

'Six' said Duryodhana hoarsely.

The Pandavas had lost once again.They took the customary vow of people going onto exile,discarded their royal robes and changed into ordinary clothes and bowing before all elders, left the palace. Kunti had stayed back with Vidura, but Panchali accompanied the five Pandavas as they walked on the roads of Hastinapur towards the forest. The ordinary people, shell –shocked from the news had lined up on the roads, climbed on the trees and roof tops to see the sons of Pandu walking away accompanied by Draupadi.

Draupadi led the flock weeping and covering her face with her hands, her hair open and dishevelled, (she had taken a vow that she would not tidy her hair or comb them till the dishonour meted out to her was avenged). Next was Yudhisthira covering his face with a cloth since he did not wish anyone to be burnt with his glances. Bhima followed him folding and squeezing his arms – impatient to use them. Nakula and Sahadeva walked with ashes and dust on their faces and bodies to control their anger. The last was Arjuna, casting earth and sand around him with both the hands, practicing scattering arrows in battle.

It was a sight not to be forgotten by all those who beheld it – reminding them of impending return of Pandavas after their exile and the contemplated revenge. They chose to exit by the south gate of Hastinapur the southerly direction being the destination towards 'Yamaloka', the abode of yamaraja, the God of death. Closely following them was the family priest Ayudhamya carrying a pot of insense and signing the verses and sama hymns invoking yama. The crowd felt the eerie effects reinforced by the dark clouds and streaks of lightning, the baying of jackals and herds of eagles flying overhead.

Pandavas and Draupadi walked as a single unit with a purpose. In fact, Kunti had asked Sahadeva to stay back with her but he had declined politely choosing to go with his brothers. When they all had come to ask for her blessings before finally departing, Kunti told them, "When you return, you would be more strong and skilled. Remember your previous stay in forests and improve upon what you had learn't then. May Gods protect you and mother earth give you the shelter and teach you the supreme patience".

Chapter-XXIII

THE AFTERMATH

There was a widespread and unanimous condemnation of the whole incident by the people of Hastinapur. The respect they had for the deceased king Pandu and all five Pandavas was only matched by the reproach they felt towards Dhritarashtra and the Kuru clan. All of them were aware that the entire kingdom belonged to Pandavas and Yudhishthira should have been handed over the reigns of Hastinapura as soon as he attained the age of majority. The fire at the house of lac, they all knew, was a planned one and not an accident. The unfair division of the kingdom in two parts and giving the undeveloped half to Pandavas was only because of the covetousness of Dhritarashtra and Duryodhana.

People are neither blind nor deaf. They were aware of the manoeuvres in the palace to win over Pandavas in the game of dice that was rigged and masterminded by Shakuni. The news of the treatment meted out to the pious Draupadi, the queen of Indraprastha at the hands of the kuru princes, Karna and Shakuni had spread like a wild fire.

Dhritarashtra summoned Vidura and asked about the reactions of the people. Vidura described the sentiments frankly. Dhritarashtra was regretting to allow the games, much against the advice of Vidura who was aware of the vile intentions of Duryodhana and Shakuni. The king was a man of weak will suffering with a lifelong complex of being blind and thus being denied his right to rule. Added to that was the soft corner he had for Duryodhana. He went out of his way to please the crown prince in agreeing to his demands which at times bordered on the preposterous. The correct thing should have been for Dhritarashtra to have put his foot down firmly and refuse the game requested by Duryodhana and his group. By agreeing to such a request, against the advice of all righteous people, the king had shown a lack of statesmanship and a serious violation of dharma to which he was duty bound to adhere.

As Dhritarashtra and Vidura were conversing, the celestal sage Narada appeared in front of them. Without observing the usual courtesies, he pronounced abruptly, "In exactly fourteen years from this day, the kuru race will disappear from the face of the earth on account of the crime committed by Duryodhana". Stating the aforesaid, he disappeared as abruptly as he had come on the scene.

Narada's prophesy shocked everyone. Even the normally unflappable Duryodhana was shaken to the core. His first thoughts went to Dronacharya who he thought might leave their camp.

Duryodhana went to the Dronacharya, and asked him politely for advice in the face of Narada's prophecy. Dronacharya was forthright. He said that even though a very serious wrong thing had been done for which the Kauravas would have to suffer grieviously, he himself would be on the side of Kauravas since he drew his salary from them and could not switch sides midstream. He then said that he agreed with Narada about the terrible consequences.

The learned guru continued, "It is known that Pandavas and Draupadi are pious people of divine origin. Our treatment to them during this entire episode has been reprehensible deserving condemnation as well as severe punishment. You have already heard the learned sage Narada. My advice to you is to do as many good deeds as possible in coming fourteen years to reduce the severity of the outcome.Pandavas had moved to the forests. Krishna arranged to move Subhadra and Abhimanyu to Dwarka while Drishtadymna came to Indraprastha and took away the five sons of Draupadi to live with him in Panchala.

During the happenings in Hastinapur, Krishna had been away to Dwarka to ward off Salva and his armies which had attacked Dwarka taking advantage of his absence. Salva was a close friend of Shishupala and the killing of latter had angered him immensely. The siege of Dwarka was defended very well by elderly Agrasena who had been entrusted the responsibility of the island city by Krishna. Krishna defeated Salva decisively and cleared the area of his troops. It was than that he heard the news about the games of dice and the banishment of Pandavas. He immediately rushed for the place where Pandavas were staying after making arrangements for Subhadra and Abhimanyu. Many other sympathizers of Pandavas and leaders of Vrishni and Bhoja tribes who were particularly close to Pandavas also went with Krishna. On reaching there, Krishna was given the first hand account of happenings. He then met Draupadi who, sobbing inconsolably, described as to how the high and mighty of Hastinapur royalty were witness to the perfidy of Shakuni, Duryodhana, Dushasana and Karna.

Krishna solemnly vowed to Draupadi that he would ensure that Kauravas were punished for their misdeed. Assuring Pandavas of his help during their exile, he returned to Dwarka.

Pandavas were also visited by the sage Maitreya who was held in high esteem by everyone, including Kauravas. After visiting them, he came to Hastinapura where he was welcomed by the royalty. He told Dhitarashtra that he had been to the forests where Pandavas were staying and had met them.

Maitreya then mentioned the game of dice, the dishonor to Draupadi and the rematch and wondered as to how, despite his presence, and that of Bhishma, Dronacharya and Kripacharya, the diagraceful venture was allowed to take place.

Dhritarashtra mumbled a few words of apology and described how the events took a serious turn rapidly. He also said that since he was not present in the hall, he rushed to the hall as soon he was informed and tried his best to repair the damage.

Duryodhana was sitting besides Dhritarashtra. He was not looking comfortable and was squirming in his seat. Maitreya looked at him and asked, "Duryodhana, you are the crown prince and the future king. How did you organize this perfidious event and order the disrobing of Draupadi, a woman and a lady of royal descent. Didn't you feel that you were committing a serious violation of 'Rajdharma', i.e. the correct conduct of a royal person".

Duryodhana did not make a direct reply, but his demenour suggested that his views differed with those of the learned saint. He was gnawing the ground with his toes, slapping his thighs and showed a clear contempt for the rishi's pronouncements.

Maitreya became extremely angry. He stood up and told Duryodhana, "For showing disrespect to the path of dharma unwillingness to make amends for the wrong deed, I pronounce that your thighs, which you are slapping indicating dissent from what I have said, would be broken by Bhima and you will be killed by him in a batttle".

Duryodhana's face lost all colour and he lost all the swagger he was displaying. Dhritarashtra, on the other hand immediately got up and fell at the feet of the great sage asking for mercy and pardon for his son. Maitreya was pacified partially. He told Dhritarashtra, "My curse will not take effect if Duryodhana mends his ways and performs good salutary deeds and pious yagyas. If however, he continues to persue the unwise path of adharma (That which is against the dharma i.e. right conduct), the curse will stay and take effect at the appropriate time". Visibly agitated still, he got up and left the king..

Despite being an ancient story and notwithstanding its mythological content, Mahabharata could be a story of modern times anywhere in the world. Human nature remains the same. Greed, avarice, anger, false pride, unusual love and affection and desire for what is not yours – are all manifesting themselves in various conflicts between individuals, families, states and even nations. Learning from its different stories and episodes could prevent a considerable amount of misery for the human beings of the world regardless of their age, status, country, race, sex, belief, religion, caste or class.True to the final exhortations of Kunti before they had departed finally, Pandavas took full advantage of their exile to become more experienced, knowledgeable, mature and skilled in different arts, particularly the weaponry. They travelled throughout Bharatavarsh, met many people, learnt many stories and made many alliances.

There was no doubt in their mind that they have to use this period of exile to prepare for a war, a fight to finish with Kauravas. The attitude of Duryodhana and his friends and advisers clearly indicated that they would leave no stone unturned to discover their whereabouts in the thirteenth year so that they could be legitimately sent for further exile for thirteen years. The Pandavas were, however, equally clear that even if their identity was not discovered in the thirteenth year, Duryodhana would resort to every trick in the book or fall back on every excuse to deny them their kingdom. Mentally, they had started to prepare for war in that event.

In fact all the younger brothers advanced arguments in support of waging an immediate war on Kauravas. However Yudhishthira stayed unmoved in his resolve to abide by the conditions of the final gambling match and to return only on completing the thirteen years with the stipulated conditions. Although he was supported in this by only a minority of his alliance partners, significantly, he had the total support of Krishna in the matter.

A large number of citizens of Hastinapur were accompanying the Pandavas. This was to demonstrate their anger at Dhritarashtra's rule and show sympathy and support for Pandavas. After a few days, Yudhishthira requested them politely to return. Apart from other things, such a large number was posing logistic problems. Yudhishthira also reminded them that many decent people including Vidura and Kunti were staying at Hastinapura and would need their support. After a number of requests, many returned to their houses and business barring a few diehard loyalists who insisted on going along with Pandavas. However, they too returned gradually after repeated pleas by Yudhishthira and his brothers. The family priest, Ayudhomya, continued to stay with them. He always built his hut a little away from the bigger hut in which Pandavas and Draupadi stayed.

There was, however, an incessant stream of visitors. Some of them came to pledge the support while others for exchanges and conversation on spiritual matters.

Yudhishthira in particular, was a mine of information, ideas and knowledge, but even his other brothers and Draupadi were equally competent.

Amongst the earliest important visitors, Maharishi Yyasa was one of them who spent a few days with them. Before departing, he told the brothers, "I can see from my divine sights that you all will complete the exile period successfully. However, despite this, there would a major conflict and a great devastating and horrible war. Your side would win but for that, you have to start preparing right from now. This is a great opportunity to improve your martial prowess, see your country, meet as many people as possible, know about them and the history of their region.

The great rishi turning towards Arjuna said, "Arjuna, you must go to mount Kailash, observe penances to please Lord Shiva and try and obtain as many divine weapons as possible".

Maharishi Vyasa also spent some time with Yudhishthira advising him on how to improve his competence in games of dice. The Pandavas were unaware that the superior competence in dice games would be very handy to Yudhishthira during his thirteenth year of their exile. Concluding his visit and once again giving his blessings to them, the learned sage left for his own ashram.

Chapter-XXIV

THE GIFT OF THE SUN-GOD

The Pandavas had settled down to their exile routine of work, prayers, penances and skill improvement. At the advice of their priest Ayudhomya, they offered special prayers to sun-god every day.On one such day when Yudhishthira was offering prayers to the sun-god, standing in the river stream, the god himself appeared in person, blessing him.The sun-god spoke, "Yudhishtira, I am immensely pleased with you and your brothers. Ask me a boon".

Yudhishthira promptly replied, "Master, grant me the capability of being able to provide for the needs of my brothers, Draupadi and our guests". He had been exercised over the previous few weeks on their only problem which was to arrange for the daily meals for everyone from their cottage. This proved to be quite a strain on Draupadi's kitchen, with the continuous stream of visitors coming to meet the Pandavas.

The sun-god showing assent, produced a pot and said, "So be it, Yudhishthira. Take this pot and hand it over to Draupadi. It will provide the desired food twice in the day in sufficient quantity till Draupadi takes her meals".

A beaming Yudhishthira returned with the pot and handed it over to Draupadi. This, under the circumstances, was the best gift to her. Not only she served the desired food to Pandavas but, more importantly, also to every visitor. At the end of the day, she sat and had her meals, fully satisfied that she had performed her most important daily duty ofproviding for her husbands and all those who visited the Pandavas their desired meals.

Chapter-XXV

ARJUNA, SHIVA AND INDRA

With things fairly settled in the Pandava camp, Arjuna prepared for his journey to Kailasha in quest of new weapons and skils. Soon, he took leave of his brothers. When he came to Draupadi, she said, "We wish you all the success. Dhananjaya. Your mission has a vital bearing on our preparations. May Shiva and other gods give you all which we need". For a moment, they all thought that it was not Draupadi, but Kunti speaking.

Arjuna had mastered the knowledge of 'Sidhastha' which enabled a person to teleport himself to a distant place through the thought process. In no time he reached the foothills of Himalayas and then, crossing a hill called Gandhamardana, reached Indrakil mountains.

Just as he prepared to proceed further, a sharp command made him stop and look at the source of voice. He found a sage sitting under a tree whose meditation was possibly disturbed by Arjuna's arrival.

The sage queried, "What are you, obviously a warrior equipped with different weapons, doing in a place here which is meant for peaceful people who wish to meditate and pray"?Arjuna paid his respects to the elderly sage and disclosed his identity and purpose.

Happy at Arjuna's sincerety and his frankness, the sage disclosed that he was Indra, the lord of devas, who had come to meet him. He advised him that he must offer penance at Mount Kailasha to the Lord of Lords, Shiva, to obtain the desired weapons. Once the Lord was pleased with him, in all likelihood, he would be sent to Indra for the needful.

Arjuna then proceeded towards Mount Kailasha. On reaching there, he was totally fascinated with the place and its grandeur. He chose an appropriate place and commenced his penance.

Up in the heavens, Lord Shiva was watching Arjuna doing penance. After he was convinced of the devotion, sincerity and hard sacrifice, the Lord decided to visit him. He transformed himself and Parvati as a hunter and his wife and, taking some of his Ganas (special soldiers) with them, descended to his favourite mountain to the place where Arjuna was.

Arjuna was deep in the meditation when a wild boar roaring menacingly approached him. As his grunt became louder and louder, Arjuna's penance was disturbed. When the boar came menacingly close Arjuna had to, most unwillingly, interrupt his penance. Lifting his bow he shot an arrow at the boar and felled him. By coincidence, Shiva also shot an arrow at the same time which too pierced the body of the boar.

The incident led to a heated argument between the two because they both argued that the other person had shot at the boar which was already killed by the first one. Arjuna shouted at the hunter arrogantly and engaged in a fight with him.

A bitter fight ensured in which all the moves of Arjuna were met and negated by the hunter, who appeared to be enjoying the fight. Eventually Arjuna gave up the fight and resumed in his prayers telling the hunter that he would deal with him once his penance was finished.

Arjuna made a Shiva linga out of snow and putting a garland of wild flowers around it, resumed his penance.

When he opened his eyes after some time he found the hunter still standing there with his wife. What was noticeable was that the garland of wild flowers was not around the snow shiva-linga, but around the neck of the hunter. In a flash, Arjuna knew that the hunter was the Lord himself. He fell at his feet mumbling apologies for having taken him on over the boar issue.

The Lord asked him to rise and then addressed him, "Arjuna, you are young and arrogant. You also need to improve your fighting skills. None –the- less, I am happy with your penance. Ask me for whatever you wish".

Arjuna respondes, "Lord, please grant me your Pashupatastra, the weapon that shoots thousands of arrows, spears and maces simultaneously".
Shiva agreed and handed the weapon to Arjuna. He cautioned him against using the weapon indiscriminately as it had the power to destroy even the cosmos. The Lord also granted him divine wisdom as well as victory over his enemies in a war.

Arjuna stood spell bound in front of the Lord. Mahadeva also told him that he would be soon visited by the gods who would give him their weapons and the words of wisdom. After blessing him once again, he, along with Parvati and his ganas disappeared.

The gods appeared immediately thereafter. Each one of them gave weapons to Arjuna and then imparted special instructions on how to use them. Some of them stayed back to pass additional divine wisdom to Arjuna.

At the end of it, Indra appeared. He informed Arjuna that his stay at Mount Kailash had come to an end and soon his special charioteer, Maitali, would come with his chariot and bring Arjuna to Indra's capital, Amravati, to do some additional religious deeds and learn some special arts and skills.

Maitali soon appeared with the divine chariot and took Arjuna to Amravati. He was given a special reception on arrival. Soon, he settled down to perform religious tasks and learn others arts. The most significiant one was of learning music and dance from Chitrasena, the Gandharva king. Although the thoughts of his brothers and Draupadi were always with him, Arjuna knew that they would not mind his stay in the Indraloka as long as it was productive, even if it stretched into years.

In fact Arjuna stayed in the Indraloka for more than five eventful years. The only blemish was his annoying Urvashi, the chief courtesan (Apsara) over there. Arjuna repeatedly spurned her amorous advances. He explained to her that in his mind, she enjoyed the status of his mother as on the earth she had been the wife of one of his gurus. When she was convinced that nothing would work, out of sheer exasperation, she left him for good. However, she also pronounced a curse on him that in view of his supposedly condemnable behaviour towards her, he would have to spend one year on earth as an eunach in company of attractive women. Later realizing that she had been extremely harsh on Arjuna who had shown an impeccable character, Urvashi modified her curse to the effect that it would help Arjuna tide over an extremely difficult crisis in the life of Pandavas.

CH-XXVI

BRIHADASWA

Not only Mahabharata is a great story depicting the victory of good over evil, it has many short stories which carry some moral or other. This was as much true in times of Mahabharata as it is in the modern times. They carry great lessons even for modern generations. The visit of sage Brihadaswa to Pandavas was one such short story with a great lesson.

Brihadaswa went to Pandava camp for exchange of ideas and views, as was customary in those days. People considered it as an honour to be in their company. Yudhishthira, in particular, was a revered person whose knowledge of scriptures was outstanding. Hence, when Brihadaswa went to the Pandavas, he expected an envigorating and illuminating spiritual dialogue.

However, on meeting the Pandavas, the learned sage found a different atmosphere. One could discern a marked degree of depression all around. The Pandavas wore a depressed look.

Yudhishthira explained to the learned rishi, "We have been cheated in a deceiptful game of dice and are here, away from our kingdom, while Duryodhana and his co-conspirers are enjoying the fruits of their deceitful action. How can the God be that unfair. Arjuna, who had left them long ago had not returned nor any word had been received from him. They were worried about his welfare and also regarding success of his mission to get weapons and to acquire new skills.

Brihadaswa listened patiently to Yudhishthira. It was obvious that Yudhishthira, generally a knowledgeable, well-balanced and mature person, could also lose his patience and be disappointed. After all, he too was human. After he had poured his heart out, Brishdaswa smiled and said, "Listen Yudhishthira, you must learn to be patient in difficult times and accept things as God's will. Never think that you are the most unfortunate person in the world. There are many people who have suffered much worse than you have. First look at your positive points. You are following dharma and are respected by all good and knowledgable people. In fact, they all come to seek your company to benefit from the interaction and discourses with you". The holy sage continued, "You are also lucky to have your brothers with you as well as a dutiful, religious and illustrious wife".

"You possibly have not heard of king Nala of Nishada. He was also deceived in a game of dice by Pushkara and lost all his treasures and the kingdom. He had to go into exile and in a fit of madness deserted his wife. For years, he roamed without any purpose all over the place. However, gradually, he obtained control over himself and started working to better his lot. In the end, he had a happy life and died with contentment".

"Sorrow, sadness and bad times are the lot of every man. Whenever, you are in difficult situations, count your blessings, show patience and fortitude and wait for the tide to turn. Nothing is permanent in this world. Bad times are followed by good ones. Your exile will be over in due course. Do not worry about Arjuna. He will return with his newly acquired weapons and new skills. Together, you and your brothers shall prevail over the decadent Kauravas and win the war". Yudhishthira had regained his composure and thanked Brihadaswa for his words of wisdom. The sage then left their place.

Chapter-XXVII

BHIMA MEETS HIS OTHER BROTHER

Despite the reassuring words of sage Brihadaswa, the brothers were increasingly getting worried about the lack of any news about Arjuna. Yudhishthira was blaming himself for letting him go. Together, the five brothers would have been a formidable group with little to worry about each other. Arjuna's absence had created an uncertainty in their minds – which resulted in their inability to plan their further moves.

One day, they were visited by sage Lomesh. He could gauge the sources of concern of Pandavas. Having been blessed with a divine vision, he could immediately locate Arjuna in the Indraloka. He gave the happy news to the brothers.

"Your brother is safe and sound in Amravati and will rejoin you after some time with required weapons and the desired skills. In the meantime, you all should see as many places as possible, meet people, sages and rishis to widen your knowledge", the holy sage advised.

They all felt mighty relieved to hear the news about Arjuna. Yudhishthira requested sage Lomesh to lead them to places which he was recommending to visit. The sage agreed and as the first leg they headed towards Badrikashram.

They were going northwards wading towards the dense forests and difficult paths. On reaching Kamyaka forests, they missed Arjuna yet more and decided to press on. On reaching Kulinda, the kingdom of Subahu in Himalayas, they accepted the king's hospitality and stayed in the capital for some time. Narayan ashrama, a charming place was the next halt.

One day when they had gone out near the river, Draupadi saw a beautiful water-lily floating in the river. Grasping the splendid flower, she could also smell its beautiful fragrance. Draupadi made a request to Bhima to fetch some more lilies so that she could present the whole bunch to Yudhishtira. She also had plans to plant some of these flowers when they returned to Kamyaka forests.

Bhima readily agreed and headed towards the north-westerly direction from which the strong smell of those flowers was coming. It was clear that it came from a place where large number of lilies had grown.

On the way, however, he found the path way completely blocked by the tail of a huge monkey who lay sleeping nearby. Not wishing to overstep the tail, he shouted at the monkey to remove the tail so that he could pass.

The monkey opened his eyes slowly, surveyed the huge frame of Bhima and said, "I am sick and unwell. You are a strong person. Why don't you just shift the tail to one side to clear the path for you to pass".

Bhima was irritated and slightly amused as well. He looked around and found himself surrounded by big plantain trees in what looked like a big banana grove. Deciding not to make in issue of the matter, he bent down to shift the tail. But, lo and behold, he found that the old and ragged looking frail tail could just not be moved at all, so heavy it was. Bhima made a few more attempts and then gave it up. He realized that this was not an ordinary monkey but some divine spirit.

Bhima folded his hands and bowing to the monkey, said, "Oh holy soul, I am sorry I spoke to you harshly in the beginning. Please let me pass and if it pleases you, please reveal yourself.

The monkey opened his eyes, smiled and got up, standing straight. He told Bhima, 'I am your elder brother, Hanuman. We both are the blessings of our father, the wind-god'. Hanuman then embraced Bhima and said, "This road you wanted to take would have taken you to the place where spirits, rakshasas and yakshas live and you would not have found the lily-flower, sugandhika, there. That is why I came here and laid down here on the way-to stop you from going ahead. Besides, to meet you in person and embrace you gave an immense pleasure. Even you will feel becoming more powerful and energized everytime after my embrace. This is because Bhagwan Shri Ram had embraced me a number of times, particularly when I had returned from Lanka after discovering mother Sita. In future, anytime you need added strength, just remember me and you shall get it. Now go down this path on the right and you will soon find a big pool of water where many sugandhikas are growing. Pick as many as you want and return to your brothers.

Bhima was not only overwhelmed from meeting his elder brother for the first time, but he was also feeling like a child in presence of Hanuman. He did not wish to leave till he had enough of him. He said, "Before I leave you I have one wish. I want to see you in the form you were in when you took off for Lanka to find Sita."

Hanuman smiled and said, "Fine, watch". He then started growing in size and in no time, became huge. After some time, he started becoming smaller till he regained his original size. He then told Bhima, "I can become yet more bigger and stronger when confronted with the enemies. Now go and get your flowers from Kubera gardens yonder. I shall always protect Pandavas and help them in their every fight. In fact, tell Arjuna that I shall be present on the flag of his chariot whenever he goes into any battle". Hanuman then walked away in a different direction and disappeared gradually.

Bhima walked down the path indicated by Hanuman and was surprised to find a pool in a big garden consisting of many plants of fruits and flowers. The garden was guarded by many guards who started closing in on Bhima as he bent down to pluck some lilies.

"Stop, or else we will capture you. How dare you pluck these flowers in the guarded territory without permission", shouted one of the senior guards."I am Bhima, son of Pandu, the deceased king of Hastinapur. I have to pluck just a few sangandhika flowers. After doing that I shall go away."

The guards closed in further and stood in the way of Bhima. Bhima was still thinking of his meeting with Hanuman. He suddenly realized that he had a problem on his hands. The guards closing on him were menacingly close. He pushed all of them with so much strength that they went away literally flying to different directions. One of them went scurrying to Kuber who was the owner of the entire stretch of the property. He narrated the entire incident to him. Kuber understood the whole matter and asked the guards to let Bhima have the flowers.

Bhima plucked the flowers and rushed back to Draupadi with them. The latter was extremely elated seeing the whole bunch. She presented them to Yudhishthira and told him that she would take them back later to samyaka forest to plant them there.

Chapter-XXVIII

PLEASANT SURPRISE

The Pandavas were passing the days travelling, meeting learned people, having discourses with them and seeing all the shrines of different places. The whole of India is full of places where there are folk tales of Pandavas having visited there and spent some time. This is particularly true of North and Central India.

Every day, one subject they never missed discussing was Arjuna's return. Despite assurances of sage Lomesh and others about his safety and eventual return, they never missed talking about Arjuna and incidents of the past when he was there with them.

One such day when the four brothers were sitting and talking, they spotted a divine chariot slowly descending from the skies. Draupadi also came out hearing their shouts. Soon the chariot, driven by Maitali, Indra's charioteer, touched down on ground and behold, Arjuna was stepping down from it. After offloading the contents of the chariot, Maitali paid obesience to everyone and flew away.

There were shouts of joy with a dramatic change in the atmosphere as if, after a long and terrible drought, the rains had come for the first time. Everyone flocked around to see what Arjuna had brought. He gave to Draupadi all the gifts and jewellery he had bought with him. Then he explained each and every weapon, their potential and effectiveness.

In the end he told the brothers about the Pashupatastra given by Mahadeva. On the urging of the excited brothers, he was on the verge of demonstrating its use against a distant mountain, when suddenly the divine sage Narada appeared before them.

Narada said 'Arjuna, remember the warning of Mahadeva when he gifted Pashupatastra to you. This weapon has the capability of destroying even the cosmos. You must exercise discretion and restraint'. Arjuna realized his mistake and apologized to Narada instantaneously. The divine sage smiled and after blessing all of them, disappeared.

Slowly and gradually the elements of an epic battle, as foretold by Veda Vyasa, were gathering around the Kauravas and Pandavas. Kauravas were engaged in enjoying the fruits of their victory over Pandavas in the infamous game of dice. They had totally forgotten the warnings of Narada and sage Maitreya to perform good deeds and yagyas to atone for their misdemeanours. Duryodhana was in full command and at his arrogant best. Dhristarashtra and Gandhari did try and sound notes of caution at items, but all their protestatious were brushed aside by their son whose power and influence were growing by the day. He was the man in control and his father, a bare nominal head.

The Pandavas, on the other hand, were also growing though in different direction. Their reputation of fairness, adherence to dharma, power, spiritual achievements was traveling far ahead of them, as they went from place to place, making friends with all and particularly with those with potential for future alliances. Their prime relative weakness of absence of plenty of weapons was more than made up by the superb gifts from devas and particularly by the lord of the Lords, Mahadeva, to Arjuna.

They decided to concentrate on their prayers, penances, improving all that they knew, whether it was Vedas or personal and martial attributes. They knew that the end of their exile period was not far away and they would have to stay incognito somewhere for an year thereafter. They were back in Kamyaka forests where they had commenced meticulous planning to prepare for a long duration deception in different roles, quite different from that of the kshatriya heroes.Yet, they also continued to entertain the people visiting them and have spiritual discourses. True, they could not look after the guests the way they would have liked to, yet most of the visitors who went back after meeting them, had the feeling and satisfaction of gaining much more than they had expected. Most of them, of course, felt pangs of regret at the cruelty of fate meted out to an emperor, his wife and family.

Chapter-XXIX

DHRISTARASHTRA HAS A VISITOR

One day a Brahmin visitor came to see king Dhritarashtra. He mentioned that he had recently visited the Pandavas in Kamyaka forests and described their difficult life in the forests. He described how they went about doing mundane chores which even an ordinary person might not like to do.

Dhritarashtra listened to all this and lamented. He said, "Oh God, it grieves me immensely that my own kith and kin and their wife are leading such a difficult life and we cannot do anything to help. Such is the providence that the Pandavas would not accept anything from me as it would be a violation of the terms of exile. On the other hand, Duryodhana, who can waive off the remaining period of their exile would not do so because of his obstinate attitude".

(Dhritarashtra and Gandhari had in a number of times in the past suggested to Duryodhana that he should do so as Pandavas had suffered enough. The latter however, remained totally adamant and did not wish to restore to Pandavas, what, in his opinion, they did not deserve to get even at the very outset).

The brahman left the king after some time. It just happened that Shakuni had overheard the conversation between the brahmin and Dhritarashtra. He was highly elated to hear regarding the sad plight of the Pandavas and immediately rushed to Duryadhana's chamber to break what he considered as the happy tidings. Karna was also present with Duryodhana. They all rejoiced at the news and hatched a plan to go to the neighbourhood of Pandavas to laugh at and make merry of their pitiable plight.

Duryodhana went to Dhritarashtra and told him a different story. He said that since he had come to know that the Pandavas were nearby in the Kamyaka forests, they had wanted to visit them in the forests and wanted the permission of the king for doing so. Dhritarashtra was a guileless person, ready to believe whatever Duryodhana told him. He was happy that his son had made that decision. Thinking that Duryodhana had a change of heart, he readily accorded the permission to them to go. He was happy to note that his son had a change of attitude which augured well for the future.

With the visit having been cleared by the king, the three planned their excursion with glee. They also decided to take an elite group of their army, just to feel superior to Pandavas. To add to their pleasure, they also decided to take their wives as well. "Let our cousins and that haughty Draupadi feel totally humiliated" they mused.

On the appointed day they all set off for their destination with all fanfare. They camped next to where Pandavas were staying and had occasions to watch the latter doing their daily chores. In between, there were games and merrymaking, aided no doubt by the stories of the miseries of Pandavas which they had observed.

A few days thereafter, Duryadhana decided to have fun along with their wives in the river which flowed nearby. Duryodhana asked his soldiers to prepare a nice platform at the river bank.

The soldiers were in for a shock. They were challenged by the guards of the Gandharva king, Chitrasena, who was camping there. The soldiers had to back down and return to the camp. They reported the entire matter to Duryodhana.

Duryodhana was extremely annoyed and decided to teach Chitrasena a lesson. He, accompanied by Karna, Shakuni and his entire army contingent, proceeded towards the place where Gandharva guards had been reported as being present. They were in for a bigger shock. As soon as they reached the place, they were subjected to a very fierce attack for which they were least prepared. This attack was followed by the 'Sammohan shastra' used by Chitrasena. The soldiers of the army, who were retreating to regroup were all frozen at their places due to the hypnotising capacity of that weapon.

As they were recovering from the two double shocks, Chitrasena launched another fierce attack aimed at Karna. For those people who had come to enjoy at what they thought was a picnic, the level of physical and mental preparation for a serious and ferocious encounter was very low. In no time, Karna's chariot was smashed to pieces. Karna, in no position to dig in and fight back literally ran away from the battle for his survival. Duryodhana was very annoyed and disappointed at the cowardly behaviour of Karna. In no time they were surrounded by Chitrasena's army who took Duryodhana and his wives as prisoners.

To their good luck, Duryodhana's wife had acted sensibly. She sent one of her attendants to the Pandavas describing their predicament and appealing for help. Bhima and Arjuna were elated to hear the news and were in no mood to go and fight Chitrasena. "Duryodhana has got what we should have done to him," said Bhima, supported by Arjuna. However, Yudhishthira over-ruled them saying that they were still their family and should be helped in this hour of crisis.

Chastened by the sober judgement of Yudhishthira, the two hastened to the place of action.

Chapter-XXX

TOTAL HUMILIATION

Both Bhima and Arjuna attacked the Gandharva Army who indeed were no match for the Pandavas. Chitrasena, sensing the impending defeat, quickly bundled his prisoners on his chariot and rushed to escape sky-wards. Arjuna, however, foiled Chitrasena's plans using a special weapon he had recently aquired and brought him to the ground.

Chitrasena had no quarrel with Arjuna. In fact, they were quite friendly. Chitrasena had taught music and dancing to Arjuna in Amravati. Extending his hand towards Arjuna in a friendly manner, he told him that he wished to explain the reason behind his action as it had been done on instructions from Indra.

Bhima then suggested that they should go to Yudhishthira and explain the matter. Chitrasena immediately consented and went along with the Pandava brothers and his prisoners to Yudhishtira's camp that was not far away.

On reaching the Pandava's place, Chitrasena told Yudhishthira the whole story. Indra had come to know of Duryodhana's plot to make fun of Pandavas and humiliate them. Duryodhana also wished to assert his superiority in the eyes of this soldiers to make his cousins feel disgraced. He had therefore asked Chitrasena to go to Samyaka forests and teach a lesson to the Kauravas instead.

Yudhishthira thanked Chitrasena and requested him to release his prisoners He did that and also released the Kaurava soldiers of the hypnotic spell. He then paid obeisance to Yudhishthira before departing for his abode. After the departure of the Gandharvas, Yudhishthira turned towards Duryodhana and said, "You should exercise caution and discretion when advised of such silly plans which bring humiliation and indignity to the great names of kuru dynasty. If Chitrasena had killed you or taken you all as prisoners, the damage to your reputation would have been irrepairable. Now go back with your army and families to Hastinapura and avoid such indiscrete and thoughtless actions in future. Please convey our respects to uncle, the king, aunt Gandhari and mother Kunti and tell them that we are happy and well due to their blessings.

Duryodhana returned suffering the greatest humiliation of his life so far. He would not have minded being killed or taken prisoner by Chitrasena and taken to Amravati. But to be rescued by Pandavas and being lectured by Yudhishthira in front of his wives and many visitors of Pandavas was the worst thing which could happen to him. He was also annoyed at the cowardice of Karna and told him so when he returned. This loss of reputation rankled in his heart many a times in future. He also never forgot nor forgave Karna for his cowardice. Clearly, what was planned as their most successful attempt to humiliate Pandavas had boomeranged badly. Many times he wished he had died rather than face that ignominy.

Gradually, however, his mood changed. Duryodhana convinced himself that he would banish from himself any thought of regret or blame Karna for running away. "If I have to die, I shall die fighting Pandavas in the battle" he declared and was applauded by his close friends for this. Emboldened by this statement, Karna declared, "And I, Karna, declare that I shall personally kill Arjuna in the same war".

DRAUPADI'S TEST

From time immemorial, there has always been a struggle between evil and good. A good person always thinks well, does well and expects good from others. An evil person represents the opposite. He is always thinking of how to harm others. There is, however, a divine justice. Help comes from unexpected quarters tilting the scales against more powerful evil forces.

One day, sage Durvasa came to Hastinapur along with his ten thousand disciples. With the royal resources of Hastinapur, the sage and his disciples were looked after very well. No one wanted to annoy Durvasa as they were all scared of his fiery temper. Duryodhana personally attended to the learned rishi and all his disciples.

Durvasa was very happy with his reception and he blessed the king and his retinue at the effort put in by everyone. Even there, Duryodhana did not fail to play his usual tricks trying to let down his cousins in the exile. He thanked Durvasa rishi for having given the time and opportunity to look after them. Following this, he told the rishi, "Our cousins are currently camping nearby in the forests. They will be equally delighted to be blessed with the visit by you and your disciples". Duryodhana then made it a point to mention the best time for visiting the Pandavas. He knew about the bowl which had been gifted by the sun-god to Pandavas. The proposed time was much later than the time when Draupadi's meals would be over and the bowl would lose the capacity to produce more meals on that day. Durvasa noted the recommended time and made it a point one day to head towards the Pandavas to reach them at the appointed hour. He was received with due respects by Yudhishthira and the family. The holy sage accepted their salutation. Pleased with their reception, he announced that they (he and his ten thousand disciples) would proceed to the nearby river to take a bath and then return to have their meals.

They all knew they had a major problem. It was impossible to cook meals for so many people from the bowl with zero capacity to cook anything on that day since even Draupadi had finished her meals after the brothers had finished theirs.

Draupadi was exasperated totally. Eventually she fell back to her last resort – closing her eyes, praying and appealing to Krishna. Sure enough, the Lord and the master was there in person.He told Draupadi, "I am very hungry. Bring whatever you have. Make sure it is a wholesome meal because I feel as if I have not eaten for days".

Draupadi told Krishna, "We have finished eating today and cannot produce any thing more today. I am expecting thousands of disciples along with sage Durvasa to arrive any time from now today and they also want to have their meals here. I prayed to you to come and help to resolve my problem. "And now, even you want to eat. What do I do my Lord?"Krishna smiled and told Draupadi, "No excuses,. Bring the bowl here and let me see for myself that the bowl is empty. I am sure there must be something there".

Draupadi shrugged her shoulders and went to fetch the bowl. Even though she had cleaned the bowl herself and was quite convinced there was nothing in it, she never argued with Krishna. She brought the shining bowl and gave to Krishna. He examined the bowl thoroughly and almost like a magician's trick, found a grain of rice and a bit of vegetable hiding under the rim of the utensil. He brought them out carefully and said "That will satisfy my appetite. I was really hungry".

Krishna then looked at Bhima and told him, "Go and tell sage Durvasa that their meal is ready and ask them to come". Bhima too never argued with Krishna. A bit mystified, he set off towards the river where they were bathing.

Durvasa and his disciples had just come out of the river and getting ready to proceed. Bhima went to the rishi and gave him the message.

Durvasa replied, "Actually I and my people were just discussing this matter. All of us are feeling full and hence would like to proceed to our next destination. I am sorry but it is necessary. Please convey our thanks to Yudhishtira, all your brothers and Draupadi. Our best blessings to you all and may you succeed in all your future ventures". After seeing them off Bhima returned to his camp to give the happy news.

(When Krishna ate his grain of rice with satisfaction he did so as the soul of universe, the creator. His satisfaction mean't that the meal he ate satisfied every one, including the revered sage and his disciples).

Draupadi till then, was feeling bad because her imperfect cleaning of the bowl had been exposed. She attributed the slovenly cleaning to God's will. She was happy that her reputation of a competent housewife had not been tarrnished. Once again, her faith in Krishna reaffirmed itself in totality.

Chapter-XXXII

JAIDRATH-CRIME, PUNISHMENT AND PENANCE

One day all Pandava brothers had gone to for hunting and Draupadi was alone in their cottage in Kamyaka forest. It so happened that Jaidrath, king of Sindh and son-in-law of Dhritarashtra by virtue of his marriage to Dushala – the lone sister of Kauravas, was passing the same place in his chariot, accompanied by some escort soldiers. Jaidratha was surprised to see an extremely beautiful woman in the midst of that wilderness. Curious and infatuated by her extremely good looks, he sent his soldiers to find out more about her. They came back to tell him that she was Draupadi, the wife of Pandavas, who was alone as Pandavas had gone out for hunting.

Feeling bold and adventurous, Jaidrath came to Draupadi and introduced himself. Draupadi had already known his identity. Since he was her sister-in-law Dushala's husband, she welcomed him and extended to him the courtesy due to his special status in the family.

Jaidrath however, had other ideas. He sympathised with her for living in such hard conditions and then proposed to her to come with him and become his queen where she would enjoy the prestige and position becoming of her. On Draupadi's refusal and chastising him at harbouring such intentions, Jaidratha took hold of her forcibly and started towards his chariot.

Draupadi warned him of dire consquences when Pandavas would return, locate them and grieviously punish him. Jaidratha laughed and dismissed her warnings. In fact, he himself was famous for his strength and bravery. With a beautiful woman such as Draupadi in his grasp,he disregarded her warning and threw all cautions to the wind and put screaming Draupadi on his chariot and drove away.

No one of consequence was around. Some domestic staff saw the whole edisode but were helpless. Luckily, the priest, Ayudhomya also witnessed the whole drama. He chased Jaidratha and his soldiers on his own.

In a short while, the Pandavas returned and were told of the whole incident. The brothers immediately set course to pursue and find Jaidratha's party.. They closed in on Jaidratha's party soon. Yudhishthira asked the brothers to get after the soldiers first. They soon immobilised all the soldiers.

Jaidhratha also spotted the Pandavas. Realising that he was in a genuine danger, he dumped Draupadi on the way and raced as fast as he could.

Pandavas recovered Draupadi and were debating on their next move. Yudhishthira wanted the incident to be forgotten as the perpretrator of the crime was their brother-inlaw. However neither Draupadi nor the other brothers were in such a magnanimous mood. Yudhishtira had to give in and Bhima and Arjuna raced towards the fleeing king of Sindhu.

They caught up soon with Jaidratha. A bit surprised because he had thought Pandavas would not chase him once they found Draupadi, he now had to defend himself.

Jaidrath too was a famous warrior, but no match to Bhima's strength and Arjuna's arrows. A few lusty blows from the former and Jaidrath was lying spread-eagled on the ground.They tied his hands and feet by ropes and carried him to their cottage as a pig is transported. Once there, they dumped him on the ground in front of Yudhishthira. Jaidratha caught hold of Yudhishtira's feet and begged for forgiveness. When Draupadi entered the cottage, he pleaded forgiveness from her, addressing her as his sister.

Yudhishthira said that he would let Draupadi decide his fate. Draupadi had, by then, regained her composure. She told Jaidrath, "Your eldest brother-in-law wants you to be forgiven since you are Dushala's husband. What you have done is a shameless act and I would not like it to be totally forgiven. In fact, you deserve to be punished in such a manner that you would remember for a long time and desist from repeating such a disgraceful act.

She then looked at Bhima and said, "Let him go after shaving his head". The brothers were too happy to do that. Jaidratha, inwardly seething with shame and anger, was outwardly calm. He thanked all of them and set off on foot from the cottage with everyone looking at him with an amused expression.

He did not go back to his capital out of shame and disgrace. Instead, he headed towards mount Kailash to do tapa and pray to Lord Shiva to seek revenge from the Pandavas.

He prayed long and hard. Ultimately the Lord appeared in front of him. He said, "Jaidratha, I am pleased with your penance. Ask me for a boon".

Jaidratha got up with the folded hands and said, "Lord, I thank you for granting me one boon. Give me the powers to defeat Pandavas in a battle".

Shiva replied, "This is impossible as the Pandavas are invincible and shall remain so. However, I grant you such powers that on a particular day, you would be able to check four of them". Saying this, the great Mahadeva disappeared.

Disappointed and dejected, Jaidratha headed towards his capital. He had so much hope that the Lord would grant him his wish. However that was not to be proving once again that the almighty is fair to all.

Chapter-XXXIII

THE MAGICAL POOL

Mahabharata is essentially the narrative of the tales and travails of Pandavas. Yet, in this wonderful epic, there are a number of countless pearls and gems of illustrative tales and of stories carrying some messages or teachings; some connected with the main theme and others, not connected, but carrying a distinct lesson or moral. This wonderful epic is a perennial source, a living fountain of the culture and ethics of our country. One such tale is of the magical pool.

One day the Pandavas found a brahmin rushing towards them and urgently pleading for help. His fire-kindling mortar had accidently been carried on the horns of a deer while it was rubbing itself against the mortar. While turning, the mortar got entangled with the deer's horns. The frightened deer ran away deep into the forest carrying the mortar.

Pointing his fingers at one direction, the brahmin shouted, "A deer has run that side carrying my fire-kindling mortar. Without it, I can neither light a fire nor can I perform my fire sacrifice. Please get my mortar back for me. The Pandavas rushed into the forest, but despite their best efforts, they could not capture the deer.

They were lamenting on their helplessness. It was obvious that the twelve year's exile, which was coming to an end soon, had taken its toll in terms of their morale. Yudhishthira was conscious of this and was thinking of a way to divert their attention. Since their immediate problem was their acute thirst and hence to locate a source of water, Yudhishtira asked Nakula to climb upon

a tall tree and see if he could locate an appropriate likely source of clean water.
Nakula climbed on the tree and could locate a place which would definitely have water since a number of birds were hovering around that area. He quickly climbed down and rushed to fetch the water in his quiver. Sure enough, he found a big pond with a lot of vegetation around it and birds flying in and out of it after drinking water.

Nakula descended on the edge of the pond and decided to drink first and then fill the quiver for his brothers. As he stooped down to the water, he heard a voice, which said, "Stop. Oh son of Madri, Do not rush to drink the water. First answer to my questions and then drink water".

Nakula laughed and scooped some water and took the first gulp. As soon as he did that he fell on the ground unconscious.

Sahadeva, Arjuna and Bhima were sent by Yudhishthira one by one to find about the rest, but they too met the same fate. Arjuna, contemptuous of the demand for answers to the questions even shot an arrow in that direction which was of no avail.

Yudhishthira was definitely worried. He rushed to the pool only to find the bodies of four of his brothers lying dead on the poolside. Totally flabbergasted, Yudhishthira could not understand what and why it had happened. Being very thirsty he stooped to scoop some water to have a drink, when suddenly the same voice spoke loudly,

"Yudhishthira, do not do that. Your brothers died because they preferred to ignore my warnings not to drink water before they had answered to my questions. If you answer my questions and then drink the water, you would come to no harm. This pool is mine and you must follow my instructions".

Yudhishthira knew that this was the voice of a Yaksha. Seeing the evidence of the damage already done, he decided to retrieve the situation rather than confront the Yaksha. He said to the bodiless voice, "Please ask your questions".

The voice started its quickfire questions with Yudhishthira answering them promptly with ease. The questions and answers were as follows:

"Who or what is man's greatest ally?"

"Patience".

"What enables the sun to shine everyday?"

"The power of Brahman.

"What rescues a man in difficulty"?

"Courage"

"The study of which science makes a man wise?"

"Association with great people makes a man wise, not by reading any shastra".

"What is more ennobling and sustaining than the earth?"

"The mother".

"What is higher than sky and what is fleeter than wind?"

"The father and the mind".

"What is worse than a withered straw?"

"A grief stricken heart"

"What befriends a traveller?"

"Learning"

"The friend of one who stays at home?"

"His wife".

"What alone accompanies a man in death?"

""Death"

"Which is the biggest vessel?"

"The earth, which contains all within itself,"

"What alone results in happiness?

"Good conduct"

"What is the loss which yields happiness, not sorrow?"

"Anger"

"What that, abandoning which, man is loved by all?"

"Pride"

"What is that giving which one becomes wealthy?"

"Desire"

"What makes one a real brahmana? Is it birth, good conduct
or learning? Answer clearly"

"One does not become a brahmana by birth or learning. Even if a man may be learned in all the four Vedas, if he displays bad conduct or falls slave to bad habits, he falls to a lower class. Good conduct is an absolute must for becoming brahaman".

" What is the greatest wonder about man?"

"Even though he sees people dying everyday, he keeps planning for life and not death".
There were many more questions which were promptly replied by Yudhishthira. Yaksha appeared to be totally satisfied. Finally, he asked Yudhishthira as to which one of his brothers, he would like to be revived, if only one was to be brought to life without the least hesitation, Yudhishthira, pointed out to Nakula.
On being queried as to why he didn't choose Bhima or Arjuna who were more dear and useful to him, Yudhishthira, responded, "Oh Yaksha, Dharma is the only shield I respect. My two mothers Kunti and Madri had three and two sons respectively. Since I shall live, it is fair that my other mother, Madri's one son also lives".

Totally pleased, Yaksha granted the rest of the brothers to be revived. He then revealed his true form which was that of Yamaraja, who had earlier taken the form of the deer in order to test his son. He embraced Yudhishthira.

Yama, the Lord of Dharma told Yudhishthira, "Your exile of twelve years is going to end and all of you will be able to pass the thirteenth year without being discovered of your true identity. I direct you to go to king Virata and pass a year's service secretly. You will remain safe and untraced there"

After saying this, he embraced Yudhishthira, blessed him and then disappeared.

The Pandavas went into a secret conclave to decide on the different strategies and tactical manoeurves to ensure absolute secrecy regarding their true identity during their stay at the Virata Kingdom. They knew that Duryodhana would have already pressed into service scores of spies to get information on them.

It was decided that each of them would try separately to get into jobs on different assignments within the royal household. Yudhishthira would go as the brahman adviser to the king of Virata. Bhima, to ensure that he got enough to eat, would go as the cook. Arjuna would utilize the curse given by Urvashi on him was to act as an eunach for an year and use his expertise imparted to him by Chitrasena of music and dancing to be a teacher for the princess Uttara in fine arts. He would get enlisted as an eunach named "Vrihannala'. Nakula would act as the syce to train and look after the horses in the royal stable. Sahadeva enlisted himself as a caretaker for the royal cattles. As far as Draupadi was concerned, she had no trouble in being accepted as the queen's maid-in-chief. Her two conditions, one not to wash the dirty dishes and second, not to eat the left-overs of the people there were readily accepted. She gave her name as 'Sairandhri.

They had no problem in getting the respective assignments on account of the mastery they had on their respective skills. Both the king and queen were very impressed with all the Pandavas and Draupadi on account of their impressive personality. Draupadi was an instant hit with the queen on account of her stunning figure and looks as well as her all round competence. Managing the household alone for the five brothers during the twelve year exile, had made her a perfect person in all these chores, a quality she did not have earlier.

The Pandavas quickly settled in their new jobs. Soon they made themselves indispensable to the kingdom due to their steadfast commitment to the work and their honesty and forthrightness. Draupadi too had settled down in her role as the maid-in-chief to the queen Sudeshana. Above all, Arjuna immensely enjoyed his new role as the teacher for Uttara. Before they realized, many months had slipped away and the end of twelve month period was fast approaching. Life was going on smoothly and relatively incident free. However, suddenly, they were all shaken up with the Keechak incident and the events following it.

Chapter – XXXIV

KEECHAK MEETS HIS NEMESIS

Keechaka was the commander-in-chief of the king Virata and queen Sudeshana's brother. He was a great warrior and was mentioned along with the likes of Bheema and Duryodhana. Since, the king of Virata and Uttara, his son, were weak people, many people considered Keechaka as the virtual ruler of Virata. He, at least, did not miss and opportunity to emphasise this fact.

One day, when Keechak had come to visit his sister, his eyes fell on Sairandhri (Draupadi) and instantaneously he felt greatly enamoured of her radiant beauty and wanted to possess her. He accosted Draupadi at the first available opportunity. He told Draupadi that a talented beauty like her had no business to be the maid in the palace. He invited her to be his consort. He went overboard to promise her the moon and grabbed her to get her consent.

Sairandhri looked at him straight in the eyes and told Keechak to take his hands off her. "I am a Gandharva woman," she said, "do not harbour your evil designs on me. You do it and you will be severely punished by the Gandharvas who are always around".

Keechak went away but his obsession with Sairandhri became more and more as the time passed. For a virtual ruler of the kingdom, it was unthinkable that an unattached maid could repulse his advances. Eventually he told his sister, queen Sudeshana, of his infatuation and solicited her help. Sudeshana promised to help him indirectly but refused to go beyond that. In her heart, she was herself scared of Sairandhri. One day when there

was a religious function in the queen's palace, she asked Sairandhri to go to Keechak's
house to fetch some puja material which the former had brought on the previous day for the function but had left it in Keechak's house. (This was Sudeshana's version. In actual fact, the queen had deliberately connived the whole thing to enable Keechak to meet Sairandhri in private at his house).

Sairandhri reluctantly went to Keechak's house which was next door. Keechak was alone at his house. He again tried to talk to her into a liaison with him. When whe refused again, he tried to force her into submission. Luckily, Sairandhri was prepared for it. She slapped him hard and before he could recover, ran away to the king's court. Keechak was mad with anger. He followed her to the king's court and in front of everyone, profusely abused her. Sairandhri shouted and shaken ran straight to Bhima's room. She found him there and told the entire story. Bhima was livid with anger and wanted to go and punish Keechak straightway. However, knowing that end of their exile was a few days away,

Draupadi counseled him patience. They decided to punish Keechak all the same, but without blowing up their cover. Bhima asked her to lure him one night in the dance-hall where he, Bhima, would do the rest. Draupadi got her opportunity soon. Keechak was visiting his sister when he found her alone. Cornering her, he asked her if she had changed her mind and if not, why not. Draupadi demurred and after a bit of no-no, said yes and suggested they meet in the dance-hall at midnight.

Keechak felt he had scored a big victory. He got ready early evening and helped himself to a number of drinks before starting for the royal dance-hall. Bhima had moved in the dance hall where he sat on the bed covering himself with a sheet of cloth. Keechak arrived at the stroke of the mignight, very excited and very intoxicated. Looking at someone seated under cover, he presumed it was Sairandhri. As he reached the bed, he slowly lifted the sheet. He was surprised to find someone other than Sairandhri there. His reactions were a bit slow on account of the drinks he had consumed. Suddenly, the huge figure of Bhima rose like colossus. In no time, he lifted Keechaka high in the air and banged his body on the ground. Keechaka was trying to recover from the shock when he saw the huge fist of Beema coming at him. It broke his crown and killed him instanteously.

Next morning, a household staff discovered Keechak's body. Entire royalty was shocked beyond imagination. Keechak was no ordinary man and that is why the death was all the more very mysterious and attracted considerable publicity and gossip.

Although Sudeshna had no evidence to link Keechak's death to Sairandhri, she suspected that the latter, or her mysterious connections, were somehow connected. She had definitely started fearing Sairandhri. After some deliberations, she summoned Sairandhri and told her she had decided to dispense with her services. Sairandhri requested for a few days before she could leave. The queen agreed for a thirteen days' reprieve.

Keechak's death opened a pandora's box of problems. Many rumours were afloat concerning Keechak and Sairandhri.

Only a few days earlier, those who were present in the royal court had seen the unfortunate incident when Keechak had badly misbehaved with Sairandhri. Sairandhri's beauty and speculation on Keechak's killer were also being publicly discussed. The king's main worry was that there was no worthy replacement for Keechak. Since he himself and prince Uttara were weak people, there was an obvious vacuum in the ruling hierarchy of Virata. This could prove disastrous for the kingdom as many of its neighbours were troublesome and were kept in check only by Keechak's powerful reputation.

The happenings of Viratanagar reached the ears of Duryodhana at Hastinapura and king Susharma of Trigarta. Both were immediate neighbours of Virata, one at north (Hastinapura) and the other at south. Both were also eager to grab their neighbour's kingdom but had been held at check due to Keechak's strong presence. Kauravas had also harboured a faint suspicion that Keechak's brutal murderer could be none other than Bheema and Sairandhri might be none other than Draupadi. The Pandavas, they speculated, could be hiding in Viratanagar and if their cover was blown open, they would have to go for another twelve years of exile.

Duryodhana was seriously contemplating an attack on Viratanagar when king Susharma of Trigarta came to meet him. He proposed that they both attack Viratanagar from north and south and once the King was subdued, they would divide the kingdom between themselves. Duryodhana readily agreed and asked Dushasana to ready the army to attack Viratanagar from north. Next day, Susharma would also do the same from south. At the sunrise on next day both armies launched the attack from north and south respectively.

Chapter-XXXV

THE INVASION ON VIRATANAGAR

King Susharma's soldiers moved quickly in Matsya territory capturing large no. of castles and livestock as well as the villages in the outskirts. A few border guards rushed to the Viratanagar to give the news of attack. With Dushasan attacking from north, further bad news of the invasion poured in. King Virata confessed to his brahamin counsel, Kanka (Yudhishthira) that they were ill prepared to meet the challenge. Yudhishthira assured him that he, with the help of Bhima, Nakula and Sahadeva, would lead the soldiers and repulse the attacks.

Reassured, though skeptical of the help from his counselor, the king prepared himself for the fight and launched the counter-attack. Trigarta soldiers and those from Hastinapur were astonished to find the counter-attack so fearsome. They were preparing to retreat when Susharma cunningly captured Virata king. This was a demoralizing blow to his soldiers.

Yudhisthira told Bhima to go after Susharma and release the Virata king. The day was coming to an end, but Bhima, rallying some soldiers, attacked the section in which Susharma was directing the fight. The Viratanagar soldiers attacked with determination in the fading light and broke the chariot of king Susharma. Susharma and Virata, whom the former was carrying as a prisoner, jumped on the ground and the latter, taking advantage of the diversion snatched the sword of Susharma and tore his way through the enemy cordon to rejoin his forces.

Bhima rushed to Susharma in the same instant and picked him up, raised him high up in the air and threw him down on the ground. As Susharma lay on the ground, Bhima raised his mace to kill him, but checked himself when he heard Yudhishthira's command to spare his life. He sat on Susharma's chest nonetheless and promised to spare his life if he in turn, promised to leave Matsya and not to attack in future; as well as release all captured asets and get back to Trigarta. Happy from being spared a sure death, Susharma vowed never to venture into Matasya territory. Returning all the captured booty, Susharma rapidly retreated to Trigarta along with his surviving soldiers.

Next day, buoyed by the success, the Virata army launched a fierce attack on Dushasan's columns. The Kaurava army could not defend itself against such lightning onslaught and fled helter-skelter leaving all the captured live stock of Virata kingdom.

In another front, Karna was moving in the Matsya territory and heading towards Viratanagar. The frightened citizens quickly retreated to the capital with some of them going to prince Uttara and reporting on Karna's advance. The prince was a very weak person. He developed cold feet and knew that he could not go and fight such a strong person as Karna. Also, his charioteer was away on some other work. However, when Sairandhri mentioned that the eunach Brihannala (Arjuna in disguise) was also an expert charioteer, Uttara agreed to go and fight.

Uttara led a column of his soldiers to meet Kauravas invading from North under Karna, but his courage took to heels with the first fearsome volley from Karna. He ordered Brihannala to return to Viratanagar. Arjuna told him that this would not go well with his troops who expected Uttara to put up a big fight. Uttara admitted his inability out of acute fear. Arjuna then suggested that they exchange their places and roles something which

Uttara immediately agreed. Arjuna told Uttara to take him to his secret hide-out in the forest where he had stashed his weapons – including Gandiva, his bow, and Devadutta – his conch. Retrieving the weapons he came to the fighting front and launched a fearsome attack. Once again, the kaurava soldiers, who were expecting a cakewalk, found a real mayhem wrecking havoc on them.

Arjuna and other Pandavas had also known that their one year of incognito exile was over on the previous day. However, Duryodhana was under the impression that the last day had yet to be passed. It is for this reason that he was consistently advising Karna to concentrate on exposing Pandavas their true identity so that they could be sent on yet another twelve year exile.

The Kaurava army was amused to see a eunach poised to lead the fight against them. They were shocked, however, when the barrage of arrows and other projectiles started from Arjuna's bows. There was an immediate recognition that this enuach was no ordinary warrior. The advancing soldiers halted and then decided to run away. In the meantime, Guru Dronacharya who was closely watching the eunach's actions, turned to Bhishma and said, "That is Arjuna. Having been his guru, I can recognize him very clearly".

The tide was now turning against Kuru soldiers. Arjuna formally announced his presence by blowing Devadutta, his conch gifted by the brahmin. When he pulled the string of Gandiva and gave the loud 'Twang', there was no doubt at all of his presence.

Duryodhana was overjoyed to discover Pandava's identity before what he thought was the expiry of thirteenth year. He also turned to Bhishma and said, "There. This is Arjuna's Deva Dutta and the twang of his

Gandiva. The Pandavas have been discovered before the end of the thirteenth year. Now, they have to go to exile for another twelve years.

Bhishma turned towards Duryodhana and said, “You will never mature, Duryodhana. The thirteenth year has already finished yesterday. Now, as per the terms of gambling game, you have to give back the territory you took from them or else risk a war”.

Duryodhana laughed at Bhishma’s reply and said, “Pitamaha, I shall not part with the slightest bit of my land. If we have to go to war, so be it. This has been our territory and my land. Uncle Pandu was temporarily handed over the reigns till I, son of the eldest son of Dhrishtrashtra, became a major. Anyhow, these discussions can wait because right now, due to entry of Pandavas in the side of Virata, We have no alternative but to retreat”.

He rushed towards Hastinapura with Arjuna, anticipating Duryodhana’s intentions, going after him at full speed. On the way, Karna tried to block his way. Arjuna sent at Karna such a massive barrage of arrows that the latter had to flee from that place to save himself. Duryodhana, realizing the difficult situation he was in, released all the Matsya livestock including milch cows. Neither Arjuna nor Uttara was keen to prolong the fight, with the return of captured livestock and retreat of kuru army away from Matsya territory.

Arjuna went to hide his weapons at his selected place and after that, dressed as Brihannala headed towards Viratnagar with prince Uttara in the prime seat and himself as prince’s charioteer.

King Virata had already returned to the capital. Along with being overjoyed with his success, he was already feeling extremely grateful to his adviser Kanka and he told Kanka of his extreme gratitude to him and his hand-picked friend. Although earlier he had felt a bit intrigued when Yudhishthira referred to Bhima, Nakula and Sahadeva as his friends and brothers, after the battle and seeing how well all the four of them had combined and fought the invading enemy, he felt convinced that their being friends and referred as brothers was not an accident, but born out of a genuine and close friendship.

While the king and Yudhishthira were playing their usual game of chess, some runners came to give the king the happy news of Uttara's victory. The king's joy was boundless. He told his deputies to arrange for a memorable welcome to the prince. Arches were to be erected, the roads to be swept and watered, and flowers and garlands to be positioned to be showered on the prince and his soldiers.

However, when Virata told Yudhishthira that the prince had scored an amazing victory over the Kaurav army invading from the north, Yudhishthira smiled and replied that it was to be expected since Brihannala was his charioteer.

The king flared up and said, "You talk as if it is Brihannala who has achieved this victory. How dare you insult me and the prince in such way". Out of rage, he picked up some chess pieces and threw them hard at Yudhishthira's face with such a force that it was cut at a few places. Saurandhri saw this and rushed to clean and dress the cuts.

In a short while prince Uttara also arrived in the palace. He came straight to the king and touched his feet. The king too got up and embraced his son. His joy, love and affection were overflowing. After all, his son, who was considered as a bit of timid boy, had returned after repulsing the invasion of a major adversary.

Uttara then turned towards Yudhishthira and showed concern over his bruised face. His father explained, "He is like this because I lost my temper and threw chess pieces at him when he made a stupid remark that your victory was achieved because Brihannala was with you".

Uttara, looking shocked, went to Kanka and paid obeisance to him. Then he went to his father, who was looking confused and rattled, and said, "Oh father, you should not have hurt him. Apart from anything else, he was supposed to be a brahmin. As regards his remarks regarding eunach Brihannala, he was absolutely right. It was not your fault because Kanka and Brihannala are in fact the two of the five Pandava brothers living their thirteenth year in our kingdom incognito, Yudhishthira and Arjuna. The other three who helped Kanka in your fight against Susharma are Bhima, Nakula and Sahadeva. Lastly, empress Draupadi has been with us as Sairandhri".

King Virata was incredulous for a few moments. Then he went to Yudhishthira, touched his feet and profusely apologized for his indiscreet behaviour. Yudhishthira smiled, got up and embraced the king. He told the king that it should be him who should be thanking the king for keeping the whole family in his employ for a year enabling them to pass the thirteenth year without being discovered of their true identity.

The king immediately restored to the Pandava family all the respect due to an ex-emperor living with them. He also offered the hand of princess Uttara for marriage with Arjuna. Yudhishthira however declined the proposal. Since a teacher is considered like a father to a pupil, the Pandavas made a counter-offer of the marriage of their son Abhimanyu which was readily accepted. Abhimanyu was called and was married to Princess Uttara in the presence of a number of royalty and guests including Krishna, Balarama, Drupad and Drishtidyumna.

The Pandavas had completed their part of the bargain as per the conditions of the dice game and rightly expected to be restored to the status quo-ante i.e. the rulership of previously held half of the kingdom. The Kaurava, however, had other ideas. Duryodhana, who was calling the shots and virtually ruling the kingdom, had made it very clear that he was not inclined to concede even single needle point head of grass of his territory. He also invented a new argument for his claim on entire territory. According to him, since Dhritarashtra was blind since birth, the kingdom was temporarily allowed to be run by the younger brother Pandu. It should have been handed over to Duryodhana, the legal heir on his attaining the majority. Despite disputing this view by even Bhishma, Duryodhana's view was prevailed upon. This was mainly due to a weak and indulgent father who kept on condoning every act of excess, every unethical decision and even the most illogical interpretiations of Duryodhana.

Even though Dhritarashtra and Gandhari kept telling Duryodhana that his illogical interpretations and wrong decisions would lead to ruin of Hastinapura, Duryodhana just wouldn't budge. Many others advised Duryodhana that handing over the part of territory to Pandava would pave the way for a lasting peace, and hence he should show magnanimity. Duryodhana however, was obstinate, obdurate and firm in not agreeing to hand over even the smallest piece of territory to Pandavas. He didn't budge a bit even when Dhritarashtra and Gandhari walked off from the conclave warning Duryodhana of disasters, if he persisted in his attitude and decisions. Though a weak-willed person, Dhritarashtra knew the ground realities much better. He dreaded the day when Bhima, his nephew with the power of a thousand elephants, would kill Dushasana as he had vowed to after the first dice game or smash Duryodhana's thighs during the impending great war between Kauravas and Pandavas. He and his wife, Gandhari, were highly apprehensive, but had resigned to the inevitable and left the future in the hands of the fate and destiny.

Chapter-XXXVI

A CRITICAL CONCLAVE

After the marriage of Abhimanyu and Uttara, all the royal heads of states who were present decided to discuss the matter relating to the restoration of Yudhishthira's kingdom to him. At the start of the meeting, Krishna narrated the sequence of events leading to the present situation and said that fairness demanded that the kingdoms should be restored to status-quo-ante, prior to the royal game of dice at Hastinapur. Krishna also spelt out the reported opposition of Duryodhana to this transfer of power and the latter's arguments supporting his claim. He recommended that an emissary be sent to the court at Hastinapura to convey the requests of Pandavas to the royal household.

Many kings spoke on the matter. Almost all of them supported the line adopted by Krishna. They also said that if the proposed mission was not successful, they should prepare for a war with Kauravas. However the motion was opposed by Balarama, Krishna's elder brother. He enunciated his own arguments but the main reason behind his stance was that he had never forgiven the Pandavas ever since Arjuna had eloped with Subhadra and had married her without his permission.

Balarama expressed agreement with the views of Duryodhana. He also said that Yudhishthira should not have agreed to accept the challenge thrown for the game of dice knowing fully well that Shakuni, a known manipulator would be assisting Duryodhana. Having committed the initial blunder, and then losing again, he should atone for the misadventure. His erstwhile kingdom could only be given if Duryodhana agreed to the transfer out of his own free will.

There were not many takers for this arguments. Satyaki, another yadava chieftain, was very vociferous in opposing Balarama's views. After an extended debate, Krishna's views prevailed. It was decided to send Sanjaya, Drupad's family priest to the court of Dhritarashtra carrying the request of Pandavas. Since the chances of acceptance were slim, the kings accepted the inevitability of war and agreed to gradually start preparing for the same.

As directed and briefed, Sanjaya went to Hastinapura and after paying regards to all present, narrated the request of Pandavas. Bhishma was first to speak after Sanjaya. He endorsed Pandava's views and said that since they had successfully fulfilled the two conditions set for the loser of the dice game, the Kauravas should honour their pledge and return the erstwhile kingdom of Pandavas to them. Duryodhana, however, pooh-poohed the idea and again reiterated his views on accession vide which on achieving majority, he was the rightful ruler of kuru dynasty. He made it abundantly clear that he had no intention to part with any part of his kingdom, not even a small portion of the size of the point of needle. Since Duryodhana wielded the real influence and the power, the elderly members who were for a peaceful resolution, just sat, listened and acquiesed, including Dhritarashtra and Gandhari. The kingdom was being put in a state of war with terrible consequences.

Duryodhana had rightly surmised that in the event of war, there would be powerful armies and warriors on his side and if handled properly, he stood a fair chance to win. Bhishma Pitamaha will be on his side on account of his vows to defend the Kuru Kingdom. Dronacharya and Kripacharya were paid servants of the Kuru throne. He himself, Karna and Shakuni were acknowledged mighty warriors, not to mention his ninety nine brothers and scores of other rulers who would be fighting under the kuru banner.

Sanjaya went back and reported the failure of his mission. The situation was hopeless. Yet, it was decided that to avoid a war, Krishna should go to Hastinapur to make one last effort. Pandavas were even prepared to settle for just five villages. Yudhishthira was not keen on the proposal. He was concerned about Krishna's safety since the Kauravas were known to be preparing for the war and Duryodhana would be too keen to eliminate Krishna who was perceived as a formidable threat to Kauravas. Krishna, however, brushed his reservations and promised to them to be extra careful.

He arrived in Hastinapur in due course. Dhritarashtra accorded him a grand welcome due to a friendly head of state. Duryodhana offered him his palace to stay but Krishna politely declined saying that he would rather stay with his old friend Vidura. When invited for a meal by Duryodhana, Krishna again politely declined stating that such things could follow the negotiations, if successful.

Krishna was received by the full court on the next day. After the preliminaries, he addressed to the royal personages the message sent by the Pandava and their friends. He emphasized that since he was close to both Kauravas and Pandavas, he wanted to do everything pssible to avert a conflict which would harm both the sides. He emphasized the need for an equitable solution so that both sides could co-exist in peace and harmony.

The arguments followed the usual pattern. Bhishma was all for a solution. Dhritarashtra agreed with Krishna but conceded nothing because Duryodhana was emphatic in not agreeing to any territory, not even equal to the tip of a needle. He, and more than him, Dushasana was rude to the elders as well as Krishna. There was even a veiled threat of arresting him. Duryodhana's close followers were so drunk with power and perceived superiority that the Lord decided to show them his cosmic self. He granted temporary vision to Dhritarashtra to see him. The king was overwhelmed and after reverting to his blindness, requested Krishna not to grant him a vision any more in future so that he could retain Krishna's grand image for ever.

The Kaurava elders and the gurus tried their best to dissuade Duryodhana in going for a war but their efforts bore no effect. They told him that Pandavas were much superior to the Kauravas in fighting skills and their cause was just but Duryodhana was adamant.He even walked out a few times from the discussions indicating his dissent.

Krishna eventually left the assembly without any concessions from Kauravas, rather Duryodhana. Even before coming to the mission, he had known that the mission was going to be an exercise in futility. Yet, he undertook it so that future generations would know that the Pandavas and their mentors tried everything to do the utmost to avoid a war but did not succeed.

(In another version, at the ending stage of the discussions, when Duryodhana and Dushasana had walked out Satyaki, spotted them talking in whispers in a suspicious manner. He came to Krishna and asked him to be careful. Krishna looked at Dhritarashtra and asked him, "Your majesty. I hope, as an emissary of Pandavas, I shall be given due courtesy and security?"

Dhritarashtra looked at Duryodhana and Dushasana who were reentering the hall. He replied, "Left to myself, I shall not allow any discourtesy or harm to befall on you.

But these days it is my sons who wield all power and influence", saying this, he shrugged his shoulders in a hopeless gesture".

Krishna smiled and asked Satyaki to go. He then looked at Duryodhana and Dushasana. The latter stepped forward and adopting an aggressive posture, said, "Krishna, you have said enough and tried our patience to the hilt. You have also stated humiliating things about my brother here. For these, the only punishment is arrest, a trial and execution". Krishna smiled and replied, 'Oh, really, Dushasana, you think this is the best way to treat an emissary who himself is ruler of a kingdom'.

Dushasana, emboldened more, laughed and said, "Whose emissary? Pandavas, who own or rule over nothing. As far as your own ideas about yourself are concerned, you have a highly inflated ego based upon what has been talked or told about you. As far as we are concerned, you are just a cowherd who has grown up amongst the yadava maidens.I think a time has come to deflate this ego. In the name of the state, I am arresting you for misbehaviour today".

Krishna, already anticipating this, smiled, and then turning towards the courtiers, showed his Virata swarup and divinity in the full dazzling form. There was a hush in the hall. Both Duryodhana and Dushasan took a step back, looking confused.

Dhritarashtra, temporarily regaining his sight by the grace of the Lord, was able to see Krishna in his vishwarup, in every form. With folded hands, he told Krishna, "Govinda, having seen you in your dazzling divine form, I request that I should be blind again. I regret that my efforts have failed. Duryodhana is obstinate and unrelenting." Krishna shrugged his shoulders and, with Satyaki and Vidura on either side of him, slowly walked out of the court.)

He prepared to return from Hastinapur. Although he knew that the war was inevitable, he genuinely wanted to do his best to avert it. He knew that the majority in the Kaurava camp were against war and for concessions to Pandavas. He was related closely to both the sides and wanted to avoid the bloodshed if he could. But, this was not to be, given the inflexible position Duryodhana had adopted.

Disappointed, Krishna went to meet Kunti before finally returning to Pandavas. Kunti had a message for Yudhishthira which she wanted Krishna to deliver personally, "Krishna", she said, "tell Yudhishthira that time has come for which every kshatriya mother waits for. He has tried his best to avoid a conflict but has not succeeded. He has shown enough restraint and now it is time to fight for his just rights. Draupadi's humiliation should be duly avenged. As always, my blessings will be with him and his brothers". Her mood was somber and grim. On his return, the message was duly delivered to Pandavas.

Chapter-XXXVII

PREPARING FOR WAR – WOOING ALLIES

Even though every sane person was convinced that war should be avoided at any cost, the Kuru dynasty was moving towards major internecine clash. Wise people speculated that this would spell a disaster for the whole region. Under the then existing culture and traditions, hardly any state, region or kingdom, big or small, would be able to stay neutral in the conflict. It was horrifying to even imagine the deadly consequences of the war.

The two parties were quietly sending messages and emissaries to obtain the consent of the heads of kingdom to join their sides in the impending war. Negotiations and bargaining, direct and indirect pressures and relationships were all to being put to effect. While Duryodhana was known to be the head of a strong empire and the likely favourite in the eyes of many, the people close to Pandavas and the ones relying on ethical considerations chose the latter for the obvious reasons. Even when some parties had made a clear choice, the wooing parties did not give up their efforts and tried to wean the adversaries to their side. Those who know about the happenings prior to the first and second world wars would be better able to appreciate the events prior to what was subsequently called as 'Mahabharata' or the great mega war of the Indian nation.

Amongst the few top kingdoms at that time, Dwarka, under Krishna and Balarama was one which both the warring parties would have liked to have on their side. Duryodhana set course for seeing Krishna in Dwarka and so did Arjuna, almost at the same time. The stakes were high because yadavas were considered to be very powerful warriors.

Duryodhana reached at Krishna's palace in the afternoon. He was taken to Krishna's chambers. The latter was asleep after the afternoon meals. Duryodhana decided to wait in the chamber and took his seat just behind the headrest of Krishna's bed.

Arjuna also reached Dwarka almost at the same time but a shade later than Duryodhana. He chose to sit at Krishna's bedside.

After a while, Krishna's sleep was over. On opening his eyes, the first person he saw was Arjuna, but when both Arjuna and Duryodhana greeted him simultaneously he became aware of presence of both.

He heard from both of them. Their pleas were similar. Both of them wanted Krishna and his army on their side. Being closely related to both of them, Krishna was in a bit of dilemma. He asked Balarama for his advice. The latter was always the one who avoided complicated problems which required too much analysis and thinking. He promptly suggested that in view of their proximity to both, they should stay neutral. This was not a decision to the liking of any of the other three, i.e. Duyodhana, Arjuna or Krishna. When they started explaining their points of view in detail to Balarama, the latter left the decision to Krishna stating that he would abide by the same and that in any case, he was going for a pilgrimage.

Krishna, on the contrary, was a highly clear-headed person. He summed up the situation to both Duryodhana and Arjuna.

"Both of you are close to me and closely related. Although it is true that I am more attached to Pandavas, and particularly to Arjuna, I am going to be absolutely unbiased in this particular issue". Krishna continued, "I am going to ask for your choices, Arjuna first, because he is younger of you and I saw him first. Both of you have a choice of either getting the Yadava army to fight on your side or to have me alone with you. In my case, I have decided to be unarmed, without any weapons. Arjun, you have to choose first".

Duryodhana was a bit restless as he was fearing that Arjun would chose the strong, courageous and well-renowned yadava army. He waited with baited breath to hear the choice of Arjuna.

Arjuna was prompt and very clear and specific. He looked at Krishna and said, "I choose you, Krishna".

This was like a windfall for Duryodhana who was waiting for what he thought was worst, i.e. Arjuna choosing the yadava army. When Arjuna chose the unarmed Krishna, Duryodhana's joy knew no bounds. He thanked his lucky stars that Arjuna, out of his personal loyalty to Krishna, forgot the basic principle of war to have a substantial increase of men under his command and thus had made an incredible gift to Duryodhana. Extremely happy, he got out of Dwarka as quickly as possible and headed towards Hastinapur. In reality, he felt as if he had already won the war.

After Duryodhana's departure Krishna wore an amused look. He turned towards Arjuna and asked, "Partha, why did you chose me and not my army"?

Arjuna replied, "Lord, like the eye of the fish in Draupadi's swayamvar, I have just one objective in the coming war, to win it. It is unthinkable that we can achieve this objective without your wise counsel, guidance and blessings". Saying this, he too made preparations to return to his brothers.

The clouds of war were gathering thick and fast. Every king was choosing the sides of Kaurava or Pandavas. The whole atmosphere was transformed from a sevene and peaceful one to a war-like one.

Shalya was one such king who was also proceeding with his troops towards the war zone to join the Pandava camp. He was the king of Madra, brother of the queen Madri, mother of Nakula and Sahadeva. Little did he realize that the fate had willed him to fight against Pandavas on account of a trick played on him by Duryodhana and his friends.

Duryodhana had his eyes on him from the very outset. The momemt he heard about his impending arrival, he, Shakuni and others ensured that he and his army were accorded an extra-ordinary welcome. The welcome party made it look like they were being welcomed on behalf of Pandavas throughout the route. When Shalya had been welcomed enough to become overwhelmed, he expressed his desire to meet their
leader, expecting one of the Pandava brothers to meet him.

To his extreme surprise, it was Duryodhana who greeted him with folded hands. Inwardly Shalya blamed himself for not confirming at the very outset on the identity of the host. The damage had already been done. He quickly regained his composure and thanked Duryodhana for looking after him and his soldiers throughout the route. Knowing that he was morally bound to return the courtesy, Shalya asked Duryodhana what could be do for him.

“Please fight on my side”, Duryodhana replied. Shalya realized that he had been tricked due to his own foolishness and he would have to fight against his own nephews, the Pandavas, whom he had resolved to help when he started from Madra. He, however, had no choice but to agree to fight on the side of Duryodhana, much to the glee of the latter.

Later, he went to Pandava camp and met Yudhishtira and his brothers. Explaining his stupid faux-pas, he apologized to Yudhishtira for having to fight against him. Yudhishtira laughed at the whole thing and told Shalya “Uncle, it does not matter really. What is needed are your blessings and we are grateful for having them from you. Yours is not the first instance of having been tricked by Duryodhana. Sooner or later he will be punished by the almighty. Please do not feel aggrieved on this score and carry out what you have committed to do”.

Shalya left a sadder man because he could see and appreciate the big-heartedness of Pandavas and contrasted it with the bigotry and trickery of Kauravas. The die, however, been cast. He would have to do something for which he had not an iota of desire to do.

Not without reason, Mahabharata has been described as the greatest epic describing human history with all the passions and emotions in it. It does not appear that the events happened thousands of years ago. It reads like something which was happening in our own time and in our own neighbourhood. No wonder, someone has described it as “What is not in it, will not be found any where else”.

Chapter-XXXVIII

AN UNUSUAL MEETING

Right from the time the war started getting really imminent, Kunti had been uneasy about her son, Karna. So many times in the past, she had felt guilty about not letting him know that whe was his real mother. She felt that Karna should know about their true relationship and about Pandavas being his real brothers.

Ever since Karna joined Duryodhana, his behaviour has been biased and at times really bad against Pandavas. The extreme example of this was the dice game and the decision to disrobe Draupadi. Being the mother, Kunti attributed this to his upbringing under the patronage of Radha and the weaver father and to a great extent her own misconduct in willing for a son through the sun-god before her marriage.

Hence, one day, she really made up her mind to see him and talk to him. She went to a place where Karna used to come to worship every morning. Karna was in meditation with closed eyes and when he opened his eyes, he was surprised to find Kunti there.

After the usual exchange of greetings and pleasantaries, Kunti came to real purpose of her visit. She disclosed their biological relationship and the fact that Pandavas were his real brothers.

Karna accepted the news with mixed emotions. He was happy to know that he indeed was a kshatriya and had the royal blood running through his veins. Yet he felt bitter that he had been humiliated so much throughout his life on account of his lowly status. The feelings were confused. He paid obeisance to her once more and then asked her if she had come for a special purpose.

Kunti replied in affirmative. She said that since a war was imminent it would be inevitable that sometime or other, he would be facing the Pandavas. She wanted to disclose his relationship with them for that reason. In this battle, whoever gets killed or injured from whichever side, she would be the loser as mother. She asked him if it was possible that this battle could be avoided so that she, as a mother, was spared an extreme agony.

Karna was known as a 'Daanveer', a person who never refused any thing asked from him. Here was his own mother asking for something which he was incapable of agreeing.

He replied, "Mother, I have already pledged to Duryodhana my life and to fight on his side. I cannot therefore agree to do what you ask. However, I do promise to you that in any case you will remain a mother of five sons. You know I and Arjuna are sworn adversaries. Whether I die or Arjuna, you would remain a mother of the five sons.

Kunti blessed him, but returned disappointed. She had hoped against hope that there would be no fight between Karna and herr five sons. She was, however, relieved that Karna had been told the truth at last.

Everyone in the hierarchy of Kauravas and Pandavas was doing his or her utmost to muster more forces and strength on their side. Comparatively, Pandavas were much more ethical in their approach, strategy and tactics. However, in the crunch time, we would see that many norms and agreements were forgotten or ignored, proving the age old dictum that all was fair in love and war.

CH-XXXIX

THE FINISHING TOUCHES AND COMMENCEMENT OF MAHABHARATA

After clearing the initial hurdles and ironing out the last minute problems, both the sides were transformed into welloiled machines poised to strike at each other. Yudhishthira had stopped wishing, or even talking about any conciliatory gesture from Duryodhana. With his totally inflexible attitude, the war was considered inevitable. Any further talk about reconciliation or avoidance of war would only dent the resolve of the leaders and soldiers alike. Henceforth, both the sides realized that their objective was only to win the war and nothing else.

The Pandavas and their allies were reorganized into five units with each unit being led under seven able commanders. These included some great names like Drupada, Satyaki, Bhima, Dhrishtadyumna, Virata, Shikhandi and Chekitan.

By common consensus, Dhrishtadumna was elected as the supreme commander of the entire Pandava Army. Not only he was a powerful and renowned fighter, but he also had the confidence of everyone.

In a formal ceremony, watched by all key unit commanders, he was announced as the Supreme Commander of the Pandava Army. Naturally, he too became a key member of the higher war council which included Krishna and Pandavas.

On the Kaurava side, similar confabulatious were gong on. There was a unanimity amongst them that Bhishma Pitamaha would be their supreme commander. He had the stature and experience. Everyone knew about his loyalty to the crown of Hastinapur and that he had taken a vow to defend it at all costs. He, however, made it clear that he would not kill any of the Pandava brothers since all the children of Dhritarashtra and Pandu were dear to him. He however reiterated that this abstinence did not apply to Pandava allies or soldiers.

Pitamaha laid down another condition. In view of the critical attitude of Karna and the history of his differences with Bhishma, he would not like Karna to participate in the war as long as Bhishma was in command. There was no problem in agreeing to this since Karna himself was not keen to fight under Bhishma.

The kuru army also had numerous chariots elephants, cavalry units and foot soldiers, ably under some famous names like Dronacharya, his son Ashwathama, Kripacharya, Shalya, Shakuni etc. Numerically, both the sides were equally matched.

Both the armies had assembled at Kurukshetra with a large number of sheds, tents and stables springing up overnight. The excitement was just too much; sound from cronch shells, trumpets, elephant calls neighing of the horses, swords hitting the shields in the mock-fights filled the atmosphere. The action was awaiting the formal announcement with everyone primed and ready to fight.

As was the custom those days, the representatives of both the parties met immediately on declaration of the war to decide on the modalities of the war, the 'dos and don'ts'. The present day wars are of the type 'No holds barred', (Even these days, though, the red cross society or representatives of other bodies as well as United

Nations broker temporary peace or halt to fighting). However, things were different those days with more emphasis on ethics. Even then, as the fighting became more intense, rules were given a go-by for short term advantages but the instances were few and far between. Each day, the battle would be suspended at the sun-set. Warriors and soldiers from both the sides could and did intermingle with each other as friends.The conflict would be resumed at the sunrise on next day. Combat could only between equals e.g. warriors, charioteers, horsemen, elephants and soldiers. Anyone who was down, injured and had surrendered was not to be attacked.Those who were employed for playing drums or bigoules or conches were not to be attacked. Non-combatants were also immune from attacks.

Duryodhana dispatched Ulook to Yudhishthira with the message that the Kuru army had arrived at Kurukshetra under the command of grandpa Bhishma and was ready for the battle with Pandavas.

The day before the war began, the leaders of both the sides gave a pep-talk to then key commanders. Bhishma addressed the leaders of Kaurava army and reminded of the great battles they had won in the past. He exhorted them to fight with the sole aim of winning the war even if it meant their death in the battle field, reminding them that a soldier does not wish to rot in the old age, but aspires to die as a hero in the battle field.

Yudhishthira and Dhrishtadyumana also gave a similar talk to their leaders. Since the Kaurava army was slightly numerically superior in numbers, it had been decided that they would follow the principle of concentration of forces so that the forces are not dissipated. The 'Needle' formations were the preferred strategy in such situations. The leaders emphasized on high valour mixed with ethics and morality, stating that these factors were to fetch the victory for them eventually.

There was, however, one problem, totally unanticipated, relating to the star fighter of Pandavas, Arjuna. When he saw the armies arrayed on both the sides, facing each other, questions started to arise in his mind. Some faces, particularly of commanders, were known familiar faces with whom he had excellent relations.

Then there were known elders. Some of whom had bestowed the best of love and affection on Arjuna. For example, the Grandsire Bhishma Pitamaha was the person whose favourite grandson was considered as Arjuna. Guru Dronacharya had declared Arjuna as his most competent and favourite disciple. Kripacharya too had always shown excellent feelings towards Dhananjaya. Many of his kuru brothers literally adored him.

Mounted on his chariot and driven by Krishna, Arjuna surveyed the battlefield. He abhorred the very thought of having to fight and kill those dearest to him. And for what gains? Some pieces of land so that they could rule. A furious battle arose within him with questions and counterquestions. Totally exhausted, he threw his Gandiva away and kneeled before Krishna with a highly agitated face and troubled eyes. He confessed to Krishna that he just did not have the stomach to fight his nearest and dearest ones for gains he did not consider as worthwhile considering the harm, he would be doing to his so-called adversaries.

Krishna then spoke to Arjuna to allay his doubts and misgiving. His clear and crisp analysis on 'do's' and 'don't's "is known as 'Bhagwad Gita' which till date is not only a superb moral and spiritual treasure of human literature, but also considered by the millions of people as the word of God.

Its emphasis on adherence to Dharma, devotion to duty without expectation of reward has inspired people and cleared their misgivings in their deepest hours of crisis. Equally applicable to all, rich and poor, learned or ignorant, it is the song of the Lord which clarifies, uplifts and guides men from all part of the world.So deep has been the impact of Bhagwad Gita even on the minds of the modern men that it is worthwhile going through the comments of some great men and philosophers of the twentieth century.

Gandhi wrote that "when disappointments stare me in the face and I see not one ray of hope on the horizon, I turn to Bhagwad-Gita and find a verse to comfort me : I immediately begin to smile in the midst of overwhelming sorrow. Those who meditate on the Gita will derive fresh joy, and new meanings from it every day".Thoreau writes, "In the morning, I bathe my intellect in the stupendous and cosmological philosophy of the Bhagwad – Gita, in comparision with which our modern world and its literature seem puny and trivial".

Emerson adds, "I owed a magnificient day to Bhagwad- Gita. It was the first of the books; it was as if an empire spoke to us, nothing small or unworthy, but large, serene and consistent. The voice of an old intelligence which in another age and climate had pondered and disposed of the same questions which exercise us".

After Krishna's discourse, Arjuna got up with a bright lit smile and confident gait. There was no uncertainty in his eyes as existed before. Rather, it was an unwaivering glint indicating his firm resolve. Arjuna picked up his gandiva, and took out his cronrch-shell, Devadutta ready to blow.

Yet again, there was a twist in the tale. With the armies arrayed facing each other and everyone keyed up for the start of fighting any moment, everyone saw Yudhishthira giving a gesture of stopping to the soldiers, getting down and taking off his armour and weapons and walking to the chariot on which Bhishma stood. The Pandavas were baffled with their misgivings with no one knowing what Yudhishthira was upto. Was he going to ask for truce or was it to negotiate? Even Krishna appeared to be quite confused.

Yudhishthira stood before Bhishma with folded hands and said, "Respected Pitamaha, we have been forced to wage a war against Kauravas much against our will. I stand before you to obtain your forgiveness before the beginning of this war. You remain our Pitamaha (Grandman). We seek your blessings for a victory of our side".Bhishma was moved. Everyone knew that he too had opposed the war and counselled peace and reconciliation. He was fighting for Kaurava in order to fulfil his vow to defend the crown of Hastinapura at all costs. He smiled and lifted his right hand in benediction and said, "Ashirvad. Vijayi Bhava". ("Blessings. May you be victorious").

Yudhishthira then moved towards Drona and then Shalya, his maternal uncle and obtained their blessings too. He then returned to his chariot and put on his armour, crown and weapons. With a confident gleam on his face, he indicated to his chieftains that he was ready. They all picked up their bows and raised the battle cry, "Death to the enemy. Hara, Hara, Mahadeva". Arjuna lifted his conch shell, Devadutta and blew it long and loud. He was joined by many others raising a deafening sound that momentarily paralysed the enemy soldiers. Bhishma launched a fearsome attack on Pandava army. Abhimanyu rushed to defend their beleagured column and counter-attacked Bhishma. Both sides moved in to defend their chieftains. All through the front, attack and counter attacks were taking place. The first day of Mahabharata war had begun.

Chapter-XL

THE FIRST DAY

A war on such a large scale had not taken place earlier. Then, the battles fought by the either side were on a much amaller scale and participated by comparatively small number of soldiers. To that extent, both the sides were inexperienced.

The front column of Kaurava army was being commanded by Dushasana while Bhima was commanding the leading column of Pandavas.

Bhishma fired a huge salvo at the Pandava soldiers and started advancing menacingly towards Pandavas. Abhimanyu who was nearby, counter – attacked with equal ferociousness. Unsuccessful attempts were made to surround Abhimanyu who was causing havoc. He cut down the flag of the chariot of Bhishma. Pandavas had in the meanwhile, advanced to form a security ring around Abhimanyu. It was Bhishma's turn to retreat.

Elsewhere too, fearsome battles were raging with more show of courage and power and less of proper strategy and tactics.

Virata prince Uttara attacked Shalya crippling the horses of the latter's chariot. Uttara himself was on an elephant. He kept raining arrows at Shalya's soldiers Shalya was enraged and threw a spear powerfully killing Uttara but not before Uttara had injured him badly.

The death of Uttara enraged his brother Shweta who, not finding king Shalya (who had been evacuated due to injury) took on Bhishma and soldiers surrounding him. Shweta too was proving to be a dangerous adversary. After hours of battle, Bhishma managed to deal a fatal blow at him but not before he had killed a disproportionately large number of Kaurava soldiers. For his age and experience, Shweta excelled in the art of war but could not match Bhishma's experience and skills.

At the sunset, the end of the day of fighting was sounded. The soldiers returned to their respective camps with some later crossing over to meet their friends. There were no foes in the night.

The leaders in the two camps confabulated to take a stock and plan for the next day. All in all, Pandavas had lost more than the Kauravas.

Chapter-XL-I

THE SECOND DAY

On the second day, the Pandava chieftain, Dhrishtadyumna implemented his previous evening's plans with precision to make his forces most effective. Chastened by the previous day's experiences, they wanted to avoid a repetition.

Duryodhana, on the other hand, was on a high note. In the morning he addressed his chieftains and exhorted them to continue the good work they had done on the previous day.

"Total annihilation and defeat of the enemy should be out aim. If necessary, give your life to overpower the enemy and deal a crushing defeat on him", Duryodhana thundered.

Despite their preparedness, the Pandava army again was under pressure mainly because of the massive ouslaught launched by Bhishma. One by one, the columns were breaking down. Seeing this, Arjuna told Krishna, "At this rate, our army shall disappear in a few days without achieving any success. We must stop Bhishma, otherwise, it is going to end up as a one-sided contest".

Krishna manoeuvered the chariot in the direction of Bhishma and said, "Partha, in that case, fight the Kaurava Chief".

Arjuna's offensive put Bhishma on the depensive momentarily and what followed was a magnificient and sustained fight between Bhishma and Arjuna. Even the Gods descended in the sky to witness the magnificient spectacle. They fought with arrows, maces, spears head on as well as from the sides. The middle ranks of soldiers and their leaders became only the spectators of this sustained fight. Reinforcements were rushing in from both the sides and for the first time, Bhishma was on the defensive, feeling the heat.

Duryodhana was not relishing this battle. "Pitamaha and Drona have become old and can't fight Arjuna" he thought. "One person whose presence could have tilted the scale in our favour, Karna, is waiting at the sideline, not being the part of the fighting elements," he lamented.

Pandavas were pressing at the other fronts as well. Dhrishtadyumna went after his sworn enemy, Dronacharya. It was a ding-dong battle on the chariots, from the ground with arrows and maces aimed at adversaries, chariots, horses and charioteers. When Drona was under the pressure, Bhishma sent the Kalinga units to augment his forces. Dhrishtadyumna got injured but continued to fight, ably supported by Pandava brothers. Bhishma also shifted his attention to help Drona. Noting this, Bhima, Satyaki and Pandava soldiers launched a fierce attack on their enemies inflicting heavy losses.

So concentrated was the barrage of weapons against Bhishma that his charioteer, hit by a shaft from Satyaki, was killed on the spot. The horses, uncontrolled, sped away from the main scene of the battle. This was a signal for a more fierce attack on Kauravas. The situation became a reverse of what it was on the previous day.

Bhishma came back with a replacement charioteer but was fighting from the position of weakness. The demoralized Kauravas and their allies suffered heavy losses. Fortunately for them, the sunset brought the fighting to a halt.

Bhishma told Drona after the fighting had ceased,"It is just as well that the sunset came, otherwise our losses would have been much more severe. Arjuna and Bhima were magnificient. We will have to do far better to win the war ultimately. In the meantime, let us call the others to plan for tomorrow".

Chapter-XL-II

THE THIRD DAY

For Kauravas, the first day's joy had turned into total gloom on the next day. Duryodhana was an impatient person who could not take setbacks lightly. Besides, in the back of his mind was also a conviction that Bhishma and Drona had a soft corner for Pandavas. Time and time again, he brought up this argument.

Bhishma's reply was steady and calculated, "Ever since the war began, my loyalty, skill and plans have always been to win the war for the Kaurava crown and the flag of Hastinapur and to defeat the Pandavas. However, before the start of war. I had warned you that the Pandavas would be a formidable lot bordering on invincibility. This war has been against my recommendations. I do love your Pandava cousins as much as I love you and your own brothers. However, all this has become immaterial since the war started. I have taken a vow to be loyal to the Hastinapur crown. I am doing it now and shall continue to do it till we achieve victory or till I die fighting for our flag. It is true, I have grown old and you all are young and strong. Notwithstanding this, there will be no lack of commitment. What my body cannot deliver, will be compensated by my brains and the experience".

A chastened Duryodhana admired the words of the ageing Kuru. Much as he liked Karna for his fighting prowess, he knew very well that the latter was no match for Bhishma or even Drona.

Kauravas arranged their army in the eagle formation with Bhishma leading from the front and Duryodhana guarding the rear. The Pandavas had anticipated this move end had arranged their forces in a crescent formation. Bhima was leading the right and while Arjuna was at the left. Pandavas and Kauravas fought fiercely on that day. No side could breach the other, but as the time passed Kauravas were pressed more and more. Duryodhana once again berated the Pitamaha for not fighting hard.

Elsewhere, Shakuni, leading his Gandhari forces attacked Satyaki and Abhimanyu. Satyaki's chariot was broken into smitherens. He moved to Abhimanyu's chariot and they fought together from the same platform. Eventually, they started getting an upper hand over Shakuni's forces. Satyaki was a known great warrior. What was also becoming clearer was that Abhimanyu, a much younger person, was no less a fighter. He was already making a mark as a great warrior.

Bhima invoked Ghatotkacha, his son from demoness Hidimba. He appeared immediately and was pressed into battle by Bhima. Ghatotkacha's huge body frame and raw power played havoc with Kaurava soldiers. Even Bhishma and Drona were at a loss to decide what to do, so terrible was the one-man onslaught by Ghatotkacha.

Bhima located Duryodhana and attacked him head-on. The attack was so sudden and so powerful that Duryodhana, despite himself being a great fighter, could not withstand the blows of Bhima's maces and fell unconscious. His charioteer sped away with him to enable him
to recover. Duryodhana, on regaining consciousness, was angry with his charioteer and went to the battlefield immediately. However, his soldiers were quite demoralized seeing him being taken away from the battle field. Sensing this, the Pandava army pounced on them and inflicted heavy casualties.

Bhishma then decided to launch a counter-attack bringing all his martial experience to use. The attack was so strong that a surging Pandava army had to backtrack and had started getting dented at key points.

Krishna told Arjuna that the time had come to put his (Krishna's) teachings to practice. Though Arjuna did ask Krishna to manoeuvre the chariot to fight Bhishma, it was clear that Arjuna was not putting in his full effort to stop Bhishma. At this, Krishna became so exasperated that he himself jumped from the chariot and prepared to launch his sudershana chakra at Bhishma. Arjuna ran to persuade him to return and promised to counter Bhishma himself effectively, when he faced him next.

Buoyed by their success, Bhishma and Drona attacked Yudhishthira as well as Nakula and Sahadeva. It was a ding – dong battle with even honours. At the close of the day when fighting ceased, it was clear that while the forenoon belonged to Pandavas, the last few hours of the day went to the credit of Kauravas. Kauravas were worried on account of Ghatotkacha and were planning on how to stop him. Pandavas, on the other hand, had realized that Bhishma was causing havoc and had to be silenced if the war to be won. Clearly, they were maturing and had started taking war seriously, certainly placing the head over the heart.

Chapter-XL-III

THE FOURTH DAY

Bhishma Pitamaha, the commander-in-chief of Kaurava army wanted to seize the initiative right from the very ouset of the battle on the fourth day. He had planned the regrouping of the forces with this aim in view. The Kauravas, accordingly, attacked on all the fronts.

Pandavas had anticipated such a move and were ready. They counter-attacked ferociously at the different fronts and heavy fighting ensued.

It was also clear that the Kauravas had identified Yudhishthira their key target as he was the head of Pandavas, Dhrishtadyumana, their Commander-in-chief, Bhima, because he was the most powerful amongst the brothers and the prime threat to Duryodhana, Arjuna, as he was the most skilful and feared on account of that and Abhimanyu on account of his youth, bundles of energy and fighting prowess worthy of a super-class fighter. These names were already become synonymous with fear as well as envy and respect.

Kauravas, in a planned move, tried to isolate and corner Abhimanyu. Surrounded by Kaurava chieftains from all sides, Abhimanyu fought magnificiently to counter this attack and made the Kauravas fall back and, in some cases, run away from the scene of the battle. Noticing that Abhimanyu was fighting many single-handedly, Bhima and some others also joined him to attack Kauravas, who had already started withdrawing.

Duryodhana, harbouring a notion momentarily that that day would be the last day of Abhimanyu's life, was disappointed to see him fighting back superbly and being helped by Bhima and others. He asked a herd of rogue elephants to be brought there and to be launched against Bhima. The latter, himself was reputed to be having the power and strength of one thousand elephants jumped down from his chariot with his mace in his hands and attacked the elephants in the front. Eight elephants were badly injured. The others turned back and ran halter-skelter through Kaurava ranks and file causing huge devastations.

Bhima noticed a concentration of brothers of Duryodhana engaging the Pandavas. He ran towards them and killed eight of them.

Duryodhana was mad on seeing all the above mentioned reverses, particularly the killing of his eight brothers. He took out a secret weapon, read the appropriate mantras and launched the same at Bhima, who, on being hit, fell down unconscious. Pandava warriors surrounded to protect him till he regained senses, of which he was already showing signs.

Ghatotkacha, finding that Bhima, his father, was injured, gave a loud roar and attacked Kauravas with the strength of a demon. He created a havoc wherever he had turned to. Bhishma and Dronacharya tried to put him out of action, but were not successful. Bhishma told Drona that, "Being the son of a demoness, his strength and maya powers increase with the setting sun. Let us not engage him today but plan a strategy to finish him tomorrow as soon as possible. Just then the trumpets and conches sounded to announce the cease-fire".

The Kaurava camp was sad and gloomy mainly on account of the killing of eight Kaurava princes. Duryodhana, in particular, was very sad and disappointed. Although he was a valiant fighter himself, he, by nature could not stomach even a minor defeat. He was in a foul mood. When they sat to discuss the days fighting, performances, gains and losses he bemoaned and berated Bhishma for being soft on Pandava brothers, Abhimanyu and Dhrishtidyumna. The Pitamaha listened to the moans of his Yuvaraja and the virtual king patiently till the end. He then replied, "Duryodhana, it is not correct for you to blame me and Drona for being soft on Pandavas. We are true professionals and have vowed to fight to attain the victory for the kingdom of Hastinapura. However, you have to expect reverses. Remember what I had warned you at the very beginning. The Pandavas are not only stronger lot, but their cause is just. This, therefore will be an extremely difficult war to win". Duryodhana sat speechless for some time and then walked away.

Chapter-XL-V

THE FIFTH DAY

Sanjaya, Dhritarashtra's secretary was a student of Vedavyasa. The latter had granted Sanjaya the powers to envision the battle at Kurukshetra where Mahabharata was being fought. Whenever queried by Dhritarashtra, Sanjaya would tell him the exact happenings at the battles. The killings of eight sons of Dhritarashtra was reported to Dhritarashtra by Sanjaya which made the old and blind king very despondent.

"Why do you keep telling me all sad news? I am sure there would be some good news of significant victories by Kuru," asked Dhritarashtra.

"Oh king, I cannot report incorrect things to you," said Sanjaya and continued, "I, as well as Vidura, Bhishma, Krishna, Drona had advised you strongly against the war but you gave in to Duryodhana's stubborn refusal. We had said that Pandavas are invincible and would become more formidable due to their cause being just. Kurukshetra, the site for Mahabharata, is also known as 'Dharmakshetra', a place known as the holiest of holies from time immemorial. It is not surprising that the Pandavas with Krishna on their side, are emerging as victorious. I am sorry but I cannot manufacture wrong news and report to you".

Disappointed and the despair writ all over his face, Dhritarashtra lamented, "Vidura was right. I could and should have stopped this war. However, I still believe in the fate. Who knows, Duryodhana might succeed in turning the tide and claim eventual victory". His bias for his famous son was quite evident.

On the battle front, Kauravas appeared to have organized themselves much better, having benefited from the experiences of reverses of the last four days, they had thought that their defences were foolproof till they found the highly motivated Pandava forces, on the heels of the successes on the fourth day, piercing the ranks and breaking down defences at many points.

Bhishma tried to check the advance by showering thousands of arrows on Pandavas but Arjuna was following him like a shadow nullifying most of Pitamaha's attack. The added advantage was that Shikhandi too was in the forefront and whenever Bhishma faced him, he stopped fighting as he had declared that he would not fight a eunach. Kauravas, in such instances had to institute emergency makeshift measures.

Bhima and Shikhandi had led the forces in the morning closely followed by Satyaki and Dhrishtidyumna. Arjuna was supporting them from different positions as well as taking on Bhishma, whenever the latter went on offensive.

Duryodhana decided to check the Pandava onslaught by sendng Bhurishrava to neutralize Satyaki. Bhurisharava was a famous warrior and known as a swordsman of repute. He attacked Satyaki with fury. He got the better of Satyaki and was pressing his advantage when the ten sons of Satyaki attacked Bhurishrava to defend their father. Bhurishrava turned his attention on the ten siblings and eventually slaughtered all of them. In the meantime, Bhima, had rescued Satyaki who was unconscions, and took him safely to their ranks.

Very heavy fighting was going on all the fronts with both sides suffering heavy losses. Only one thing was noticeable and was talked about by everyone. This was the mighty Arjuna's skill as a great warrior.

Suddenly, without any notice, the sunset crept in, heralded by the conch-shell blowers. The leadership from both the sides met in their respective groups to assess the situation. While Kauravas were disappointed that barring the first day of the war, they did not have any significant successes. Pandavas, on the other hand, were happy that the momentum was very slowly shifting towards them. They knew that the fighting in coming days was going to be crucial and very bitter.

Chapter-XL-V

THE SIXTH DAY

Following the losses on previous days, Kauravas organized a regrouping but Pandavas were not complacent either. The fighting was getting intense and it was important to win local battles. Equally important, there was an overall need to minimize the losses. Kauravas organized their forces in a Kraunch (A heron) formation while Pandavas did so in a Makra (crab) one. These formations were well known tactical manoeuvers in the military doctrine accepted those days. What is worth noting however is that all important leaders were expected to be well-versed in them. Those manoeuvres were taught to all princes, kings and kshatriyas by the Gurus, most competent amongst whom were Dronacharya and Kripacharya. Even today, there are accepted types of formations and manoeuvres, not only in the land army, but also in the airforce and navy.

Surprising everyone, the battles were bitter and intense from the first wave of fighting in the morning and throughout the day, a virtual slaughter was inflicted on both the sides.

Yet, on this sixth day, one man who was at his martial best was Dronacharya. He was brilliant, attacking enemy warriors and switching from front to front. There was no term in vogue in those days to describe such a person, but one could say that on the sixth day Dronacharya was the most outstanding fighter.

Drona launched his own assaults. He neutralized Bhima who was bent upon inflicting damages to the Kaurava princes. Even Dhrishtidyumna was checked when he came to assist and reinforce Bhima. The former unleashed a secret weapon (Taught to him by Drona when he was his disciple) putting the Kaurava forces in a stupor. Duryodhana countered its effects by launching another one capable of undoing it.

As the evening approached, the Pandavas under Bhima and Dhrishtadyumna were reeling. Fortunately, a contingent sent by Yudhishthira arrived and checked the Kaurava advance. The momentum of fighting was so strong that it continued till nearly an hour after the sunset.

Only once, Duryodhana and Bhima, the traditional arch rivals came face to face. After an exchange of words, there was a fight, not with the maces, but with bows and arrows. Duryodhana was losing ground slowly and also getting badly injured. To his good fortune, Kripacharya arrived at the scene and extricated the Kaurava chieftain with serious wounds.

There were smaller heroes all through the day, but clearly the 'Man of the day' was Dronacharya. However, there were huge losses on both the sides and almost all the leading warriors had more than one wound to attend to.

Chapter-XL-VI

THE SEVENTH DAY

Duryodhana had been medically attended to in the previous night. He was an extremely fit and robust person, hence the recovery was quick and complete. In the morning, he was already on the side of Bhishma, Donacharya and Kirpacharya chalking out the operations of the day and the various strategies.

The war was gathering momentum. Signs of that were visible from the fact that intense fighting, which used to start around mid-day, had started commencing from the mornings itself. The ferociousness of single combats and fights between groups of soldiers was visible from the beginning of the day itself.

The battles were being fought on various fronts. Both the sides had organized their troops and formations as per the plans. Ghatotkacha ran headlong into king Bhagmal and a bitter battle ensued. Ashwaththama had engaged Shikhandi. It was clear that unlike Bhishma, he had no qualms about taking on Shikhandi. Old and traditional friends turned foes, Drupada and Drona were fighting it out between themselves. Satyaki was trying his best to defeat the Kaurava's demon ally, Alambash. Cries, screeches, blood, sounds of maces hitting each other were all there. The vultures knew that those were the days of abundant food and were constantly hovering in the sky.

Yudhishthira engaged Shatayu and killed his charioteer. Shikhandi was defeated by Ashwaththama. Bhagmal proved to be better than Ghatotkacha who had to be protected. Satyaki beat back Alambash Drona killed Drupada's son Shaukha and drove Drupada away.

Elsewhere, Bhurishrava fought Dhrishtaketu and wounded him badly. He was however, a made of different metal. He fought on and made Bhurishrava flee. Kripacharya had fought on with Chekitan inconclusively. Abhimanyu showed a different class putting Kaurava princes to sword. He could have killed some of them specially Dushasana, but spared their lives leaving them for Bhima who had vowed to kill latter and get his blood to wash the hair of Draupadi. Abhimanyu swiftly turned to attack Bhishma. As Bhishma prepared to fight back, other Pandavas rushed in to support the youngster. Just then, the sun set in and the cessation of fighting was announced.

Chapter-XL-VII

THE EIGHTH DAY

In the review of the seventh day, Duryodhana looked dejected and resorted to the baiting of Bhishma.

"Our soldiers are dying all over and our losses are mounting, yet you are not doing anything. At this rate our armies will diappear in a matter of days. This is not the war, I had contemplated. With our overwhelming superiority, I had thought that we will advance like lightning and defeat the Pandavas in a matter of days," he said.

The grandsire knew Duryodhana much too much to get ruffled. He tried to comfort Durodhana. He said, "In a war of this magnitude, losses are bound to happen on both the sides. Pandavas and their allies may be numerically less than us but they also have strong warriors who can give a real fight".

The Pitamaha added, "But, look at our side. We have leaders, warriors and soldiers, mounted as well as foot fighters, chariots, horses, elephants weapons and skills to use them. Any one who has these people should be proud of his position and certain of a victory. We have declared a war and should fight it out till the bitter end. If in the efforts to achieve the objective, we even lose our life it should not matter because this is what every kshatriya aspires for".

Bhishma carried on, "The war has gone on for more than a week and all our top leaders are all there giving a good account of themselves in the battle field. Drona, Kripacharya, Ashwatthama, Vikarna, Salya, Kritavarman, Bhagdutta, Shakuni, the two brothers of Avanti, the

Trigarta chief, and the king of Magadha are all there ready to give their life to you and fight to the finish. There is no reason for you to feel despondent. Let us have faith in ourselves and in our ultimate victory. Cheer up and get ready for the day's battle. Believe me, with these leaders and soldiers, even the Gods will hesitate to take you on". He then gave the orders for the deployment and the objectives for the day .

Kauravas had organized their armies in kurma vyuha (Turtle fortress). Noticing this, Dhrishtidyumana organized the Pandava forces in three arrow-like formations with arrows intended to pierce the enemy fronts. Each arrow formation was headed by Bhima, Yudhishthira and Satyaki respectively. On the Kaurava front, Duryodhana, in his glittering armour, was seen moving around making a magnificient sight.

Although quite different from the modern warfare strategies, our ancestors had a very well developed military doctrine with strategies and tactics suited to the then available resources. These sciences of war had not been reduced in writing but were preserved and passed on from Gurus who taught extensively the successive kshatriya generations of shishyas since the military affairs were considered as exclusive preserve of the military order, kshtariyas.

Bhima charged like a bull with his forces and made deep inroads in the every ranks. Within the first hour, he killed another eight of the brothers of Duryodhana who was a witness to that battle. Bhimasena that day was like a fighter possessed and it appeared that he would take his revenge that very day – the revenge which he swore in the hall of games on Draupadi's humiliation.

Elsewhere, Iravan, the son of Arjuna from his Naga wife Uloopi, was in full flow when he was challenged by rakshasa Alambasa, deputed by Duryodhana to stop Iravan. A fierce fight ensued resulting in Iravan's death. The news made Arjuna very sad. On the other hand, Ghatotkacha made such a loud cry on hearing about Iravan's death that the entire body of soldiers trembled. Ghatokacha, along with his division caused huge destruction of Kauravas. Duryodhana personally came to stop Ghatotkacha and caused a considerable damage to his soldiers. This was a great day for Duryodhana as he fought magnificiently, perhaps at his best till then. Fortunately for him, he also escaped from getting killed by a javelin thrown by Ghatotkacha at an amazing force. At the very last minute the Vanga chief intervened and came with his elephant to block the blow. The javelin pierced through the elephant's body which was instantaneously killed. Duryodhana, however, was saved.

Bhishma sent additional reinforcements to assist Duryodhana while Yudhishthira deputed Bhima to assist Ghatotkacha. It was near mayhem at many fronts with unbelievable slaughter of the forces of both the sides. Even though the cessation of fighting was announced at the sun set by blowing of cronches, some battles carried on for some more time due to sheer momentum.

When the fighting finally halted, both sides were sad for their losses. On that one day, Duryodhana lost a total of sixteen of his brothers. Arjuna lost Iravan, his dear son, a young lad who had come to join Pandavas and fought brilliantly till the bitter end. He confessed to Krishna that how right was Vidura when he had forecasted huge losses and destruction on both the sides. Although he had opposed Yudhishtira's scaling down of demands to only five villages, he confessed that, from hindsight he and his three brothers were wrong while Yudhishtira was to be commended for his courageous decision to avoid the war as far as he could.

Chapter-XL-VIII

THE NINTH DAY

When Sanjaya, who had been granted the divine sight by Vedavyasa so that he could report the war situation to his king Dhritarashtra, informed the latter of the losses, specially sixteen of his sons, to the king. Dhritarashtra was very perturbed and sad. He turned around to Sanjaya and said, "What is the use of hearing your reports. Every day there are more and more losses on our sides. Now you tell me that sixteen of Duryodhana's brothers have lost their lives. Can't you give me some news which can cheer me up? Where will it all finish?

Sanjaya replied to his king, "Your honour, I cannot manufacture good news to cheer you up. I can only report the actual happenings of the war as seen by me. What is happening is as a direct consequence of your inability to stop Duryodhana in his unjust deeds. Unless the latter changes his minds and does what is right, the Kauravas will suffer tremendous losses. Have you forgotten the curse of sage Maitraya when he had warned Duryodhana that his thighs will be smashed by Bhimasena and he shall die on the battle field. Truly someone has said that one's right thinking and wisdom deserts when he approaches his destruction".

The king had had enough of it. He stopped Sanjaya from lecturing to him further. He did, however, tell himself, "Vidura's warnings are coming true. I am like a ship wrecked man desperate to save himself in a storm ravaged ocean."

On the battle front, Duryodhana walked inside the Pitamaha's tent before the commencement of the battle and pleaded with him for some positive results.

Bhishma smiled and tried to comfort Duryadhana. "I am doing my best in fulfilling my vow to protect and bring glory to the crown of Hastinapur. Except for not killing Pandavas and not raising arms against women, which includes Shikhandi, I have not given quarter or concessions to any of the enemy. Once again, I am advising you not to feel dejected, desperate or impatient. Let us all fight the enemy in the true sprit of kshatriyas. If we waiver or have doubts in our objectives, we shall not achieve the victory. Cheer up and do your bit".

Duryodhana, reassured, went back to his own tent to get ready for the day's battles. He, however, summoned Dushasana and asked him to pass the word to be extra vigilant to protect Bhishma, particularly when he is engaged by Shikhandi.

Alambasa's prowess was put to test by Abhimanyu, proving quite equal to his illustrious father and uncles. Alambasa had to run away on foot to save himself. Drona fought against Arjuna, Satyaki against Ashwatthama and all the Pandavas against Bhishma. The latter, however, retaliated with such alacricity and force that Pandavas suffered huge losses.

Krishna halted the chariot on the way and told Arjuna that the time had come when he had to go for a kill against the Pitamaha, notwithstanding his affection and regards for Bhishma. "You are not fighting as you should and you can", said Krishna. He even jumped down again from the chariot, taking up his discus, and advanced towards Bhishma to attack the latter, himself seeing this, Arjuna too jumped down from the chariot and held Krishna. He told Krishna, 'Very frankly, I do not mind continuing in the exile rather than killing my teachers and the grandsire, whose favourite son I myself was.

However, I shall do now what you advise, that is perform my duty as a soldier. I shall kill the grandsire myself.

The battle had been resumed. In all Pandava had suffered substantial losses when fighting ended for the day with the sun setting in the west.

Chapter-XL-IX

THE TENTH DAY: FALL OF A TITAN

It was a momentous day. Arjuna had decided to go after Bhishma at the very outset. Keeping Shikhandi in his front, he planned his attack. Duryodhana had asked Dushasana to protect the grandsire from Shikhandi, since Bhishma had declared that he would not fight a woman, nor even an eunach.

"Even a hound can take on a lion, when the latter is not willing to fight", Duryodhana had said to Dushasana asking him once again to be extra careful in defending Bhishma. Dushasana had made adequate preparations but was not prepared to face Shikhandi and Arjuna together. Shikhandi started his onslaught of arrows and other missiles on taking position. Every arrow or missile wounding the body of Bhishma made the latter wince in a boiling rage. He, however, also remembered the injustice meted out to Amba, Shikhandi's previous incarnation and continued in his resolve not to fight back at him.

(Readers will remember that Bhishma had forcibly abducted her along with her two sisters during their swayamvar ceremony at their father, King of Kashi's, palace. He had brought them forcibly to be the wives of Vichitra Vira. However when she (Amba) pleaded with the queen Satyavati stating that she had already pledged herself to king Salva, she was allowed to go to the latter. Salva refused to accept her stating that she had been defiled at Hastinapur. When she returned to Bhishma and asked him to marry her, Bhishma refused. Eventually, totally disappointed she committed suicide vowing that in her next birth she would be the cause of Bhishma's death).

Arjuna too was attacking Bhishma, standing behind Shikhandi. He also simultaneously attacked others who were trying to protect Bhishma by attacking Shikhandi, Bhishma also recognized the arrows hurled by Arjuna as they were much more powerful and lethal. "These arrows are not from Shikhandi as they burn my body like a crab's young ones tear their mother's body. He then smiled knowing that his end was near.

Yet, as a true kshatriya, he resolved to fight till the bitter end. He threw a javelin powerfully at the person dearest to him in the world and one, who sitting as a child in his lap, had given him maximum satisfaction. Arjuna, however, sent three arrows which cut the javelin in the mid air and destroyed it totally. Bhishma then took his sword and shield and jumped down the chariot to advance towards Arjuna with his body riddled with arrows. Arjuna destroyed the shield first and then the sword while showering more arrows on the grandsire. It was a gory sight with not an inch of Bhishma's body without the arrows, Bhishma staggered and fell on the ground.

The gods above who had witnessed this battle paid obeisance to the greatest warrior of the world as well the greatest human being. Thus fell Bhishma, the spotless hero who renounced his rights to make his father happy and thereafter maintained his pledge to defend the kingdom and crown of Hastinapur. The son of Ganga lay grieviously on the ground under the scorching sun.

A hush fell on the entire battle field and all fighting ceased with the chieftains moving in to surround Bhishma and to pay obeisance to him. They knew they would never witness another man of principles as well as fighting prowess of highest caliber.

Bhishma's body was straightened resting on the arrows. However, his head hung precauously since it did not have any arrows to support. As Bhishma said feebly, "My head needs a support", Duryodhana and other warriors shouted for the cushions to be brought quickly. As they were brought, Bhishma smiled and rejected them all. He turned towards Arjuna and said, "Dearest Partha, give me a cushion a warrior deserves".

Arjuna, with tears streaming down his face took out three arrows out of his quiver and placed them appropriately to support Bhishma's head. The latter then addressed people around him, "Princes, I shall lie comfortably resting my head on Arjuna's arrows which would give me the greatest of comfort. I had been granted the power to choose the time of my death by my father and I shall do so when the sun reverses its course and proceeds northwards. When I pass away, those who are still alive may come and see me. Again, with his head turning towards Arjuna, he said, "I am very thirsty. Get me some drinking water".

Arjuna raised his bow and drawing it to the ear, fired an arrow near the right side of the grandsire. At once, through the gaping hole, a stream of pure sweet water rushed out and fell on the perched lips of the dying man. Vyasa, the poet says, it was Ganga who came up to quench her son's burning thrust. Bhishma drank and was happy.

Karna came rushing in. After paying respects to Bhishma he told him, "Pitamaha, do not leave us at this juncture. I know you do not like me because I am from a lower caste and we have had differences on other matters too. But, in the heart of hearts; I always had the highest regard for you".

Bhishma gestured to Karna to come closer to him. He then said, "Karna my son, you are Kunti devi's eldest son and Pandavas are your brothers. By allying with Duryodhana you are supporting unethical causes. In fact, your support has made him more arrogant. Go back in the service of Dharma. There is still time".

Karna shook his head and said, "I am glad that you are aware of my true identity. However there are still many who are not aware of it. Duryodhana gave me a tremendous support believing me to be a weaver's son. I am under too many obligations from him and cannot turn back on him, even when I know that I shall have to fight my own brothers".Bhishma then turned towards Duryodhana. "Duryodhana, "he said "Even now there is time to end this war and make peace with Pandavas. This war will bring disaster for us. You have just seen Partha's prowess with archery. Only he in this world could shoot an arrow in the ground to have sweet water falling in my mouth. Make Pandavas your allies, not enemies. Hastinapur will be stronger than ever before. Even now it is not too late".

Duryodhana's demeanour clearly indicated that he did not intend to follow grandman's advice. He did not however, reply back as he used to do earlier, in deference to the state of Pitamaha. He, however, did ask Bhishma as to who should take over the mantle from him. Bhishma suggested Karna's name adding that he was best leader amongst those who could be considered for this responsibility.

One by one, the kings and princes retired to their places of stay. As the sun was setting, Bhishma was left lying alone surrounded by a few attendants.

On his return, Karna, however went straightaway to Duryodhana and told him that it was not prudent to appoint him the Commander-in-chief when many others too senior and equally experienced leaders were available. He expressed the fear that this would cause heartburns and bickernings. Duryodhana agreed with Karna and decided to give the mantle to Dronacharya. They all went to Drona to inform him of this decision.

Chapter-L

THE NEW COMMANDER-IN-CHIEF OF KAURAVA ARMY

Drona was happy to learn of the decision of Duryodhana. Next day, early in the morning, he was duly appointed in the presence of the Princes and Kings. They were all happy to see Dronacharya as their new chief. After all, he was the Guru of most of them and an expert on the military strategy and tactics.

Dronacharya was even more happy when Duryodhana, Dushasana and Karna formally requested him to treat the capture of Yudhishthira alive as his highest priority task. The venerable guru also did not favour the killing of Pandavas who were his favourite pupils.

Duryodhana, however, had a special reason too, which, much to the annoyance of Dronacharya, was disclosed to him much later. Duryodhana knew that his side was doomed for a certain defeat. If somehow they could somehow capture Yudhishthira alive, there was a chance that, with him as a king, they could trick them again in a game of dice and deprive the Pandavas of the throne. If it was not the game of dice, then in some other way, the Pandavas could be tricked. This was a long-shot objective of the wily person bent upon improving his bargaining position.

The presence of Karna on the battle front was yet another morale-boosting factor with Kauravas and their allies. As long as Bhishma was in command, Karna did not take part in any battle. With Bhishma not in the field now and put out of action, there was no reason for Karna to stay away. In fact, he was over eager to make up for the lost time. The troops and their chieftains were extremely elated at seeing the illustrious and a great young fighter in their midst. If there was anyone who could match Arjuna, weapon for weapon, it was Karna, they knew. All of them looked forward to taking part in great battles in the coming days.

Chapter-L-I

THE ELEVENTH AND TWELTH DAY OF WAR

Drona organized the fighting units in a circular formation. He led the Kauravas by personal example. Notwithstanding his advanced age, he was omnipresent in the battle area and showed agility and energy of a young warrior. During his tenure he took on the famous and powerful warriors and gave them a challenging fight and some time even defeated tham and made them flee. These included Drupada, Dhrishtadyumna, Arjuna, Bhima, Kashiraja, Abhimanyu and other Pandavas.

Both sides had an elaborate spy system. Pandavas had already come to know of Dronacharaya's mission to capture Yudhishthira alive and they had organized adequate counter- measures for protection of Yudhishthira at all cost.

At the start of the day, Drona tore through Pandava lines seeking Dhrishtadyumna. Nakula was engaged in a duel with his uncle Shalya while Sahadeva and Shakuni were having a mace combat. Bhima was wreaking havoc, wherever he turned to, scaring the Kaurava soldiers.

Abhimanyu was in a most belligerent mood. He was showing that he was not inferior to any of his uncles. Satyaki and Virata too were in a great spree of destruction of Kauravas. Abhimanyu was taken on by four warriors, Shalya, Kritvarma, Jaidratha and Paurava. Even then, most of the time the latter were on the receiving end fighting with the young dynamite. Situation took a definite turn for the worse for the four allies when Bhima joined his nephew. Eventually Shalya was felled by Bhima through a very powerful blow by the mace. The Kaurava soldiers fled to all the directions.

Suddenly Drona got a window of opportunity to get Yudhishthira. He raced his chariot towards the Pandava chieftain. Yudhishthira too was alert and tried his best raining arrows on Drona. The Guru, however, got better of shishya and almost managed to reach him. However a counter-attack of great ferocity from Arjuna made Drona to retreat post-haste. They realized that unless Arjuna was taken away from helping Yudhishthira, their objective of capturing Yudhishtira will remain just a pipe-dream.

The task of diversion of Arjuna away from Yudhishthira was accepted by Susharma, the king of Trigarta. Next day, he regrouped a task force of suicide warriors who took a vow that they would not leave the battlefide till Arjuna was killed. He then attacked Arjuna and personally challenged him. Entrusting the responsibility of defending Yudhishthira to Dhrishtidyumana, Arjuna concentrated on fighting Susharma.

Drona again raced towards Yudhishthira with a formidable force but was again stopped by the Drupad prince. The battle for 'Yudhishthira' raged throughout the day. Dhrishtidymna lost his two brothers and a son of Virata. The conflict was raging high. Bhima, realized the need to help his commander- inchief as well as Arjuna's forces. He rounded up Satyaki, Drupada, Virata, Nakula and Shikhandi. When Duryodhana and Karna came with trained elephants, Bhima beat them back. Bhugdutta chipped in to help Duryodhana's forces and pressed in his famous elephant 'Supratika' to counterattack. Bhima lunged forward, caught hold Supratika's trunk and banged him down on the ground. Being an expert on anatomy of elephants, Bhima got under the elephant and speared soft and critical parts of its underbelly to cause him maximum agony. Supratika, shrieking with pain ran away from the scene with Bhugdutta on its back.

Susharma was losing his troops by dozens, Desperate, he launched two divine weapons at Krishna and Arjuna. The latter launched four arrows, three to counter missiles and one to attack the Trigarta king. He then attacked Bhugdutta and Supratika. The former lost his life while Supratika's armour was shattered allowing Arjuna's arrow to sneak in and pierce his body killing him. Seeing his blazing form, Vrishaka and Achala, Shakuni's sons attacked Arjuna but were no match for the great warrior. They died there. Maddened by this loss, Shakuni counter-attacked Arjuna, only to be beaten back making him flee from the battleground.

The battle for 'Yudhishthira' was won by Pandavas but was clearly inconclusive. There were huge losses, more suffered by Kauravas than Pandavas.

Chapter-L-II

THE THIRTEENTH DAY

Dronacharya was unhappy. Neither he could capture Yudhishthira on the previous day nor prevent major losses to the Kaurava army. He was already sulking when Duryodhana added fuel to the fire by remonstrating him for the failures.

The learned Guru gave a wry smile and replied, "Duryodhana, you have still not assessed Arjuna's prowess so far. Even when fighting elsewhere, he is still carefully planning all the moves to protect Yudhishthira. Today, however, is another day and we will again try to achieve our objective, capture Yudhishthira alive, turn the scales on Pandavas. They are all strong. Above all, Bhima and Arjuna are great fighters. Then again, amongst the younger generation, their two off-springs, Abhimanyu and Ghatotkacha are also wrecking havoc. We are also fighting with all our might. Let us hope that we succeed today.

The strategy of engaging Arjuna away from Yudhishtira was again implemented and Susharma continued to fight with Arjuna with fresh vigour drawing him farther away from the focus on that day – Yudhishthira.

Drona had organized his forces in the 'Chakra Vyuha' or 'A circle within the circle' formation.

With Arjuna away, Drona sensed the opportunity and launched a very strong attack to break the Pandava lines and reach Yudhishthira. The attack was so swift and formidable that despite the defence provided by none others than Bhima, Kantibhoja, Satyaki and Virata, there were visible signs of Yudhishthira being in the imminent danger. The Kaurava chakra-vyuha was closing in like a juggernaut. The only person who could breach in and get out was Arjuna, who was fighting his battle miles away with Susharma and his crack troops. It was not possible for him to leave that place and switch to the breach-point of the chakravyuha.

It was then that Abhimanyu decided to counter-attack the Chakravyuha formation. He had learnt how to pierce it, but did not know how to come out of it. In fact, he was in Subhadra's womb when once Arjuna was describing to her as to how to pierce a Chakravyuha formation. However, when Arjuna took on the strategy of getting out of the vyuha, Subhadra had dozed off and was fast asleep depriving

Abhimanyu of this vital information. Abhimanyu asked Bhima to follow him when piercing the chakra-vyuha and assist him in exiting from the Vyuha. Sumittra, his charioteer, however described the planned operation as too dangerous and was reluctant to take him in. Abhimanyu, would have none of it, with Yudhishthira being in danger, he was determined to go in and asked Sumittra to do as he was ordered.

Arranging with Bhima to assist him in the exit operations, Abhimanyu asked Sumittra to race on inside. In no time, he created mayhem in Kaurava lines. The outer ring of the vyuha started getting breached in face of the relentless attack of Abhimanyu. Duryodhana realized that Abhimanyu must be checked. He himself attacked the latter. What he had not anticipated was a personal counter-attack by the young hero on him. In his dare-devil attack, Abhimanyu's intentions were clearly to take Duryodhana as the prisoner. Fortunately for the latter, Drona noticed

Duryodhana's predicament. A fresh contingent was sent which saved Duryodhana who, otherwise, would have surely been captured. Duryodhana's luckly escape in front of his own forces was a matter of deep humiliation. At that instant, he took the decision to get Abhimanyu by fair means or foul. Even Dronacharya, a protagonist of ethical fighting looked the other way. Duryodhana's evil plan of having seven top warriors to capture or kill Abhimanyu got underway. Kripacharya, Shalya, Karna, Jaidratha, Ashwatthama,Shakuni and Drona were to destroy this daredevil son of Arjuna.

In the meantime Abhimanyu kept on his rampage. He killed a king called Ashmakh, sent Shalya to sleep with a sharp arrow, killed his brother with just one arrow and gave such a mighty blow to Karna that his armour got smashed. Before Karna could string his bow, Abhimanyu cut the same down. Someone who ran in to help Karna got felled. Duryodhana's son, Laxmana, seeing his father's predicament, chipped in to try and stop the onslaught. His effort was short-lived as a single arrow from Abhimanyu went straight into his heart.

Laxmana's death was the last straw. In utter violation of the agreed codes where only one-to-one combats were permitted, the dirty sevens attacked Abhimanyu from all sides, even from behind.

Jaidratha successfully blocked the advance of Bhima and other Pandavas to help Abhimanyu. He invoked Shiva's boon to block the four Pandava brothers while Arjuna was far away. Closing in, Karna attacked Abhimanyu from behind and smashed his armour. The youngster fought and went on his rampage.

This was indeed the lowest point of Mahabharata. Abhimanyu's chariot was smashed by the multi-sided attack by many. He picked up a wheel and killed many Kauravas with it alone. Dushasana's son dealt a mace blow on Abhimanyu who in turn snatched the same from him. Abhimanyu, however, checked himself because his adversary was unarmed. But, someone from Kaurava side dealt a mace blow to Abhimanyu from behind. He fell with a thud and died. While Kauravas rejoiced, the Pandava camp was filled with gloom.

Yudhishthira cried in his tent. He was comforted by sage Vyasa who had just arrived. He comforted them by saying that in the war they should not grieve over an honourable death of a brave warrior. As more information trickled in, it was clear that Kauravas had broken all agreed codes of conduct and Jaidratha was the master-mind. When Arjuna arrived, the sad news was given to him and Yudhishtira gave a full account of the Kaurava treachery to trap the young warrior. Although all the seven warriors, lead by senior people like Drona, Kripa and Duryodhana were guilty, the main perpetrator was Jaidratha who master-minded attacks on Abhimanyu first along with others and then went to outer ring to stop Bhima and others of breaching it and help Abhimanyu.

Arjuna got up after listening the reports. He took a vow that he would slay Jaidratha before the sunset on the next day.

The end of the thirteenth day marked the end of one phase of observing honour codes and decent fighting. Kauravas broke the rules blatantly with the approval of no less a person than Dronacharya, their commander-in-chief and the most revered guru of the Kaurava and Pandava royalty alike. Drona had agreed to the vile plans of killing Abhimanyu because he himself was under tremendous pressure to show some results in the war which was slowly turning against them. What Drona and his other warriors did not realize that the incident gave a kind of moral sanction to the other party to bend the rules, or even break them in a crunch situation.

Chapter-L-III

THE FOURTEENTH DAY

The Pandava camp was baying for revenge of Abhimanyu's death through foul means. The news regarding Arjuna's vow to kill Jaidrath before sunset had a deep unnerving effect on Jaidrath. He pleaded with Duryodhana and Drona to let him return to his capital for a day but the request was turned down. The two top guns assured Jaidrath that he would be given full protection.

The fourteenth day actually became the 'Defence of Jaidrath' day for Kauravas. Their entire strategy revolved around defending Jaidrath on that day till the sunset. Duryodhana knew that if they could defend Jaidrath on that day there would be added reward of Arjuna laying down his life out of shame of not fulfilling his vow. With Arjuna out of picture half of the battle of Mahabharata could be safely considered as won.

The day began with Jaidrath and his personal army at the centre. The other armies were positioned around them in concentric circles. Dushasana's army was positioned right in the front as the first line of defence. As soon as he spotted Arjuna, Dushasana challenged him. Arjuna accepted the challenge and the fight began. In no time, Dushasana and his army was driven away. Arjuna was looking for Jaidratha. When he couldn't find him he went to Drona to enquire about his whereabouts. Drona decline to reveal Jaidratha's position saying that the latters protection was his mission and he could not divulge his location. Arjuna prepared to take on the Guru when Krishna advised him not to waste his time but took him instead to the left flank for breaching the Kaurava defence and moving towards the centre where they were certain to find Jaidratha.

Kaurava's outer defence was breached quickly. Drona gave a divine chest shield to Duryodhana and asked him to go and fight Arjuna to stop him. Arjuna attacked Duryodhana ferociously but soon realized that the latter was wearing a divine shield or armour. He then invoked his own divine weapons and attacked Duryodhana. Duryodhana's horses of the chariot got killed and wheels got smashed. Sensing danger to himself Duryodhana fled from the battle.

Bhima too was in a murderous spree. Vikarna challenged him but was killed by Bhima in no time. Bhima felt sorry because Vikarna was the only one who was ethical and an ardent follower of dharma amongst the Kaurava brothers. Bhima, however continued his ouslaught killing several other Kaurava princes.

Karna tried his best to get even with Bhima and was driven away every time. That day eighteen of his bows were smashed. When he came back again Bhima attacked with his bow and arrow. Karna smashed them and continued to attack Bhima, even though he was unarmed. Krishna pointed out to Arjuna of Karna's misdemeanour. Karna, however, was in a bind. He knew that if he stopped, Bhima would kill him with his bare hands. On the other hand, if he killed Bhima, he would not be able to kill Arjuna in accordance to his pledge to Kunti.

Fortunately for him, Arjuna's attack on him came as a blessing. Incensed by the cowardly attack of Karna on unarmed Bhima, Arjuna fired such a barrage of arrows at Karna that the latter had to flee from the fight.Worried about Yudhishthira's safety, Arjuna found that Bhurishrava, a formidable foe, had been fighting Satyaki and had taken him away from his chosen position near Yudhishthira. Krishna also noticed that Satyaki was looking weak and tired and Bhurishvara was gaining an upper hand. He pointed the same to Arjuna. As Arjuna was closing in on Bhurishvara, he found that Bhurishrava was raising his hand with dagger to slaughter Satyaki who was unarmed and looked extremely exhausted. An attack on such an enemy who was unarmed, down and out, was against the code of conduct of war. Arjuna saw this and sent an arrow cutting off Bhurishvara's dagger wielding hand. When the latter protested, Arjuna explained that the reason for this was his violation of code of conduct. However, immediately thereafter Satyaki got up and taking the dagger of Bhurishrava from his severed hand, killed the great old warrior. This also was an act of serious misconduct for which Satyaki came in for a considerable condemnation from all the quarters. What, however, was evident that with fighting intensifying, even reputed fighters, known for their fairness, were turning a blind eye to these violations. Abhimanyu's killing was an extreme example.

As the time was running out and sunset time closing in, Arjuna closed in on the defences of Jaidratha. Arjuna was in a dangerous mood.

Smashing all the defences, Arjuna came face to face with Jaidratha. Jaidratha, noticing that the sun was kissing thehorizon and not much time was left for the sunset, used all his guile to defend himself. Arjuna mounted a devastating barrage which Jaidratha could somehow survive. Next moment, it became dark.

A wave of cheer went up amongst the entire Kaurava contingent while, stunned and sad, Arjuna's eyes were downcast. Jaidratha too was celebrating, having survived a sure death.

When shouts and cheers were in full swing, Krishna told Arjuna, "Arjuna, the sun has not set. I have created an illusion. Very soon it will reappear again. This is the time you should cut off Jaidratha's head and make it fall in his father's lap. (Jaidratha's father, Vriddhakshatra, was doing a penance in the far away forest. It had been ordained that if Jaidratha's head fell from some one's lap on the ground, that person's head would burst into hundred segments). The moment sun reappeared, Arjuna raised his bow and shot an arrow at Jaidratha, who was celebrating with his chieftains, cutting off his head. He then shot many arrows which in relays took the head to his father, making it fall in the latter's lap and fall out.

As the Kauravas were surprised and dismayed at the supposed dastardly act of Arjuna, breaking his vow and murmurs of protest started all around, they were flabbergasted at seeing the sun reappearing on the horizon, getting ready to set, but not yet set. For a moment, Duryodhana too was debating whether his decision to opt for Yadava army, and not Krishna, was correct.

Later, even when the sun had really set, the fighting continued. Kauravas were agitated at the unethical killing of Jaidratha while Pandava armies were still agitated and baying for revenge for Abhimanyu's killing.

Two more significant actions were taking place causing considerable worry to the respective enemy camps. Ghatotkcha was in his rampaging mood with his weapons and appeared to be unstoppable. Unable to stand any more, Duryodhana, asked Karna to stop and kill him at whatever cost. With the son of Bhima in such a murderous form, Karna knew that he would have to use the shakti which Indra had given to him, but which had been reserved by Karna for his fight against Arjuna. However, with Duryodhana's exhortation, he had no choice but to use the shakti. He confronted Ghatotkacha initially with other weapons. Finding them ineffective, he used Indra's shakti to kill him. When Ghatotkacha fell, dozens of Kaurava soldiers lost their life by being crushed under the monster-person's body.

The other action was Drona's ouslaught against the Pandava army. Despite repeated attempts of Dhrishtidyumna, Drona was unstoppable that day. It was clear that something special had to be done.

Krishna knew that Drona's weakest point was his near fanatic love for his son Ashwaththama. He made a plan through which Drona would be rendered powerless on hearing that Ashwaththama was dead, though not actually, so.

Accordingly, Bhima killed an elephant named Ashwaththama. Simultaneously a rumour was spread that Ashwaththama, the son of Guru Drona was killed. The rumour spread like a wild fire. When Drona heard it from a number of people, he wanted to confirm it from the most reliable source, his disciple and current adversary the, truthspeaking Yudhishthira.

Drona went to Yudhishthira and asked him if the rumour regarding Ashwaththama was correct. Yudhishthira had been briefed by Krishna. He replied, "Yes reverened Guru, the rumour is correct. Ashwathama has been killed and is dead. However, it is not your son, but the elephant".

It was already planned that the Pandava soldiers around Yudhishthira would celebrate with a deafening sound of cronches and cymbals the moment Yudhishthira finished his first part of the reply, i.e. Ashwaththama was dead. The rest of the reply was inaudible to Dronacharya nor was he, expecting a twist of any sort in Yudhishthira's report.

Totally non-plussed and shocked, the old man literally collapsed on the ground grieving for his son. Dhrishtidyumna, who had been stalking the Guru throughout the day, lost no time and attacked him. Guru Drona had no will to fight left in him. The person who had been retaliating and punishing Dhrishtidyumna throughout the day, accepted the death from his hands, now that his son had been killed (at least he thought it was so). He was beheaded by Dhrishtidyumna.

Loss of their three most formidable warriors, Drona, Bhurishrava and Jaidratha and a large number of Duryodhana's brothers dealt a body blow to Kauravas. Was this the beginning of the end, many wondered. Dhritarashtra, who was getting the first hand account of the battle from Sanjaya, was cursing Duryodhana for his stupid decisions. When Sanjaya retorted that even he, Dhritarashtra, could have prevented all this slaughter, had he not been so indulgent, forgiving and at times encouraging towards Duryodhana, Dhritarashtra was speechless.

As the passions rose to a crescendo on fourteenth day, the codes, rules and restraints were ignored. Even, Yudhishthira committed knowingly the cardinal sin of lying to Dronacharya because that was the only way to stop the murderous guru.

When he uttered the words of untruth, the wheels of his chariot, which always stood and moved four inches above the ground, at once came down and touched the earth and never rose anytime later.

Chapter-L-IV

THE FIFTEENTH DAY

On the fifteenth day, the Kaurava army had a new, the third, commander-in-chief – Karna. Shalya had been asked to be his charioteer. Kauravas felt happy and encouraged because Karna was an icon for younger elements a great warrior and an inspiring leader for all. Everyone knew that his confrontation with Arjuna would also be decisive.

Pandavas had already consulted astrologers for the most appropriate hour for Arjuna's engagement with Karna. Even Dhritarashtra was nervous and excited. He was asking Sanjaya to concentrate on those two. The king knew that even at that late stage, if Arjuna was eliminated, the Kauravas stood more than a fair chance of achieving the ultimate victory.

The two titans entered the battlefield from the opposite sides accompanied by their armies. In the background, the drum beats added to the excitement. Karna was accompanied by Dushasana while Arjuna had Bhima and his expert chosen warriors. Arjuna rained a volley of fierce arrows on Karna and the latter gave a befitting response.

Suddenly, what should have been the side show, occupied the mainstage. The Bhima-Dushasana fight burst upon the scene. Dushasana, taking an offensive and to support Karna, sent a heavy barrage of arrows. Bhima, in a flash, realized that the time for fulfilling his vow on the floor of the palace of games more than thirteen years ago had arrived. Years of hatred had reached a crescendo and he knew that the time had come to redeem his pledge to Draupadi who was disgraced in front of the entire royalty after the gambling match.While Dushasana was preparing for his next volley of arrows at Bhima, the latter jumped down from his chariot and ran towards Dushasana with a roar. The entire battlefield, including Karna, literally froze with their eyes on the two.

Bhima raced to Dushasana, braving the arrows, and in a flash, pulled Dushasana out of his chariot, lifted him bodily and threw the body with such a strength that it must have broken at many points. Bhima then lifted his mace and smashed the skull of Dushasana followed by smashing of the entire body breaking all the bones.

In the macabre aftermath, covered with dying Dushasana's blood all over, Bhima then tore open Dushasana's chest and drank his blood to the horror of all. Wiping his face, he collected some blood in the earthen pot he was carrying, to give to Draupadi to wash her hair by which she was dragged to the centre of the gambling palace by Dushasana. Bhima then rose like a titan and shouted a challenge to Duryodhana whose thighs too he had pledged to break. Fortunately for Duryodhana, he was not there at the scene of the battle. The entire battlefield, with Karauvas and Pandavas alike including Arjuna, Karna and Shalya stood frozen witnessing this macabre event. Yojana's away, Dhritarashtra's body gave a shudder when Sanjaya recounted the killing of his dear son to him.

Bhima walked back to his chariot to resume his role of reinforcing the defence of Arjuna. Shalya slowly nudged Karna to get out of his trance and recommence his fight with Arjuna. Shaken by Dushasana's cold blooded murder, the Kaurava army took some time to muster courage to fight their enemies.

Duryodhana, fighting elsewhere, received the news of Dushasana's death with horror and disbelief. Yet, when Ashwaththama, who was next to him, suggested that they should sue for peace with Pandavas, Duryodhana summarily rejected the suggestion and attacked the Pandavas with more determination and passion.

Karna, regaining his composure, resumed fighting with Arjuna with increased vigour. He shot an arrow that rained fire. Krishna manouvered his chariot in such a way that the front portion dipped nearly a foot. The arrow missed Arjuna's head, but took his crown away leaving him hugely embarrassed.

Arjuna retaliated and an intense duel ensued. Considering its criticality, many ceased fighting to watch the encounter. Suddenly they saw Karna's chariot lurching precariously to the left. When he found that his left wheel had got stuck in a hole. He shouted at Arjuna saying, 'Wait Arjuna, let me pull this wheel out of the hole'.

Arjuna paused a bit but Krishna retorted, "Karna, did you pause when you were planning the burning of Lakshagraha with Pandavas in it? Where was your great sense of chivalry when Panchali was being disrobed? In fact, you were one of the prime cheer leaders. And, where was your sense of fairness when you attacked Abhimanyu from the rear and your half a dozen colleagues from all around, the lone young warrior? This is not a demonstration match, but a war with most unscrupulous persons of your kind. You do not deserve any mercy, nor even some time to pull out your wheel".

Karna was speechless. After trying for one more time, he got up and shot an arrow at Arjuna. The powerful missile hit Arjuna's chariot making it shudder. He then again bent down to pull out the wheel. He tried to remember the advice given by his guru, but just couldn't, (His guru, Parashurama had put a curse on him to the effect that he would not be able to recall the guru's advice and use brahmastra when he would need it most critically).

It was a most unusual sight to see one of the greatest warriors of the world not able to move and looking totally confused and indecisive, Krishna signaled to Arjuna to finish Karna. Arjuna was ready and shot the arrow which neatly sliced off his head from the body. The third Kaurava commander-in-chief collapsed on the ground and lay dead. Shouts of victory came out from the Pandavas from all over the battlefield.

Duryodhana received the sad news with a stony silence. His most loyal, most powerful friend and the supreme commander, was dead. He knew that the defeat was closing in. He went to Guru Kripacharya and sought his advice. He advised Duryodhana what others had done – seek a peace with Pandavas. "A peace for what?" asked Duryodhana. "During the rest of my life I shall carry the feeling of humiliation and will blame myself for all the death and destruction of people loyal to me. No, I would rather die in the battle field with my head held high in the true traditions of kshtriyas". Kripacharya nodded in agreement. Clearly, Duryodhana had run out of all honourable options.

There were not many experienced warriors left. Shalya, the uncle of Nakula and Sahdeva, was given the mantle for leading the Kauravas.

Chapter-L-V

THE SIXTEENTH DAY

Shalya, the new Commander was a brave and experienced warrior. He organized the Kauravas in the best possible formations. There was little doubt that Pandava army was confident and itching for the ultimate victory. Yet, the battle was fierce with neither side ready to concede defeat.

That day, Yudhishthira led the attack personally. It was a strange sight because Yudhishthira was always considered as a peace-loving and non-violent person. But that day, he was excelling himself equally well in the art of war. The battle between him and Shalya was a prolonged one and on equal terms. The end came suddenly when a spear was hurled straight at Shalya by Yudhishthira and it went straight through the great warrior's body. Shalya's ramrod straight body fell on the ground like a fallen pillar. The last generalissmo of Kauravas was also gone.

The Kaurava army, scattered here and there, defeated and dejected, was withdrawing where it could. The others were mercilessly slaughtered by their enemy. The crimson colour was visible everywhere. All the surviving brothers of Duryodhana surrounded Bhima and attacked him together in a last ditch attempt to have some worthwhile revenge. Bhima, however, was in a murderous mood. Remembering once again the great dishonour perpetrated on Draupadi by the Kaurava princes, he smashed and killed each and everyone with great glee. In the end, he shouted, "I have redeemed my pledge made to all in the hall of games. Only Duryodhana is left who shall also be punished and killed".

Shakuni, the maternal uncle and the arch schemer was still left. He was also a competent fighter which was evidenced by the attack launched by him on Sahadeva. After a few equal exchanges, Sahadeva launched a sword headed arrow at Shakuni, shouting, "Take your medicine, you foulheaded scheming monster and the perpetrator of all foul deeds of Kauravas," The neck of Shakuni was neatly sliced with his head falling a few yards away.

Duryodhana, shocked and despondent was looking for a place to cool off his burning body, "Vidura was right, after all, in advising me against the war. I did, however, what I thought was right thing to do". He spied a pond nearby and, walking towards it, entered the water to take a samadhi.

Chapter-L-VI

THE SEVENTEENTH DAY

Sanjaya, recounting the final reverses of Kaurava, told Dhritarashtra, "There it is, Oh king, we are seeing the ignoble and humiliating end of your army of eleven Akshawhinis (An army formation consisting of 21870 chariots, 21870 elephants, 65610 horses and 1,09,350 foot soldiers) with greatest stalwarts on the earth. I can only see Duryodhana walking towards a pond while Kripacharya, Kritavarma and Ashwaththama are not in the battle field. Your ninety-nine sons are all dead and so are your son-in-law Jayadratha, Shakuni and Shalya. Too late to lament over the wrong decisions taken ignoring the right counsel from the proven wellwishers.

The Pandava brothers, led by Yudhishthira, had been looking for Duryodhana all over the battle field without any success. Eventually, they came to the pond on getting the information that Duryodhana had been seen entering that pond. At the edge of the pond, Yudhishthira shouted for Duryodhana, asking him to come out of his hiding.

Duryodhana slowly emerged out of water carrying his mace denying that he was hiding in the water. He added, "I was cooling the fire raging inside me. I have no desire for a fight anymore nor any more desire for any kingdom. Go and enjoy your conquest and leave me alone to myself".

Pandavas were in a belligerent mood. Yudhishthira, normally a peaceful and adherent of non-violence, was scathing in reply, "Now that is very magnanimous of you, but where was this great quality when you tried to poison Bhima, or burn us at the lac-house, or playing games.

And indeed where was the magnanimity when you refused even the ground occupied by the pointed ends of five grass weeds against our toned down request for just five villages. Sorry, Duryodhana, your pot of sins is overflowing. You, against all the wise counsel and sane advice, insisted for a war and you will have to finish it yourself. We challenge you for a fight with anyone of us. Do not be a coward and go back to the water hiding your true self behind the façade for suing peace when you have lost everything."

Duryodhana, sufficiently aroused and inflamed, rose to his full height with the mace. He then roared back, "I accept the challenge and will fight with the mace, since I am alone, I shall duel with all the five of you one by one". He then braced up for the fight.

Before Yudhishtira could go himself or depute one of his brothers, Bhima responded to the challenge and jumped to fight the Kaurava crown prince with his mace. "Come, you rat, show your fighting prowess. I have been waiting for this moment for the last thirteen years", he shouted.

The fight was fierce and on equal terms. Duryodhana was a known fighter, particularly with mace. The fight was getting intense and prolonged and Krishna was getting impatient. He told Arjuna in a voice loud enough to be heard by Bhima, "This is time for Bhima to redeem his vow to smash the thighs of Duryodhana after he had declared his intention to make Draupadi sit on his thighs".

Bhima heard Krishna's words. Remembering Kaurava's violations of the rules of war, the last one being the dastardly murder of Abhimanyu by eight of Kauravas, including Karna who attacked from behind, a rush of blood came to his head and he charged at Duryodhana with his mace aimed at both the thighs smashing them in quick succession. Duryodhana collapsed, grievously injured with his broken thighs.

As Pandavas prepared to depart from there Balarama appeared on the scene, having returned from the pilgrimage. Balarama was well-versed on the rules of fights. Finding that Bhima had smashed the thighs of Duryodhana he turned to Pandavas and rebuked them for indulging in an unfair fight. (In a duel with maces, one was not supposed to hit below the waist).

Situation was turning into an ugly one when Krishna, intervened on behalf of the Pandavas. He explained to Balarama that till that day Bhima had always fought fair duels with his opponents. However the battle with Duryodhana was different. Bhima had taken a vow to smash Duryodhana's thighs, thirteen years ago after the despicable act of Kaurava princes who had tried to disrobe Draupadi in full public view. It is in fulfilling that vow that Bhima had done the smashing act.

Krishna continued using his best persuasive skills with Balarama. He recounted to Balarama how the violations of rules began with Kaurava and with the war intensifying everyday they all saw the norms being ignored. The worst was the attack on Abhimanyu resulting in his death, which could be better described as a cold blooded murder. He advised Balarama that since he did not have a total picture on the breakdown of rules of the war from both the sides and from warriors and soldiers, he should not judge Bhima too harshly. Eventually Balarama did, what he had been doing throughout his life i.e. giving in to the highly persuasive skills of his younger brother. After rebuking the Pandavas, he went away. Pandavas too, relieved at Balarama's change of stance, went away to their camps as there was no one to fight with and the sun was setting.

Duryodhana lay there, bleeding and slowly approaching death – a hero's death nonetheless, since he would die on the battlefield. Suddenly, Ashwaththama came and stood by him. Remembering his father's death through trickery by Pandavas and Duryodhana's death through the blows below his waist he took a decision. He told Duryodhana, "Most revered crown prince. I promise that I shall avenge your death and that of my father by those wicked Pandavas. I promise you that I shall murder all the remaining Pandavas so that no Pandava rules over the Hastinapur. In the typical 'Do as I say not as I do' mood which had set in the crumbling norms at the fag-end of the war, Ashwaththama found nothing wrong in his decision to carry out the stealth operation in the night when no fighting was expected to take place.

Duryodhana too was pleased to hear of Ashwaththama's resolve. In his last gesture of defiance, he put a tilak on Ashwaththama's forehead and told him, "I have full faith in your capability to do what you have told me just now. I am pronouncing you as our commander-in-chief. My blessings are with you and till my death, I shall be praying for your success".

As Ashwaththama walked away, he realized that he did not really have a plan which would enable him to do what he wanted. The night had already set in. He was feverishly thinking of a way to keep his pledge with Duryodhana when he spied an owl which was sneaking in a bird's nest to kill and eat all its occupants as well as the eggs.

The owl's example gave the idea which enabled Ashwaththama to carry out his plans in the night itself. He proceeded immediately to Kripacharya and Kritavarma and disclosed his plans and sought their help. Kripacharya vehemently opposed the plan on the basis of its being much too much unethical. Kritavarma went along with him. However, when Ashwaththama countered with his own arguments quoting deliberate violations by Pandavas and stating his firm resolve to go alone, if need be, the two grudgingly joined him in his plans.

They moved in stealth in the cover of darkness towards the Pandava camp. Unknown to them, Krishna had taken the Pandavas to another place. In their place, the five sons of Draupadi were fast asleep. Systematically, they slit the throats of all five of them presuming them to be Pandavas. Then they moved and gave the similar treatment to next set of tents which housed Dhrishtadyumna and all Panchala soldiers. Thereafter they moved in a random manner, destroying, killing and setting fire to whatever they could put their hands on.

The trio then went back straight to dying Duryodhana and reported the completion of the mission and that all Pandavas had been eliminated. Duryodhana heard the report and died with a satisfied smile on his face.

Chapter-L-VII

THE EIGHTEENTH DAY

The news about the massive mayhem spread quickly and was received with shock and horror by one and all including the five Pandavas. Draupadi's grief over the cold blooded murder of all her five sons was uncontrollable. Pandavas were shocked and then very angry. They immediately set out to find the culprits. Soon it was clear that Ashwaththama had masterminded the entire operation.

A search was on and soon the Pandavas located Ashwaththama near the hut of sage Vyasa. As they approached Ashwaththama, the latter, seeing them realized his mistake. As his last act, he picked up a straw from the ground, invoked it with a mantra and sent it away. The straw had become a sword which was rushing towards the Pandava camp. Ashwaththama had, through his invocation of mantra, ordered the sword to go and kill any seed of Pandavas which might be in the womb of any of the women. Fortunately, Krishna was also there with the Pandavas. He understood the intention of Ashwaththama and immediately deactivated the straw-turned-sword. The sword, headed for the child in the womb of Uttara, widow of Abhimanyu, flew to a target elsewhere harmlessly. The child, who later became king Parikshit, continued the Pandava dynasty.

Bhima challenged Ashwaththama to a mace duel and defeated him after a brief struggle. Ashwaththama took out a jewel from his forehead and surrendered it to Bhima. This was the divine jewel that was granted as a boon to Ashwaththama to make him immortal. The son of Dronacharya went away to forests for penance.

With the surrender of the last Commander-in-chief of Duryodhana, the 18-day war of Mahabhata came to an end with Pandavas emerging as the undisputed winners.

Bhima carried the big jewel surrendered by Ashwaththama to Draupadi. Giving it to her, he said, "Purest amongst women, this belongs to you. This has been surrendered by the man who has killed your sons. We have defeated Kauravas. Duryodhana is dead. Dushasana has been killed by me and his blood has been tasted by me. Your dishonor has been avenged. You can now wash your hair and make them as you desire".

Draupadi, still sad but satisfied, walked over to Yudhishthira and said, "Purest among humans, this actually belongs to you. Take it and wear it on your crown".

Chapter-L-VIII

GRIEVING OVER THE DEAD

Hastinapura was a city of mourning. Dhritarashtra, accompanied by Sanjaya and thousands of mourning women and children went to the scene of battles. He openly wept for the dead, more so for his sons. Sanjaya consoled him and told him about the urgent need for proper funerals of the dead.

Vyasa also arrived there and consoled Dhritarashtra. Speaking tenderly, he told the king not to grieve over the dead as the war was predestined to reduce the burden on the earth. He advised Dhritarashtra to treat and love Yudhishthira and Pandavas as his own sons.

Yudhishthira was present nearby. He came and bowed before Dhritarashtra who embraced him. One could not blame him for the lack of warmth in his embrace.

Bhima came to the blind king. Krishna stopped him and quietly pushed a metal statue of Bhima instead. When Dhritarashtra embraced the statue, the memories of all his sons killed by Bhima overwhelmed him and in his grief, his embrace became a fatal clasp and the statue was crushed to pieces. The king shouted in horror, 'I lost all control and have been deceived by my wrath. I have killed Bhima'.

Krishna informed him of the switch and advised him to be more forgiving. The blind king, chastened by his folly, embraced the remaining four Pandava brothers, and blessed them. They then proceeded to meet the queen to seek her forgiveness and blessings.

Sage Vyasa had already conselled Gandhari over the need to let bygones be bygones and treat Pandavas as her own sons. Gandhari admitted that the evil has perished and the war was as a result of the misdeeds of Dushasana and her brother, Shakuni. She did, however, regret the war on two counts. One was the unethical killing of Duryodhana and the other was that not even one of her sons' life was spared on whom the old couple could have depended in the old age.

Bhima admitted that he broke the rules to defeat Duryodhana who otherwise was invincible and unconquerable. He added that Duryodhana was also aware of Bhima's vows on the floor of the hall of games and to that extent, should have protected his thighs too. He (Bhima) recounted the misdeeds and unethical actions of Duryodhana, culminating in the murder of Abhimanyu. He was, however, frank enough to admit that he broke the rules primarily to save himself. Gandhari listened calmly and though still agitated, asked for Yudhishthira.

The eldest Pandava came and bowed before Gandhari and said, "Dear mother and queen, the person responsible for the killing your sons stands before you ready to accept your curse, for I have no desire for the life or the kingdom".

Gandhari turned her blindfolded face away but even while doing so, her strong gaze, filtered through cloth and incensed through anger fell on the toe of Yudhishtira which instantaneously turned into a charred block of wood.

Regaining her composure, the queen blessed all the Pandavas and sent them to Kunti. Who could blame the royal couple who had lost their hundred children.

Gandhari turned towards Draupadi, who was standing by her side, and said, "Dear child, I and you have lost all our children mainly due to my stupidity in not stopping my errant sons when, with a little firmness from my side, I could have done so".

The Pandavas went to Kunti and paid obeisance to her. Not much was spoken nor there was too much of joy and happiness. They were now gradually realizing the huge loss of men and other fighting elements which both the sides had suffered. From what could have been a tremendously large and formidable army in both the sides, combined or separate, only seven men were left in the Pandava's side and just three on Kaurava's.

Next day they went to the bank of Ganges and performed last rites of all the dead, praying for peace for their souls. Only Pitamaha was still there waiting for the appointed day when the sun would enter "Uttarayan' and he would achieve his desired death, the 'Ichacha Mrityu' as per the blessings and the boon given by Shantanu. Pandavas camped on the bank of Ganga for a month.

Chapter-L-IX

AGONY AND THE ECSTASY

The month at the Ganges provided a depressing environment. While others came out of it and became normal, the Dharamputra, Yudhishthira, had been continuously gloomy and was even contemplating refusal to accept the throne.

One day the celestial rishi, Narada, appeared before him and congratulated him on the victory over Kauravas. What, however made Yudhishthira still more sad was the information provided by the learned sage that Karna was Kunti's eldest son and their eldest brother. Yudhishthira became yet more depressed when Narada revealed that Karna had spared them, particularly Bhima in the battlefield in keeping his pledge to Kunti that he would not kill more than one brother of his in the impending war. The very of thought that Karna was their eldest brother who was killed mercilessly by Arjuna drove Yudhishthira to the precipice of gloom.

Noticing Yudhishthira's extreme sadness, Narada told himn in detail the story of Karna's life starting from his birth.

Narada narrated the two curses pronounded on Karna one by his guru and other by a brahmin. The first was when the Parashuram discovered that contrary to what Karna had told him, when he came to learn the art of weaponry from the learned rishi, Karna was not a brahmin, but a kshatriya, Parashuram had shouted at him, saying, that when the most critical moment in fighting would befall him, his knowledge of weapons, learned from Parashurama would fail him.

The second curse had been pronounced on Karna by a brahmin living near Parashuram's hermitage. Karna had accidently killed a cow of this brahmin while practicing with his bow, "Just as you have slaughtered this innocent animal, "the brahmin said, "You too will be killed in a battle when your wheel of the chariot will get stuck in the; mud in a battle and you will be trying to unsuccessfully wrench that wheel out of mud".

Narada told Yudhishtira that thus the latter was not the sole person responsible for Karna's death. Apart from the two curses pronounced on Karna, there was yet another instance when he had to part with his divine earrings and the cloak which he was wearing from his very birth. Although he had been warned by the Sun-god that Indra would try and take away these divine accountrements, he could not refuse to give them when Indra came dressed as a brahmin and asked as alms the two protective apparels. This reduced Karna's effectiveness. Added to that was his pledge to Kunti that he would not kill more than one Pandava. Narada continued, "Karna's misdeeds and misadventures are also known to you and indeed, everyone. His worse attribute was his misplaced loyalty to Duryodhana, which was carried to extreme limits. You may not know but it is a fact that both his father, Surya, and I myself tried our best to argue him out of his alliance with Duryodhana but he just would not budge even a wee bit from his declared stand to support Duryodhana till the very end. His death was a will of destiny. You are not to be blamed for it. Karna brought his end through his own actions".

Yudhishthira had regained his composure. He saw things in proper perspective, yet he could not totally forgive his mother for concealing the secret of Karna being her eldest son. He told Kunti, "Mother, by your suppressing information on Karna, we have killed our own eldest brother and committed a great sin. pronounce a curse on all womanhood that henceforth, they will not be able to conceal their pregnancy and keep it secret.

Despite the aforesaid, Yudhishthira was still in no mood to accept the throne despite pressure from everyone, big and small. He expressed his desire to give up the desires, retire to forests and do penance to seek the forgiveness of his sins. All his brothers, mother and Draupadi tried unsuccessfully to persuade him to accept the crown. It was only when Vyasa came and spoke to him, citing precedences, emphasizing that his duty lay in going to Hastinapura, accept the throne and govern the nation, that he agreed to return and take over the reins.

Before starting to perform his duties he went to Bhishma Pitamaha, still lying on the bed of arrows. Bhishma not only gave him his blessings but also extensive instructions on dharma. Pitamaha's discourses form the famous 'Shantiparva' of Mahabharata.

Bhishma died at the appointed hour. They performed the last rites to seek peace for his soul. When the rituals were finished, Yudhishtira walked to the bank of ganges and stood thinking of the tragic events of the recent past and loss of the lives of millions, including many who were his good friends and followers in both the camps. His sadness was so intense that he passed out and fell senseless on the ground. They all knew that Yudhishthira, the most righteous person in the world was going through a most traumatic period of his life. Bhima came and caressed him tenderly till he regained his consciousness.

It was, however, Dhritarashtra, whose words were really the healing balm. He said, 'Son Yudhishthira, arise and assisted by your brothers and friends take up your duties of the king. You have won a war in accordance to the dharma of the warriors. Go now and rule the kingdom you have rightly won.

Dhritarashtra continued, "This war was entirely my folly. Instead of listening to the wise advice of Pitamaha, Krishna and Vidura, I relied on Duryodhana's foolish words. It was like a bad dream where gold was everywhere with nothing left on waking up. Leave the grieving to myself and Gandhari for the loss of so many near and dear ones including our hundred sons who disappeared in the world of no where. We now have you as our son. Do not grieve and feel sad.

With his job done, Krishna bade farewell to Pandavas and started for Dwaraka.

Chapter-L-X

KRISHNA EXPLAINS UTANGA REGRETS

Mahabharata is full of many stories which carry a message on some aspect of personal conduct, behaviour, action or dharma. One such story relating to Krishna and his old friend, brahmin Utanga.

After bidding farewell to Pandavas, Krishna sought his old friend on the way. Utanga was a wandering monk who moved from place to place, mountains and deserts, offering penances, and thus not fully up-do-date on what was happening in the region or the country.

They exchanged the usual pleasantaries and then settled down for the usual chat. Utanga enquired from Krishna about the latter's cousins, Pandavas and Kauravas. The Brahmaan was evidently totally unaware of the events leading to the great internecine war. Krishna stood for a moment thinking of what to tell and then related the entire story.

Utanga was highly agitated after hearing about the macabre war and the events. It was beyond his comprehension that Vasudeva (Krishna) had let all this happen despite his being present and in the know of what was happening.

The Brahmin got up with an angry glint in his eyes and an unfriendly stare. He said to Krishna, "How could you let all this happen despite your being present there. I know that if you had wanted, you could surely have stopped this destruction. I am sorry but I have to pronounce a curse on you. Get ready to receive it".

Krishna held up his hand smiled and said, "Revered Brahmin and friend, calm down and listen to my explanation. If, even after listening to me you still feel like pronouncing the curse, by all means, you are welcome to deliver it. I shall receive it with all humility. Till the time you have listened to me, do not waste what you have earned through your penances in a hasty decision".

Utanga becalmed himself and waited to hear from Madhava (Another name of Krishna, the other prominent ones being Keshava, Govind, and Murari etc). Then Krishna appeared to him in his divine, all embracing creator's Vishwarupa in all its magnificence.

"Whenever there is a serious threat to Dharma and evil descends on the earth, I am born in various forms to save it and establish the good. In whatever form I am born, I have to behave as per the nature of that rupa or body. If I am born as a deva or rakshasa or yaksha or a human being or even a beast, I do what is expected and natural to that body", he said.

Krishna continued, "I pleaded with Kauravas to give up their path of confrontation but, drunk with their arrogance and power, they rejected all my peace overtures. I warned them of dire consequences and in a desperate move, appeared before them in this form. They dismissed all this, attributing to my powers of illusion, Maya. They were bent upon a war and continued their evil doings. Finally, they waged the war and perished, killing a large number of Pandava soldiers as well. Oh, best among brahmins, you have thus no reason to be angry with me, "Krishna thereafter became a normal human being.

Utanga had recovered his original composure. Krishna was happy and delighted. He then told Utanga that he wanted to give him a boon and asked for his choice. The brahmin initially declined saying that seeing Krishna's divine form was more than what he had ever wished. However, on Krishna's insistence, he relented and asked for getting water to drink, wherever and whenever he felt thirsty and suffered acutely from its unavailability. Krishna granted it readily and moved on.

Utanga resumed his penances wandering in deserts and mountains. One day in the scorching heat in the desert he felt acutely thirsty with no source of water anywhere around. He remembered Krishna's boon and willed for some water.

Suddenly an outcast, a nishada, clothed in dirty clothes, having five snarling wild dogs on the leash and carrying water in a leather container with a bamboo spout, appeared before him and offered him water from the spout. Utanga became very unhappy at the filthy sight and firmly refused the offer. Despite repeated offers from the Nishada, Utanga persisted in his refusal. Eventually the nishada and his dogs disappeared. Utanga was unhappy even with Krishna for playing what he thought was a cruel poor joke on him.

The brahmin, however, was intrigued by the mysterious and sudden disappearance of nishada. Soon he understood that it was a test of his gyana (True knowledge) and he had failed in it due to his sheer arrogance.

In a moment, the Lord appeared in his regalia. He said, "Friend Utanga, when you tested my boon, I prevailed upon Indra to send you amrita (The nectar of immorality) as water. He resisted a great deal but eventually agreed with the condition that he will carry it as a chandala to test your complete gyana and the power to have transcended externals. I am sorry that you refused and failed me. Indra won because he was right and sadly I have lost to him".

The aforesaid tale illustrates two points. To deserve the best, total gyan and transcending of externals is an absolute must. Secondly, rarely, but surely, even the Lord can be wrong. His decisions are, however, open to review and modifications.

Chapter-L-XII

PANDAVA RULE AND DEPARTURE OF ELDERS

Hastinapura flourished under Pandavas and became an ideal welfare state being ruled under tenets of dharma. King Yudhishtira was universally respected and his four brothers helped him to administer the various functions of the state. Many yagyas including Ashwamedha yagya were organized and successfully carried out.

With passage of time Dhritarashtra and Gandhari gradually forgot the sadness due to loss of their sons. What gave them the healing balm was the total devotion with which they were looked after by the five Pandavas, Kunti and Draupadi. Bhima, due to his abrasive tongue was, however, at times, slightly impertinent while speaking to Dhritarashtra which pained the elderly couple. They, however, accepted and tolerated those remarks and insults as something they deserved. These hurts were made up by total reverence of rest of the people, particularly Yudhishthira.

However, gradually the elderly royal couple found a growing desire to renounce the worldly comforts and go to the forest for offering penance. They mustered up enough courage and went to Yudhishthira to disclose their wish. Yudhishthira rejected the suggestion outright and even anxiously enquired, if something was lacking in their being looked after. Dhritarashtra insisted that they had been looked after in the best possible and most courteous manner. Knowing that persuading Yudhishtira was going to be a difficult task they solicited the help of Vidura, Kripacharya and even sage Vyasa, who happened to be visiting them, to make the young king agree to their wish. Eventually, Yudhishthira agreed and arranged for their departure. Both Dhritarashtra and Gandhari thanked the king for looking after them as well as ruling Hastinapura in the best possible manner. Wishing them the very best, they left the palace in their forest attire. Sanjaya too prepared to go along with them.

At the last moment, Kunti too desired to go with them. Yudhishthira resisted initially but had to give in at the end. It seems that the mood for going for penances had set in after fifteen years of absolute enjoyment under the new dispensation.

Prior to her departure, Kunti spoke to Yudhishthira expressing her total satisfaction at his rule and conduct. She however specially emphasized two things to him.

"Look after your brothers, particularly Nakula and Sahadeva, Madri's sons and never forget to give due respects to the memory of your eldest brother Karna. He never really got his due; something which did have a bearing on his changed attitude and behaviour".

They left for the forest and settled down in their routine of prayers and penances.

Nearly three years after leaving Hastinapura, they were caught in a huge forest fire. Realising, that the end was near, they advised Sanjaya to go away and look after himself. Thereafter they themselves sat calmly in a samadhi. As the fire engulfed them, they surrendered to it perishing, but content to meet the maker.

Chapter-L-XII

KRISHNA TOO DEPARTS

Krishna ruled over Dwaraka for thirty six years. The yadavas, however, became a decadent lot living a life of loose morals, drinking, feasting and frolicking.

One day, a group of sages arrived in Dwaraka. The yadavas decided to play a prank. One of their princes, named Samba, went to them dressed as a pregnant woman. He asked the sages, "Oh great sages, please tell me whether I will have a son or a daughter?" The question was followed by a hilarious laughter of the bunch of other yadavas behind Samba.

The leader of the group, an elderly sage saw through the ploy. He became very angry at the sheer discourtesy and replied, "You will not have a boy or a girl, but a mace which will destroy your entire dynasty". The fiery curse of the elderly sage chastened the crowd which went away a bit shaken. There was a further cause of alarm when on the next day samba's stomach got bloated and he delivered not a human being, but a mace.

Terrorised at seeing the mace, they ground the object and when it became powdery, they scattered the powder over the sea. They got relieved that they had got rid of the problematic mace and soon forgot all about it.

The mace powder particles had, however, been swept inland and in a few seasons grew into a crop of sturdy maces.

One day the yadavas decided to have a picnic at the beach. As usual, there was a considerable amount of drinking and revelry. Soon this gave way to minor arguments leading to major ones. They divided themselves into two groups, one lead by Satyaki and the other by Kritavarma. The former called the latter as a coward who murdered the Pandavas in the forbidden hours in the dark. Kritavarma retorted by saying that Satyaki was no better as he had killed Bhurishrava when he had lost an arm and was sitting in a yoga pose.

There were no arms but surely thousands of maces which had grown on the beaches. Pulling them out they used them as clubs and started attacking each other. Soon it became a major war and when it ended not a single yadava was left living.

Balarama was shocked by the news. He could not recover from the grief and died from sheer remorse. Krishna too knew that the end was coming. Some say that after Mahabharata, Gandhari, shocked by the loss of all her hundred sons, had pronounced a curse on Krishna that he too would lose his entire tribe as a punishment for complicity in the Mahabharata war.

Krishna shocked beyond limits went to the forest and was resting under a tree where he fell asleep. A hunter who was passing by, mistook the sole of his foot as an organ of a deer. He shot an arrow at it. The arrow hit the aim powerfully. Krishna could not recover from the injury and departed for his heavenly abode.

Krishna had served the purpose for which he was borne in this world. The fourth Yuga, Kaliyuga, had already commenced. Men were beginning to lose their sense of Dharma. He knew he would have to be born again at the end of the age of Kali.

Prior to his death, Krishna had sent Daruka to Hāstinapur to call Arjuna urgently to Dwaraka. Arjuna, shocked to hear about the events at Dwaraka, rushed to Prabhasa. They were all dead. He collected the surviving women and children and headed back towards Hastinapur. On their heels, the sea, which had been rushing in and retreating broke the rules of nature and rushed to cover up entire Dwarka, its wonderful palaces, mansions and buildings. Then, in a few moments, it was all quiet with the sea covering what Dwarka was. The beautiful city was now just a memory, a name.

When Arjuna reached Hastinapur, he stood before Yudhishthira, totally speechless. Physically and mentally exhausted, he collapsed in a dead faint..

Chapter-L-XIII

PANDAVAS FOLLOW SUIT

Pandavas were shaken by the news from Dwaraka regarding the destruction of yadavas and death of Balarama and Krishna. They too thought it was time for them to depart for their final journey to the after-world. Yudhishthira handed over the reins to Parikshit, son of Abhimanyu. All the five brothers and Draupadi set off for the pilgrimage enroute to the Himalayas. On the way, a dog also joined them and travelled with them from then onwards.

They travelled to many auspicious places and even installed statues of gods and goddesses (whole of Himanchala and Uttaranchala is full of temples and other noteworthy landmarks still bear the marks of Pandavas having travelled there). Even now many stories are told locally regarding Pandavas visiting different places within the region.

The travel through valleys, passes and forests was getting progressively difficult. When they reached Himadri hills, all they could see was a white sheet of snow all the way upto the horizon. The party of six humans and a dog walked on bravely through the snow. It was freezing cold and at places the ground was extremely slippery. Surprisingly Yudhishthira was most steady while others went through many falls and tumbles. At times, death seemed just round the corner.

It was evident that this kind of trecking could not carry on for long without accidents and falls. Sure enough, Draupadi was the first one to slip down a deep gorge and died. As others went through the glaciers and snow valleys, Arjuna, Nakula, Sahadeva and Bhima lost their lives, one by one.

Only Yudhishthira and his dog had survived. What Yudhishthira did not know that the dog was, in fact, Dharmaraja in disguise to test the Pandava elder.

After some more determined walking, one day, Yudhishthira spotted a chariot flying in from the sky. It was Indra, who had come in his personal chariot driven by Maitali, his personal charioteer.

Indra got down and approached Yudhishthira who paid obeisance to former. Indra blessed him and said, "Yudhishthira, I have come to take you to heavens alive since you have been an incarnation of Dharma on earth. Your brothers and Draupadi have already reached their appointed place. Please step on the chariot."

Yudhishthira was starting to mount the chariot. Right behind him as the dog also tried to follow his master, he was shouted upon by Indra with an emphatic "No". Indra turned to Yudhishthira and said, "We cannot take him to heavens".

Yudhishthira looked surprised and shocked. He slowly got down from Indra's chariot and told the lord, "This dog had joined us during our journey. Since then, it has stuck to us through thick and thin. If it is not acceptable to you, I would rather stay on earth than go without him".

Indra tried his best to persuade Yudhishthira to leave the dog back on earth and accompany Indra to heavens, but he did not succeed because Yudhishthira stuck to his ground and did not budge an inch from his firm stand.

All of a sudden the dog transformed into Lord Dharmaraja. He expressed his happiness to have seen Yudhishthira's concern, compassion and loyalty to those who served him honestly. After blessing Yudhishthira, the Lord disappeared. A happy Yudhishthira stepped on the chariot of Indra for the journey to heavens.

On arrival at heavens, he was in for a bigger shock. To his consternation, he found that while Duryodhana and many other Kauravas were enjoying merrily in heavens, his own brothers as well as Draupadi, were going through a horrific time in hell with many atrocities being committed on them, e.g. causing burns on their bodies or rotting away of some organs etc.

Yudhishthira was aghast at the scene in the hell. He turned to the angel who was escorting him and shouted, "What kind of justice is this. Duryodhana, his kins, who have committed the evil deeds on earth are enjoying here in heavens. In contrast, my own truthful brothers and noble and pure Draupadi of spotless character are being meted out this extremely cruel and inhuman punishment"?.

The escorting angel did not reply, but when he gestured to Yudhishthira to return with him back to heavens, he said, "You go back to heavens alone because I would rather burn and rot here in the hell with my brothers and Draupadi than return to the heavenly comforts in company of those people who do not deserve it".

The angel left the hell for heavens alone. Yudhishthira stayed back dumb founded, sad, sick and pained, wondering at the gross travesty of justice in the God's own kingdom. .

Yudhishtira stayed in hell for a thirtieth part of the day with himself being put to the cruel punishments like the ones being subjected to his kins.

Suddenly there was a total transformation in atmosphere. Those cruel scenes of persecution had disappeared. In fact the hell was not there any more. Yudhishthira found once again Dharmaraja and Indra standing in front of him. The former told Yudhishtira, "You have passed all the tests we put you to. You stuck to be by the side of your brothers and Draupadi even at the risk of abandoning you place in heavens. We therefore welcome you with open arms and are proud to have such a truthful person, conscious of his dharma and the need to abide by it, come what may even in heavens".

Yudhishthira looked pouzzled and asked Dharmaraja, "Father, I am relieved by your explanation but have still two questions. Why was I put to these tests and where are my brothers and Draupadi at this moment".
Both Dharmaraja and Indra smiled as the former spoke, "My beloved son, you have been an ideal human being and a law-abiding king totally loyal to the interest of those under you. The best test was to test your ability to stick to your principles and not to abandon them even when pitted against the cruelities of hell. We are glad that you have passed this test as well. We are already in heavens and so are all your brothers and Draupadi. The scenes of hell were illusions created to test you. There comes sage Narada to meet us".

Yudhishthira heaved a sign of relief. He paid obeisance to the heavenly sage who knew all the three worlds and whose knowledge was unquestionably immense. The wise sage could feel that Yudhishthira had still questions on the nature of justice and its dispensation in the kingdom of God.

Narada told Yudhishthira, "Famous and renowned prince, I can see that you have reservations on some things you have observed here. Let me clarify these to you". Narada continued, "In swarga (Heavens) we do not harbor any ill-will against anyone. People are accepted here on the basis of their adherence to Dharma. Duryodhana has attained a place of honour by his adherence to kshatriya Dharma. He died as a kshatriya should. You have been given the singular honour of arriving in the swarga with your human body. It is for this reason that the earthly feelings are clouding your thinking and vision. Once this mortal frame is abandoned, these things of flesh and breeding of ill-will will also disappear. Do not grieve. Come and meet all the people of the swarga including your near and dear ones".

Narada further clarified, "The rules of heaven are different. A man whose good deeds exceed his sins goes to hell first. After finishing his predestined stay, he goes to heavens. The reverse is true for those whose sins are greater than the good deeds".

"We understand your anger against Duryodhana and as a human, you have a right to feel aggrieved. But, he also lived and died as a kshatriya should. He was fearless and ruled his kingdom justly. His soul has been cleansed because he died while fighting in the battle field. It is ordained that if a kshatriya dies a noble death (while fighting bravely) his all sins are forgiven. Come then and be one amongst us".

Krishna sat there in the midst of all. He was back after his mission in the world. The Lord had arranged for the gods to be born in the world of men to help Him in his task : To clean the earth of the poisons which were defiling her and establishment of dharma. Indra, Vayu, Dharma and the Aswin twins were there to help him as five Pandavas.

Attainment of truth and righteousness is the true religion. The story of Pandavas, their eventual victory over Kauravas, depicting the victory of good over evil, has become immortal. As long as the sun, moon and stars are there, their memory will always remain etched in the mind of men and their story will be read by the coming generations till the time immemorial.

At a nod from Yama, the mortal frame of Yudhishtira disappeared and he was transfigured into the form of a god. In a flash, all the agitation, anger, abhorrence and hatred disappeared from the face of the Dharamputra. There was a serene peace and happiness written all over his face. He was extremely overjoyed to meet Karna and all his brothers as well as his cousins, the sons of Dhritarashtra, who too were there without any trace of ill-will or rancour. Yudhishthira had at last attained peace, happiness and contentment in heavens.

GLOSSARY

Abhimanyu	Son of Arjuna and Subhadra. Husband of Uttara, daughter of King Virata.
Acharya	Teacher, also called Guru.
Achyuta	A synonym of Krishna, other popular ones being Madhava, Govind, Murari, Vasudeva etc.
Adhiratha	Karna's foster father, a weaver
Airavata	Indra's elephant
Akshauhini	An army formation, each consisting of 21870 chariots and elephants, 65610 horses and 109350 foot soldiers.
Alambasa	A rakashasa (demon) friend of Duryodhana. He joined Duryodhana's forces. He was forced to flee from battle field by Satyaki.
Amrita	A nectar of immorality, food of gods.
Anga	The kingdom of which Duryodhana made Karna the king.
Artha	Wealth, a key object of human life, others being Dharma (Righteous duty, Kama (Fufilment of desires), and Moksha (Spiritual salvation).
Astra	A missile for use against the enemy.
Ashwamedha Yagya	A horse – sacrifice organized by an aspiring emperor.
Ashwaththama	Ashwaththama Son of Guru Dronacharya and the last commander-in-chief of Kaurava armies.
Balarama	Elder brother of Krishna, also known as Baladeva

Bakasura	A cruel demon (rakshasa) who tyrannised the citizens of Ekachakrapuram. He was eventually killed by Bhima bringing succour to the whole village.
Bhagwan	A title used to address gods and great rishis e.g. Krishna, Vyasa etc.
Brahma	The creator of universe.
Brahmastra	A devastating weapon given by lord Brahma.
Brihannala	The name adopted by Arjuna during his incognito stay in the kingdom of Virata. Brihannala, posing as an enuach, taught dancing to princess Uttara.
Brihadratha	Commander of three regiments who ruled over Magadha, a celebrity. His son was known as Jarasandha
Bhima	The second eldest pandava, son of the wind-god, Vayu. He was extremely powerful and strong.
Bhishma	The eighth son of king Shantanu and Ganga. A famous person known for his adherence to dharma and moral values. Remained steadfast in his oath to protect the crown of Hastinapura throughout his life.
Chandala	A low-caste person. An untouchable, whose mere touch was supposed to result in defilement of the body.
Chitrasena	King of Gandharvas, the celestial beings, regarded as experts in music and dance.
Chitrangada	Elder son of Satyawati and Shantanu. He succeeded Shantanu on the throne of Hastinapura.

Damka	Charioteer of Krishna
Devadatta	Arjuna's conch.
Devavrata	Bhishma, the eighth child of Shantanu and Ganga.
Devendra	King of gods, also known as Indra.
Dharma	Righteous conduct.
Dhananjaya	Another name of Arjuna.
Dhaumya	Guru of Pandavas, who went with them during their exile. Also called Ayudhaumya.
Dhrishtadumna	Elder brother of Draupadi, later appointed as the supreme commander of the Pandava forces.
Dhritarashtra	Son of Queen Ambika. He was blind by birth. Husband of Gandhari and father of hundred sons, eldest amongst them being Duryodhana.
Dharamaputra	Synonym for Yudhishthira.
Draupadi	Daughter of king Drupada, king of Panchala. Also known as Panchali, she married all the five Pandavas, though Arjuna won her in a swayamvara organized by her father.
Drona	Also known as Dronacharya, a famous teacher on use of arms, of Kaurava and Pandava princes. Son of brahmana named Bharadwaja and disciple of Parasurama. Father of Ashwaththama and husband of Kripi.
Drupada	King of Panchala and father of Dhrishtidyumna and Draupadi.

Dushasana	Younger brother of Duryodhana who dragged Draupadi by pulling her by hair to the hall of games.
Durvasa	A sage known for his fiery temper.
Ganapati	Lord Ganesha, who agreed to write down the story of Mahabharata dictated by Vyasa without pause or hesitation.
Gandhari	Dhritarashtra's wife, the queen mother of Kaurava princes. Ex-princess of the kingdom of Gandhara.
Gandharvas	Celestial beings who are regarded as masters of music and dances.
Gandiva	Arjuna's most powerful and fearsome bow.
Ghatotkacha	Son of Bhima from demoness Hidimba.
Guru	Acharya, Teacher, revered preceptor.
Hanumana	Powerful and wise monkey devotee of Sri Rama, son of Vayu.
Hastinapura	Famous capital of Kauravas.
Indra	King of gods.
Iravana	Arjuna's son by a Naga wife Uloopi. Iravana died on the eighth day of Mahabharata, in the battlefield fighting Kauravas.
Janardana	A name of Krishna, others being Hrishikesh, Keshava.
Jarasandha	The king of Magadha known for his might and physical power. Killed by Bhima on the thirteenth day of non-stop combat, with Krishna and Arjuna as witnesses.

Jayadratha	Son-in-law of Dhritarashtra. A powerful warrior on Kaurava's side.
Kanka	Assumed name of Yudhishtira in the court of king of Virata.
Karna	Son of sun-god and Kunti, a matchless warrior. Adopted as son and brought up by Radha, wife of a weaver. Also known as 'Radheya'.
Khandavaprastha	Ancient capital from where ancestors of Pandavas ruled. Rebuilt and renamed as Indraprastha.
Keechaka	Commander-in-chief of king Virata and his brother-in-law.
Kripacharya	Another guru of kuru princes. Maternal uncle of Ashwaththama.
Krishna Dvaipayana	Sage Vyasa's another name
Kritavarma	Yadava warrior who fought on the side of Kauravas.
Kunti	Daughter of Sura, also known as Pritha and Kunti. Mother of Karna and five famous Pandava brothers, wife of Pandu.
Madri	Another wife of Pandu and mother of Nakula and Sahadeva.

Lomasa	A brahmin sage.
Madhava	Krishna. Also means Lord of Lakshmi.
Maitreya	A sage.
Mantra	An incantation with words of power.
Manasarovar	A sacred lake in Himalayas.

Matali	Charioteer of Indra.
Nandini	Divinely beautiful cow of Vasistha.
Nara	Arjuna, Dhananjaya.
Narada	The heavenly rishi of encyclopaedic knowledge whose peregrinations cover the three worlds.
Narayana	Vishnu ; Sri Krishna
Nishada	A hunter belonging to a low caste. Generally an outcast.
Panchajanya	Krishna's conch.
Pandu	Son of Ambika who succeeded to the throne of Hastinapura on his father's death because his elder brother, Dhritarashtra, was born blind. Father of Pandavas.
Parashara	A great sage. Father of Vedavyasa.
Parikshit	Son of Abhimanyu. Later crowned as the king.
Partha	Arjuna, other name Dhananjaya.
Prabhasa	The Vasu, guilty of seizing Vasishtha's holy cow.
Pritha	Kunti's name before her marriage.
Purochana	Duryodhana's architect who built a

	beautiful wax palace which was highly inflammable; part of conspiracy to burn Pandavas who were invited to live in there.
Pitamaha	Gradfather. Expression used for Bhishma.
Radheya	Karna, son of Radha.
Rajasuya	A yagya performed by a king to become entitled to assume the title of 'Emperor'.
Romapada	King of Anga which experienced severe drought.
Rudra	Another name of Shiva.
Sahadeva	Youngest of the Pandava princes.
Sairandhri	A maid in royal apartments for females. Draupadi acted as one in King Virata's female chambers.
Shakuni	Brother of Gandhari. Friend of Duryodhana and an arch-schemer.
Salya	King of Madrasena. Brother of Madri, second queen of Pandu.
Samba	A yadava prankster who gave birth to a mace due to a curse from rishi.
Sanjaya	A narrator, blessed by Veda Vyasa of divine vision to keep narrating the real time happenings of Mahabharata war to the king Dhritarashtra.
Shantanu	King of Kuru dynasty. Father of Bhishma and husband of Ganga and

	later Satyavati.
Satyaki	A yadava warrior and friend of Krishna.
Satyavati	A fisherman's daughter who later became king Shantanu's second queen.
Sugandhika	A fragrant flower.
Sabyasachi	Another name of Arjuna meaning one who could use his both hands with equal facility and effect.
Shikhandin	A daughter-turned-man of Drupada. Amba in earlier birth.
Sisupal (Shishupal)	Powerful king of Chedi who died at the hands of Krishna during Yudhishthira's Rajsuya yagya.
Shubhadra	Sister of Krishna and Balarama. Arjuna's wife and mother of Abhimanyu.
Sudeshna	Queen of king Virata.
Suka	Son of Vyasa.
Supratika	Name of a powerful elephant of king Bhagadutta.
Susharma	King of Trigarta, who supported by Kauravas, attacked Matsya of Virata Kingdom.
Swarga	The heavens ruled by Indra where mortals after death enjoy the results of their good deeds on earth.
Upaplavya	A place in Matsya Kingdom where Pandavas stayed after their exile of thirteen years.
Urvasi	An apsara of Indra's court. Her amorous overtures were repulsed by Arjuna.
Vaisampayana	Chief disciple of Rishi Vyasa who

	revealed the epic 'Mahabharata' for the benefit of humanity.
Varnavata	A forest where a wax-house was built to house Pandavas with the intention of setting the house on fire while Pandavas slept in it.
Vasishtha	A sage who had cursed the eight Vasus to be born on earth for stealing his cow.
Vishwarup	A vision of the Lord of the universe.
Veda Vyasa	A great rishi, author of Mahabharat.
Vikarna	The only son of Dhritarashtra who declared the staking and losing of Draupadi as illegal.
Virata	King of Matsya.
Vriddhakshatra	King of Sindhu, father of Jaidratha.
Vrishnis, kekayas	Tribals devoted to Pandavas
Vrikodara	Another name of Bhima
Yama	God of Death.
Yagya(Yajna)	A sacrificial ritual.
Yaksha	Demi-gods. Subjects of god of wealth, Kubera.
Yuyutsu	A noble son of Dhritarashtra, who disapproved of the unfair way in which Abhimanyu was killed.

BIBLIOGRAPHY

1	The Mahabharata of Krishna-Dwaipayana Vyasa, Vol.I to IV	Translated by Kisari Mohan Ganguli and published by Munshiram Manoharlal Publishers Pvt. Ltd.
2	Mahabharata	C. Rajagopalachari-Bharatiya Vidya Bhawan, KulapatiKM Munshi Marg, Mumbai-400007
3	Mahabharata	Kamla Subramaniam. Bharatiya Vidya Bhawan, Kulapati KM Munshi Marg, Mumbai-400007
4	Mahabharata	William Buck – Motilal BanarsiDass Publishers Private Ltd.,Delhi-110007
5	Mahabharata	Translated by Igen B. Manoj Publications, Delhi-110084.